"Vincent Smiles offers a significant contribution to the contemporary discussion of science and religion. Combining his expertise in biblical scholarship with a refined theological sensitivity and profound pedagogical concern, he has produced a work that readers at many levels will find very illuminating. Strongly recommended."

—*John F. Haught, Ph.D*
Senior Fellow, Science and Religion
Woodstock Theological Center
Georgetown University, Washington, DC

"The debate on the relationship between religion and science rages on in America. Unlike many books in the field, Vincent Smiles places science and the Bible on an equal footing, regarding each as a source of knowledge about our world and about our God. The result is a thoughtful and refreshingly balanced dialogue that will keep the reader thinking long after finishing the last page."

—*Dr. Noreen Herzfeld*
Nicholas and Bernice Reuter
Professor of Science and Religion
Saint John's University, Collegeville, MN

"When their understanding of God is challenged by new insights, some claim: God is dead! However, when their view of the world is so challenged, they seldom declare: Science is dead. In this very well-researched study, Vincent M. Smiles sketches the development in the West of the notions of science and of God, as well as of understanding itself. He shows how science and religion conflicted in the past, and he argues that they need not do so in the present or the future, as well as science is not equated with scientific materialism or religion with fundamentalism. Rather, these two very different ways of understanding can enhance each other."

—*Dianne Bergant, CSA*
Professor of Biblical Studies
Catholic Theological Union, Chicago, IL

THE BIBLE AND SCIENCE

LONGING FOR GOD IN A SCIENCE-DOMINATED WORLD

Vincent M. Smiles

A Michael Glazier Book

LITURGICAL PRESS
Collegeville, Minnesota

www.litpress.org

A Michael Glazier Book published by Liturgical Press

Cover design by Ann Blattner.
Illustration: Photos.com (top) and PhotoSpin.com (bottom).

Unless otherwise noted, Scripture quotations are from the translations listed below as amended by the author:

1 2 3 4 5 6 7 8 9

Library of Congress Cataloging-in-Publication Data

Smiles, Vincent M., 1949–
The Bible and science : longing for God in a science-dominated world / Vincent M. Smiles.
p. cm.
"A Michael Glazier book."
Includes bibliographical references and index.
ISBN 978-0-8146-5513-9 — ISBN 978-0-8146-8006-3 (ebook)
1. Bible and science. 2. Religion and science. I. Title.

BS650.S64 2011
261.5'5—dc22 2011002358

In Memoriam

Bill Smiles, 1919–2002
"a kind and gentle man"

&

Rose Patricia (Cliff) Smiles
"Her children rise up and call her blessed"
(Proverbs 31:28, RSV)

CONTENTS

Preface xi

Chapter 1: Overture 1

Essential Preliminaries for the Road Ahead 1

Debate and Confusion about Theology and Science 4

Purpose, Meaning, and Value in Human Life 9

The Relationship of Faith and Reason 10

Reasons to be Skeptical about Scientific Naturalism 13

The Bible and Science as Partners in Understanding Reality 17

Overcoming Arrogance 20

Conclusion 22

Chapter 2: The Bible 24

Introduction 24

The Problem of Content 26

The Problem of Interpretation 28

Avoiding Extreme Views about the Bible 30

Richard Dawkins 30

Biblical Fundamentalism 33

Interpreting the Bible: The Problem of Method 36

The Historical-Critical Method: Benedict Spinoza 38

The "Four Assumptions" of the Ancient Interpreters and "The Very Idea of the Bible" (James Kugel) 43

A Response to Kugel: Historical Criticism *and* Faith 49

Learning from the Bible and Science: The Assumptions behind the Combination 53

The Bible in the Context of the Science-Theology Dialogue 58

Chapter 3: God 64
The "Problem" of God 64
Origen: The Highest "Branch of Learning" 66
Symbolism and Contemplation of God 69
The Loss of Symbolism 72
A Science-Dominated World 74
The Trivializing of God and Humanity 76
Theology and Science: Sources of Knowing 81
Science's Suggestions of God 85
God of Creation and Hope 91
Conclusion: Rediscovering God 97

Chapter 4: Humanity 100
What Is a Human Being? 100
Scientific Materialism 103
The Liberation of the Human Spirit 109
The Many Facets of Knowledge 116
Michael Polanyi: Scientist and Philosopher 121
Emergence 127
Conclusion: All of the Evidence 130

Chapter 5: Types of Knowing in the Bible 134
Tacit Knowing and the Language of Scripture 134
Bridging the Distance 139
Suffering 145
The Silence of God 149
God, Creation, and Suffering 151
Miracles 154
Jesus and the Demons 159
Spiritual Experience and Theological Creativity among Jesus' Earliest Followers 165
Jesus as LORD of the Sea 169
Conclusion 174

Life after Death 175
The Old Testament 175
The New Testament 180
Near-Death Experiences 184
Eternal Life 188
Conclusion 194

Bibliography 196

Index of People and Sujects 203

Scripture Index 208

PREFACE

There is a great deal of confusion about the relationship between biblical faith and modern science. The warring factions of religious fundamentalists on one side and scientific fundamentalists on the other give the impression that there is constant warfare between religion and science. Some science writers present their personal philosophies as though they were the conclusions that everyone must draw from biology and cosmology. They blur the line between science and philosophy, use vitriolic language against religion, and so portray science as utterly opposed to biblical faith. With respect to the Bible, the confusion arises because people rarely have occasion to study it carefully, and the loudest voices tend to be those who feel they must defend the Bible against science and the modern world. Some, in fact, want to convince us that Genesis is a scientific account of the world's origins! They play into the hands of those who happily portray science and religion as mortal enemies.

This book is for those who are convinced of, or are at least open to, the fact that ancient biblical faith and modern science can get along. The challenge ahead lies in the deeply paradoxical role the Bible plays in modern society. On the one hand, it is the perennial best seller, outselling all other best sellers every year without exception. It is appealed to by politicians as well as clergy. People argue constantly about what "the Bible says," and even those who mostly ignore it often have a hidden respect for it. It stands as a symbol of ancient creeds and values. People place their hands on it and swear by it in courts of law; they give it as a gift on special occasions. On the other hand, only rarely do people spend much time reading the Bible, and so are often at the mercy of fundamentalists when it comes to the question of how to interpret it. In the context of the culture wars, some quote the Bible and imagine thereby that they speak for God, which for some others makes the Bible distasteful. The deepest paradox is that the Bible has been so formative of the Western world. Indeed, the case is sometimes made that the Bible's image of a rational God creating an orderly, rational universe was a major stimulus for the rise of modern science. And yet the notion remains alarmingly popular that the Bible and science are in complete disagreement!

But there are signs of hope. There is a rich and deep dialogue between religion and science that has been going on for many years. After about two hundred years of near complete obsession with scientific knowledge alone, it is now becoming clear to more and more thinkers, including scientists, that human existence cannot thrive without "other kinds of knowledge."[1] We sell ourselves short when we denigrate one type of knowledge at the expense of another. Not only science but also art, history, philosophy, and theology reveal the depths of reality. In the coming chapters, I hope to make that case, and to do so by bringing the Bible more directly and fully into the conversation. The Bible's simple stories, imagery, and symbolic universe need to be part of our language

and way of thought, not primarily for their own sake, but because they also, like science, reveal us to ourselves. Much of the argument of these chapters is about shuffling the furniture of our thinking to allow the Bible some space.

I am grateful to John Haught (distinguished research professor of theology at Georgetown University), an international leader in the science-theology dialogue, for reading the manuscript in a rough form and giving me much-needed encouragement. I am similarly grateful to my colleague Dan Finn (Clemens Professor of Economics and Theology), who at a crucial point read a large part of the manuscript and offered numerous valuable suggestions. My friend and colleague John Merkle (professor of theology) gave me valuable help with the chapter on "God." My thanks also to Dianne Bergant (professor of Old Testament Studies at Catholic Theological Union in Chicago) and my colleagues in Minnesota, Kathleen Cahalan (professor of theology) and Noreen Herzfeld (professor of computer science and theology), who have all, in differing ways, offered guidance and encouragement. I owe a unique debt of thanks to my colleague Chuck Rodell (professor of biology), who for several years now has been a catalyst for my venturing deeper into the science-theology dialogue.

1. Elaine Howard Ecklund (*Science vs. Religion: What Scientists Really Think* [New York: Oxford University Press, 2010], 107–8) relates that Ian Hutchinson, a professor "of Nuclear Science and Engineering at the Massachusetts Institute of Technology . . . often gives talks about the relationship between religious faith and science." Among other things, he points out that numerous "great scientists have been convinced that science and Christian faith are compatible"; he insists on the need for "other kinds of knowledge," and he rejects the notion "that the only meaningful knowledge is scientific."

There are no words to express my gratitude to Ingrid, my beloved spouse, whose support in all things is unwavering and indispensable. Our sons, Matthew, Aaron, and Daniel, are a constant reminder of what is really valuable and good in life. The dedication to my parents speaks for itself.

Vincent M. Smiles
November 1, 2010
All Saints' Day

CHAPTER 1

OVERTURE

The whole world before you
is like a speck that tips the scales,
and like a drop of morning dew
that falls on the ground.

—Wisdom of Solomon 11:22, NRSV

Essential Preliminaries for the Road Ahead

My purpose in this book is to discuss the Bible and science as two different, but complementary, ways to understand the reality that encompasses the universe. Atheists and theists agree these days that there is such an encompassing reality. In his latest book, Stephen Hawking apparently has "declared God pretty much dead," but for him, no less than for any believer, the universe is not all there is. Hawking and his cowriter say that "according to M-theory, 'ours is not the only universe.'" So, what we have to reckon with is not just our universe, but also the multiverse, and M-theory ("an extension of string theory") and, beyond that presumably, whatever it is that made M-theory.[1]

For atheists, reality stops with some set of laws that determine how universes come into and out of existence. I have no argument with M-theory or any other aspect of science. I simply think that the reality that encompasses, and accounts for, the laws is itself enfolded in a loving God; M-theory is just a recipe. For me, therefore, reality (the fullness of being) goes far beyond any scientific theory, and so a further purpose for this book is to show why it makes sense to understand reality in terms of

1. Stephen Hawking and Leonard Mlodinow, *The Grand Design* (New York: Bantam Books, 2010); all quotes are taken from the review by Dwight Garner, "Many Kinds of Universes, and None Require God," *New York Times*, Sept 7, 2010, http://www.nytimes.com/2010/09/08/books/08book.html.

God. Humans have a capacity to know God, and the Bible is one of the channels of such knowledge. Other channels include science, philosophy, art, history, and religious traditions beyond the Bible. The discussion in this book will focus on the Bible and science—science, because it so obviously dominates our modern world, and the Bible, because it represents the inspiration and revelation of ancient spiritual wisdom. Both can enable us to contemplate reality and the Eternal Mystery that gives being to all beings.

"Science-Dominated" in the title of this book is not intended as an expression of regret or complaint; it is simply a description of the world we live in. Science is a major aspect of the lives and thinking of large segments of the human population—that is just a fact. An important aspect of the coming discussion will have to do with whether science alone should determine our understanding of reality to the exclusion of biblical ways of knowing. My response to that question is no, but, as already indicated, this has nothing to do with rejecting science. To the contrary, I gladly echo John Haught in saying that science is "a *gift* to theology."[2] People of faith, to the fullest extent possible, should embrace every aspect of science, consider carefully its challenges to ancient religious ideas, and think creatively about how these differing revelations can cohere in our understanding. I take it for granted that the Bible and science equally derive from God. We can know God in numerous different ways (physical, spiritual, intellectual, artistic); the adventure is in exploring all of them.

This brings me to issues of definition. I take science to be primarily a method of inquiry into the nature of physical things that includes observation, measurement, experiment, and theory. It also includes the products of science, both the technology we take for granted (e.g., jet airplanes) and the products that we regret or fear (e.g., industrial pollution, WMDs). In chapter 2, I will discuss extensively what the Bible is, including with respect to both its genius and its downfalls. Here I need to discuss briefly how I relate the Bible with faith, religion, and theology.

Faith is not the same as belief. Belief has to do with doctrines and creeds that are particular to individuals and religious traditions. Faith is a more universal aspect of human experience; it nearly always involves beliefs, but it is not definable in terms of any of them. Abraham had faith in God and so do I, but what he, as a nineteenth-century-BC Middle

2. See John Haught, *God After Darwin: A Theology of Evolution* (Boulder, CO: Westview Press, 2000), 45; Haught actually speaks of "Darwin's Gift to Theology."

Easterner, believed about God was far different from what I believe, as a twenty-first-century-AD Westerner. Nevertheless, what Abraham and I share is a fundamental *trust* in God as the ground of all existence.

Every human culture, of every time and place that we know of, acknowledges in some fashion that behind the veil of ordinary existence there is a sacredness that undergirds all things. It is this fundamental *experience* of the sacred that evokes faith in God, but what "God" means, how this deity is named and envisaged, what obligations (if any) derive from faith, and numerous other issues are matters of belief that vary from person to person, and religion to religion. For our purposes in this book, what is most important is the fundamental experience of the sacred that leads to and is often termed "faith." The Bible gives ample witness to the reality and power of faith, as also to the fact that faith has many facets, from simple trust (Gen 15:6) to knowing, commitment, and loving action (e.g., Gal 2:16-21; 5:6). Faith is not properly defined as belief without evidence, as some critics would have it. It is an experience, and a way of being.

Not everything in the Bible and religion is of equal value. Indeed, it is well known, and an issue for discussion below, that religion is by no means only a source of good, and that the Bible contains ideas we cannot accept. It is the role of theology to examine faith and religion, so as to make them coherent and consider their ultimate meaning, and to do so with critical reasoning, in order to sort the wheat from the chaff. This is an unending process. In science—confined as it is to the realm of the physical—it is comparatively easy to distinguish the true from the false, though even in science there are numerous complexities. In the abstract realms of knowledge that concern theology, the issues are more difficult, but they are no less important, since they concern such questions as, what is existence, what is a human, and what are the transcendent values that ought to guide our thinking and behavior? The guiding question in this book is, how can the Bible and science help to make sense of human existence? I take it for granted that they can, but in our modern context, the case has to be made.

This will involve consideration of specific scientific insights, and also what science in itself is, and is not. Science has its limits. In light of the experience of faith, theology picks up where science leaves off. There is some wisdom in the old adage that science is concerned with the "how," and theology with the "why." The discussion gets complicated, however, with such borderline questions as the nature of ultimate reality and of mind, where science and theology both have things to say. At that point, mutual respect ought to be the order of the day. My guiding method is theology that has to do with reflection on faith and knowledge in the light of God as the ground of all existence. Whereas science is concerned only with the physical level of reality, theology takes it for granted that there are further levels.

Science and theology, as I will speak of them, have no necessary conflict; they are complementary ways of knowing. Hence, the Bible and faith, fundamental sources of theological reflection, also are compatible with science. Indeed, as already said, science is a gift to theology; it both enriches and purifies theological thought. But whereas science confines itself to physical evidence, theology has to consider also evidence that is not subject to scientific observations and measurements. Theology is concerned with the wider human experience, and so provides a richer background and context for human knowing than science alone can provide.

But my idyllic picture of the Bible and science as complementary lenses through which to know the world and God does not conform to the situation we encounter in modern society. To the contrary, there are extremist warring factions, some of whom wish to eliminate God and the Bible entirely, and some of whom would have us rip large pages from the book of science. This book is a war on two fronts against both extremes.

Debate and Confusion about Theology and Science

The dialogue between theology and science is complex; it takes place in many different ways and at many different levels. To a large extent, it is an academic debate conducted by philosophers, scientists, and theologians. But, as mentioned, there are also the extremists, some of whom see no hope of dialogue unless it has to do with religion's surrender to a materialist understanding of itself and the universe, while others will accept only the parts of science that agree with their religious views. Most scholars, however, do not regard science and belief in God as incompatible.[3] In fact, enormous work has been done in recent decades by

3. For example, see the 2005 survey by Elaine Howard Ecklund, a sociologist at Rice University, of which a summary is available at http://www.msnbc.msn.com/id/8916982/; see also her book, *Science vs. Religion: What Scientists Really Think* (New York: Oxford University Press, 2010); Alister McGrath, *Dawkins' God: Genes, Memes, and the Meaning of Life* (Malden, MA: Blackwell, 2005), esp. 53–57 and 139–59; and A. Flew, *There is a God: How the World's Most Notorious Atheist Changed His Mind* (New York: HarperOne, 2007), 96–112. Ecklund's book is by far the best resource, since it relies on interviews as well as statistics. For instance, she shows that while a far higher percentage of scientists (53 percent) have

scientists, who have an interest in how religious insights cohere with, and even add to, science's view of the universe, and by theologians who view scientific knowledge as both a needed challenge and valuable enrichment to religious belief.[4] But the writings of the scholars represent only the explicit, public face of the science-theology dialogue.

The dialogue is also taking place, far less reflectively—indeed, sometimes almost subconsciously—in society at large, among those who know little of the scholarship. If "in the intellectual world today," as John Haught says, "there is a widely shared belief that science is enough to account fully for everything,"[5] so also in society at large the view is common that science *alone* provides reliable knowledge, and that science and technology comprise the solution to all human problems. This perspective—often referred to as "naturalism" or "scientific materialism"[6]—fosters the view that religious beliefs are outdated, and that when entering church, one needs to leave one's intelligence at the door. Naturalism has become the default worldview in large segments of modern society, but because it goes largely unexamined, its negative effects with respect to the understanding of the Bible and science are only multiplied. This is evident in the two opposing streams of thought that so often dominate the debate about science and theology in the mass media.

---

no faith in God compared with Americans at large (16 percent), it is also the case that scientists "self-select . . . from backgrounds where religion was practiced only weakly" (26), and, among the scientists interviewed, "it is not the engagement with science itself that leads them away from religion" (17).

4. I have in mind authors like Stephen M. Barr (Catholic physicist), Ian Barbour (professor of physics and religion), Paul Davies (mathematical physicist), John Haught (theologian), Martinez Hewlett (biologist), Alister McGrath (scientist turned theologian), Kenneth Miller (Catholic biologist), Arthur Peacocke (theologian and biochemist), Ted Peters (theologian), Michael Polanyi (scientist turned philosopher), and John Polkinghorne (physicist and theologian). But these are just a small sample of the recent authors in this increasingly vigorous field of inquiry.

5. John Haught, *Christianity and Science: Toward a Theology of Nature* (New York: Orbis, 2007), 6.

6. "Naturalism" goes back at least to Alfred North Whitehead (*Science and the Modern World: Lowell Lectures, 1925* [New York: Free Press, 1925, 1967]), who says that an "interest in natural objects and in natural occurrences, for their own sakes" arose "in the later Middle Ages" (15). For recent discussion, see John Haught, *Is Nature Enough? Meaning and Truth in the Age of Science* (New York: Cambridge University Press, 2006); and Stephen M. Barr, *Modern Physics and Ancient Faith* (Notre Dame: University of Notre Dame Press, 2003), who speaks of "the materialist creed." "Scientific Materialism" is the preferred term of Edward O. Wilson, a strong advocate of this philosophy. See his book *On Human Nature* (Cambridge, MA: Harvard University Press, 1978), 190–93 and 201–9.

On the one hand, there are those whom John Haught has called "the new atheists," whose books have gained a great deal of attention in recent times. Haught primarily refers to Richard Dawkins, Sam Harris, and Christopher Hitchens, all of whom have recently written popular books that aggressively make a case for atheism.[7] These writers argue that science demonstrates the truth of a purely naturalist interpretation of reality. This view can justifiably be called pessimistic, since it maintains that the subjective perception that life has value and meaning is ultimately just an illusion. For instance, Loyal Rue (a philosopher of religion), maintains that

> the universe is blind and aimless; it has no value in and of itself; it is unenchanted by forces, qualities, characteristics that might objectively endorse any particular human orientation toward it. The universe is dead and devoid of meaning; its significance is not demonstrably one thing or another. The universe *just is.*

He presents no evidence or argument for this claim; "I shall not bother much," he says, "about its origins or whether it is true. On the contrary, I will assume its truth."[8] He can do that, because it is largely the mindset of much of modern society; if it were not, he would have to make the case.

The opposite extreme of this naturalist, essentially atheist, perspective is that of religious fundamentalism, particularly biblical literalism. This perspective rejects whatever in modern science appears to compete with or deny what the Bible teaches regarding creation. I have to write "*appears* to compete," because whether or not any such competition exists in fact depends entirely on how the texts in question are interpreted. Biblical fundamentalists can be described as "extreme," not because of their faith in God or because they believe in the divine inspiration of the Bible; most moderates also gladly affirm those propositions, as I will in this book. Fundamentalism is an extreme position because of the way it insists on a very particular way of interpreting the Scriptures. It involves the notion that the Bible, particularly Genesis 1–2, is incompatible with modern science, particularly evolution, and with the sciences of cosmology and geology, which together show that the universe is about fourteen billion years old, and the earth about five billion. Fundamental-

7. John Haught, *God and the New Atheism: A Critical Response to Dawkins, Harris, and Hitchens* (Louisville: Westminster John Knox, 2008).

8. Loyal Rue, *By the Grace of Guile: The Role of Deception in Natural History and Human Affairs* (New York: Oxford University Press, 1994), 3.

ism is perhaps best represented by John C. Whitcomb (professor of Old Testament) and Henry M. Morris (founder of the Institute for Creation Research), whose book *The Genesis Flood* (1961) remains popular.

Creationism is often conflated in popular thinking with the intelligent design movement that is mostly associated with authors like Michael Behe (biochemist) and William A. Dembski (philosopher and mathematician). And there is a historical link. When advocates of creationism lost the battle to remove Darwinism as the framework for biological education in high schools, intelligent design was proposed as an alternative "scientific" theory to evolution. This more sophisticated strategy did not appeal to the Bible as such, but its religious biases and roots are sufficiently clear that it has had no more success in the courts.[9] Nevertheless, Behe is a professor of biochemistry; his advocacy of ID, therefore, differs quite substantially from creationism. He does not advocate biblical literalism and he fully accepts the basic scientific assertions of Darwinism, a universe that is "billions of years old" and "the development and behavior of organisms within an evolutionary framework." He simply does not accept that Darwinism explains "molecular life" and insists that its "irreducible complexity" points to an intelligent designer.[10] In spite of these differences, in popular thinking creationism and intelligent design are conflated in such a way that they represent a unified front against modern science. In this popular picture, science—most especially evolution—is seen as atheistic, while religion—particularly the Bible—is seen as antiscience. The result is enormous confusion regarding both science and religion.

Most relevant with respect to the coming chapters is that from both sides the Bible is shredded, and religion and science are seen as enemies. From the side of naturalism, the Bible is made to appear an outdated and irrelevant book that sides with creationism and intelligent design against science and the modern world; the message is, "Biblical faith is unintelligent and closed-minded." Worse than that, in the hands of the "new atheists," especially Richard Dawkins, the Bible is said to present us with a God who is

> a petty, unjust, unforgiving control-freak; a vindictive, bloodthirsty ethnic cleanser; a misogynistic, homophobic, racist,

9. See Karl W. Giberson, *Saving Darwin: How to be a Christian and Believe in Evolution* (New York: HarperOne, 2008), esp. 108–19.

10. Michael J. Behe, *Darwin's Black Box* (New York: Free Press, 1996), 5 and 187–208.

> infanticidal, genocidal, filicidal, pestilential, megalomaniacal, sadomasochistic, capriciously malevolent bully.[11]

Dawkins's criticisms can be effectively answered,[12] but his books are popular and influential. Biblical literalism does not improve the Bible's image, since it goes right along with the perception that the Bible excludes evolution and other aspects of science. Further, the Bible's strongest advocates describe it in ways that are just as unbalanced as those of Dawkins. The Southern Baptist Convention describes the Bible as "a *perfect* treasure of divine instruction" and as "*totally* true and trustworthy."[13] Such a description and the attitude toward the Scriptures that goes along with it fly in the face of biblical study that has developed since the seventeenth century and that continues to be espoused, with some appropriate caution, even by as careful an interpreter as Pope Benedict XVI.[14] But while some believers proclaim the Bible to be "perfect," others are largely ignorant of it. Though the Bible is a perennial best seller, full understanding of it is sadly lacking. As TIME reported recently:

> Pollster George Gallup has dubbed us "a nation of biblical illiterates." Only half of U.S. adults know the title of even one Gospel. Most can't name the Bible's first book. The trend extends even to Evangelicals, only 44% of whose teens could identify a particular quote as coming from the Sermon on the Mount.[15]

In other words, even the Bible's advocates do not always know the texts well and are even less schooled in the nuances of their interpretation. Such a situation makes it easy both for the naturalists to deride the Bible and for fundamentalists to claim that its truth outweighs the claims of

11. Richard Dawkins, *The God Delusion* (Boston: Houghton Mifflin, 2006), 31. That is his description of the God of the OT; the NT, in his view, only makes matters worse (250–62).

12. Very effective responses have been written by John Haught, *God and the New Atheism*; and Alister McGrath and Joanna Collicutt McGrath, *The Dawkins Delusion? Atheist Fundamentalism and the Denial of the Divine* (Downers Grove, IL: InterVarsity Press, 2007).

13. The full statement is available at www.sbc.net/aboutus/basicbeliefs.asp.

14. Joseph Ratzinger, Pope Benedict XVI, *Jesus of Nazareth: From the Baptism in the Jordan to the Transfiguration*, trans. Adrian J. Walker (New York: Doubleday, 2007), xv–xvi. The pope emphasizes that "this book is in no way an exercise of the magisterium"; it is simply "a personal search 'for the face of the Lord' (cf. Ps 27:8)." One might also note that the pope does not practice historical-criticism rigorously; the book is far closer to a sermon than to investigation.

15. David Van Biema, "The Case for Teaching the Bible," *TIME In Partnership with CNN*, March 22, 2007, http://www.time.com/time/magazine/article/0,9171,1601845-1,00.html.

science. The net result is that the Bible and science are rarely seen as *partners* in the task to gain a deeper understanding of human existence, and its meaning and value.

Purpose, Meaning, and Value in Human Life

What is human existence? Does it have any intrinsic purpose or meaning, or are we merely the accidental products of billions of years of cosmic evolution? Our subjective sense tells us that indeed both the vast universe and our individual lives have purpose. Most people would probably define their particular purpose in terms of their families and relationships, their children, and their life's work. Such purpose, of course, is not always religious, but for most of us it involves at least some commitment to certain values, some sort of ethical code. However, since the nineteenth century, and with even greater force in recent years, purpose and meaning have come under attack. Popular writers, supposedly in the name of science, tell us that our sense of purpose is an "illusion," that the universe "has precisely the properties we should expect if there is, at bottom, no design, no purpose, no evil and no good, nothing but blind pitiless indifference."

That quote is from Richard Dawkins, one of the most vociferous and most popular of such writers; the book in question is *River Out of Eden* (1995).[16] Let me emphasize immediately that I will in no way dispute the science that Dawkins explains. The dispute arises with respect to the philosophy that he attaches to the science, but which cannot be derived from it. Science as such confines itself to physical reality and claims no expertise for judging the ultimate meaning of what it discovers. In claiming, therefore, that science requires us to abandon notions of genuine meaning and purpose in the universe,[17] Dawkins is straying outside the competence of science. Daniel Dennett, at the outset of *Darwin's Dangerous Idea*, asks whether "*any* version of this attitude of wonder and purpose" (whether strictly religious or more broadly philosophical) can "be sustained in the face of Darwinism." To which his book answers with a resounding no; life and its laws emerged, he insists, as "the outcome

16. Richard Dawkins, *River Out of Eden: A Darwinian View of Life* (New York: Basic Books, 1995), 133.

17. A very full description of six such writers, with careful and effective responses, can be found in Karl Giberson and Mariano Artigas, *Oracles of Science: Celebrity Scientists versus God and Religion* (New York: Oxford University Press, 2007).

of a blind, uncaring shuffle through Chaos."[18] This also is a confused blurring of science and philosophy.

On the other hand, in the Judeo-Christian tradition, the Bible and its accompanying theologies have played an enormous role in fashioning society's sense of meaning and purpose. To this day, large numbers of people—even those who are not very religious—believe that they and the universe have been created by God and that the Bible represents spiritual values and beliefs that they live by. Whether we know it or not, and whether we read it or not, the Bible has played a substantial role in our sense of ourselves and the world we live in. And yet, fundamentalists aside, many people approach the Bible, if they read it at all, with a fair measure of diffidence, if not downright skepticism. Though having a sense that it contains much that is valuable, they realize—quite properly—that it cannot all be accepted without some measure of discernment. Faith in God, we rightly suspect, is not identical with accepting uncritically everything that is in the Bible. We will deal with issues of biblical interpretation in chapter 2; for now, we need to consider the more general issue of faith in relation to reason.

The Relationship of Faith and Reason

In every society, religion, economics, politics, and other powerful forces inevitably rub shoulders. Believers are rarely just believers and worshipers; they are also involved in families, histories, economics, and politics. Religion, more often than believers like to admit, becomes embroiled in movements and actions that go against everything religion properly stands for. In the fourth and fifth centuries, when the Church gained power in the Roman Empire, it turned against other religions, especially Judaism, in violent ways, leading to horrible pogroms in the Middle Ages and contributing, in the twentieth century, to the Holocaust. Quite properly, therefore, numerous people—including religious believers—have become wary of religion's power for evil. Nevertheless, most people, me included, remain convinced that religion has a crucial role to play in human life for the sake of goodness.

18. Daniel Dennett, *Darwin's Dangerous Idea: Evolution and the Meanings of Life* (New York: Penguin Books, 1995), 18 and 185. To be fair, Dennett does write eloquently of "the beauty" of Darwinism (521); though it is a "universal acid," "what remains," he says, "is more than enough to build on" (521). The problem is that "what remains" is only Dennett's view of reality reduced to purely material stuff and laws; there is no place for any genuinely *spiritual* "attitude of wonder and purpose."

Religion has been challenged both by its own failures and by believers as they have gained new knowledge. This has caused religious practices and attitudes to change considerably over the centuries. In medieval philosophy and theology, when belief in God was largely taken for granted by everyone, there was vigorous debate about the appropriate role of science, then called "natural philosophy," in relation to faith and theology. Investigation of nature was sometimes regarded as suspect, since the concept of the universe having fixed laws might seem to compromise belief in God's sovereign freedom to act contrary to them. The skeptics, however, could not stem the tide. Adelard of Bath (twelfth-century philosopher), for instance, insisted that the world God created is orderly and open to human reason and that, in all judgments, reason has to be supreme over authority.[19] The view increasingly developed in the late Middle Ages that "if we ask questions of nature, we can expect to get answers, and to be able to understand them."[20]

This, of course, was the necessary foundation of science. At its birth, therefore, there was no question of science (natural philosophy) being interpreted as destructive of faith in God; to the contrary, Galileo (1564–1642), Kepler (1571–1630), Newton (1643–1727), and the other great founders of modern science, like their medieval forebears, saw no contradiction between their knowledge of the world and their faith in God. To the contrary, the early scientists were mostly deeply religious. But things did not remain peaceful. The new view of the universe seemed to challenge the authority of Genesis, and in 1633 Pope Urban VIII made the enormous mistake of silencing Galileo, apparently placing biblical faith in opposition to scientific knowledge.[21] Violent disputes between Catholics and Protestants, in the aftermath of the sixteenth-century Reformation, had already brought religious dogma into disrepute. The time was ripe for the Enlightenment, the eighteenth-century movement that asserted the power of reason over tradition and dogma. This story will

19. *Adelard of Bath, Conversations with His Nephew: On the Same and the Different, Questions on Natural Science, and on Birds*, ed. and trans. Charles Burnett, with Italo Ronca et al. (New York: Cambridge University Press, 1998), 97–99, 103–5, and 125–35; and Louise Cochrane, *Adelard of Bath: The First English Scientist* (London: British Museum Press, 1994), esp. 11–19 and 43–45.

20. Philip Ball, "Triumph of the Medieval Mind," *Nature* 452 (April 17, 2008): 816.

21. In 1992 Pope John Paul II accepted the findings of the Galileo "Study Commission" and acknowledged the failings of seventeenth-century theology. The full text is available at http://www.its.caltech.edu/~nmcenter/sci-cp/sci-9211.html. It originally appeared in *L'Osservatore Romano*, N. 44 (1264), November 4, 1992.

be told more fully in chapter 3 ("God"), but it is helpful here at least to note its outlines.

The roots of modern science stem from the Middle Ages and even earlier, but science as we now know it only began to be recognizable in the sixteenth and seventeenth centuries.[22] By the late seventeenth century, René Descartes provided the grounding for the modern scientific method and cemented reason as the supreme power in the search for what is "really out there . . . the measure of physical reality."[23] This was the move that was most characteristic of the Enlightenment and that set it apart from the Middle Ages and has made it suspect to many believers even today. Whereas medieval scholarship had employed reason as a *tool* of philosophy and theology, always presupposing the paramount importance of faith and spiritual reality, the Enlightenment began to set faith and spirituality aside and to define reality in purely "physical" terms, and reason as

> the authority to determine what is out there in the first place and to set the standards to which things have to measure up. That is what the "Age of Reason," the "Enlightenment" means. It all has to do with who has the "authority" and the power—faith or reason.[24]

The Enlightenment did not reject faith in God as such, but its focus on reason as *the* way to understand reality and its rejection of religious dogmatism combined in many quarters to produce the dualism (physical

22. Modern histories of science usually begin the story in the sixteenth or seventeenth century. For example, John Gribbin, *Science: A History: 1543–2001* (New York: Penguin Books, 2003) begins in the middle of the sixteenth century. A much fuller history, tracing the roots of "the scientific revolution" back to ancient times and the Middle Ages, is provided by David C. Lindberg, *The Beginnings of Western Science: The European Scientific Tradition in Philosophical, Religious, and Institutional Context, 600 B.C. to A.D. 1450* (Chicago: University of Chicago Press, 1992).

23. John D. Caputo, *Philosophy and Theology* (Nashville: Abingdon Press, 2006), 26.

24. Caputo, *Philosophy and Theology*, 26. Going along with this, Lindberg (*The Beginnings of Western Science*, 364–65) says that "the underlying source of revolutionary novelty in [the science of] the sixteenth and seventeenth centuries . . . [was] the 'mechanical philosophy' . . . In exchange for the purposeful, organized, organic world of Aristotelian natural philosophy, the new metaphysics offered a mechanical world of lifeless matter, unceasing local motion and random collisions." Of course, the "atomism" on which the new metaphysics was founded was not new; it derived from "the Epicurean atomism of the third century B.C., passed down within the classical tradition and appropriately Christianized" (366, and see 76–79).

separate from spiritual) and rationalism (reason *alone*) that suggest that faith and reason, and therefore faith and science, are mutually opposed. To state the matter succinctly, whereas reason had been seen as the God-given capacity enabling *communion* with God, in the Enlightenment it became the human capacity to *argue about* God, even about whether God exists. In the aftermath of the Enlightenment, especially in the nineteenth to twentieth centuries, atheism gained ground, and we arrived at the situation today where the view is being aggressively fostered that the universe is full of "blind pitiless indifference," it "has no value in and of itself . . . it is devoid of meaning," and so on. Notice, however, that these are not conclusions of science; they have to do with the type of *philosophy* that is made to accompany science in the hands of Richard Dawkins, Loyal Rue, and others.

Reasons to be Skeptical about Scientific Naturalism

There are a few questions about this type of philosophy that immediately suggest themselves: for instance, how can a "dead" universe evolve life? How can a "meaningless" universe evolve direction, purpose, and meaning? How can a "blind" universe produce sight, insight, the search for truth, and genuine knowledge (of whatever type)? Meaning, purpose, truth, and factual knowledge are all closely related, and they are *all* products of the subjective, human mind. Subjectivity is what the Enlightenment, in its quest for objective truth, tried to escape, but we now know that none of us can escape our subjectivity. This was argued in great detail by Michael Polanyi (scientist-philosopher, 1891–1976)[25] and, with inevitable varieties of emphasis, has only been confirmed by others. We all inevitably see even the most objective of facts from a particular angle and context; there is no value-free perception and thus faith and reason are less distinguishable from one another than the Enlightenment presumed.[26]

25. For example, *Personal Knowledge: Towards a Post-Critical Philosophy* (Chicago: University of Chicago Press, 1958); and *The Study of Man* (Chicago: University of Chicago Press, 1958). I should emphasize that Polanyi preferred the term "personal," which for him expresses both the (subjective) commitment to know and the recognition of knowledge that is independent of the subject. Knowledge, therefore, is neither purely subjective nor purely objective; it transcends such distinctions since it requires both the human search for truth and the awareness that truth is beyond human control. Polanyi's ideas will be given some detailed attention in chapter 4, "Humanity."

26. For example, Caputo, *Philosophy and Theology*, 26. His point is that the "distinction between faith and reason has become more porous" (54); both have to do with "seeing as"

Where do we draw the line between the subjective and the objective, and without subjectivity, how can we make the judgment? If we allow that objective facts tell us about the universe, what does the *fact* of human subjectivity tell us? Let me put this another way: science properly insists that our material nature, the chemical composition of our bodies and our descent from animals, are clues to the nature of the universe. But material nature is not all there is to us. As I will discuss in chapter 4 ("Humanity"), we also have unique human qualities, capacities for transcendence, meaning, and truth, as expressed in art, science, philosophy, and religious contemplation. But are not these also clues to the nature of the universe? What do those qualities tell us not only about ourselves but also about the origin and nature of all reality?

In response to the question, "Is there a purpose to the universe?" Richard Dawkins said the following:

> Why would we even want to use a word like purpose of the universe? . . . In my own field of biology, we use the word purpose in a sort of metaphorical sense—there's purpose in a bird's wing and purpose in an eye. The *illusion* of purpose is built up by natural selection in a way that's very well understood, but if you ask, what's the purpose of a mountain? Or what's the purpose of the universe? . . . it's not just meaningless, it's stupid.[27]

Is Dawkins correct? Is it indeed "meaningless" and "stupid" to search for purpose? Ironically, if he were to be correct, then he would have discovered an ultimate truth—that the universe has "no design, no purpose," and so on, but here's the problem: Dawkins's very pronouncement of such a truth implies that there *is* ultimate truth out there waiting for, and perhaps even inviting, our discovery. His claim to have discovered that ultimately there is no meaning or purpose is fraught with a profound self-contradiction, since the absence of meaning or purpose would make all statements utterly meaningless and useless, including his own.

(56–57) and cannot ultimately be totally separated from one another, though the distinction is not to be erased (68).

27. Richard Dawkins and Lawrence Krauss, Stanford University Forum on "Science Education," Q&A Part 7, March 9, 2008, accessed October 14, 2010, http://richarddawkins.net/article,2472,Richard-Dawkins-and-Lawrence-Krauss,RichardDawkinsnet. A much longer discussion of what Dawkins sees as the "illusion" of purpose can be found in *River Out of Eden*, 95–133, but there also he fails to see the problem that his own attempts to explain the truth about nature undermine his fundamental thesis that the universe has no purpose.

Still, the discussion raises an important question: could the pursuit of truth constitute a genuine purpose in life? Surely it can! In fact, if I may say so, that is the purpose of Richard Dawkins's own life as an Oxford professor who fosters the public understanding of science. There is at least one purpose in the universe—the search for genuine truth. But is Dawkins the only one who can engage in that quest? Might someone engage in it and come to a different conclusion? It is difficult to see how he can have it both ways: genuine purpose and meaning, presumably, in his own endeavors, but only the "illusion of purpose" in the quest for truth, understanding, and purpose in which others engage. Surely it is self-contradictory to claim to have acquired some ultimate truth and then claim that the truth acquired makes all other purposeful pursuit of ultimacy "meaningless" and "stupid"? Might the human capacity for truth be a genuine clue about the nature of the universe and of the reality that undergirds it?

Dawkins believes that science (specifically, natural selection) brings us to the conclusion that life has no purpose, but first, that is a philosophical, not a scientific, conclusion. There is no way that science as such can investigate purpose, which has to do with things like desire, promise, and hope, none of which are reducible to the categories of physics or biology. And second, such an idea has to face the criticism articulated by John Haught in his book *Deeper Than Darwin*. Haught directly addresses naturalists, like Dawkins, who insist that human intelligence is "fully intelligible" in terms of causes that are themselves "devoid of mind and intelligence":

> The question I have for you, then, is this: Given the avowedly exhaustive explanation of your intelligence in terms of purely unintelligent causes, why should I, or anybody else including you, take seriously the claims that this *purely adaptive* instrument is now making? Why should I assume that this adaptive instrument (your mind) is able to discover *truth*?[28]

If we assume that the mind is nothing but an "adaptive instrument," built *only* by natural selection for survival and reproduction, can it really reach out for ultimate truth? Even basic study in either psychology or history shows that humans have an endless capacity for both unintended

28. John F. Haught, *Deeper Than Darwin: The Prospect for Religion in the Age of Evolution* (Boulder, CO: Westview Press, 2003), 97.

illusions and deliberate deceptions.[29] And yet we yearn for meaning and truth, *and* we believe we can attain them, that we can rise above illusion and deception and—at least to some degree—acquire truth. In other words, we believe, indeed we *have* to believe—otherwise all inquiry is nonsense—in a truth that transcends mere physical causality. None of this is an argument against science; it is simply a matter of asking about the significance of the search for truth, to which science, as well as philosophy and theology, gives eloquent witness.

Science's ability, by observation and experiment, to distinguish between genuine and false knowledge is simply an aspect of the human capacity for truth, which is a thoroughly purposeful enterprise. Science, no less than philosophy or theology, is completely dependent on the very thing that gives it shape in the first place and enables it to function: truth and the value humans place on it. Daniel Dennett (philosopher), a strong ally of Dawkins, at the outset of *Darwin's Dangerous Idea*, says that "whatever we hold precious, we cannot protect it from our curiosity," and he is surely correct about that. Dennett, however, thinks that "curiosity" inevitably leads through science to the abandoning of "sacred myth" and to the conclusion that life is the product of "mindless purposeless forces."[30] But surely our curiosity can extend to asking whether Dennett is necessarily correct in that view. Darwinism can be interpreted in numerous ways, including theologically.[31] Curiosity not only challenges "sacred myth," it also challenges Daniel Dennett. It challenges theology and science, and the philosophies derived from them. And the truth we long for utterly escapes final explanation by any of them.[32]

Dennett accounts for "curiosity" in purely Darwinian terms, and to be sure, evolution has much to tell us about brains, instincts, and intelligence; I am not arguing here against the insights of science. Theology, on the other hand, adds that curiosity has to do with God creating humans in the divine "image and likeness" (Gen 1:26), and a large part of this book depends on my belief in that idea. But neither scientists nor theologians occupy a point so much above particular viewpoints that

29. This, in fact, is largely the substance of Loyal Rue's book *By the Grace of Guile*, which I quoted above.

30. *Darwin's Dangerous Idea*, 22 and 520.

31. Among numerous possible examples, see Haught, *God After Darwin*; and Holmes Rolston III, "Does Nature Need to be Redeemed?" *Zygon* 29:2 (June 1994): 205–29.

32. Some might reasonably object that theology does provide "final" explanations, but my point is that theology never reaches the end of that quest for understanding God and God's purpose. All theologies and creeds are provisional.

they can claim to be beyond the search for truth, and to have attained ultimate understanding; both are completely dependent on subjectivity. What Dennett says about "whatever we hold precious" being subject to our "curiosity" holds for Dennett's views on evolution, as surely as it holds for the convictions of theology. Science, like theology, is shaped by its purpose of trying to discover the truth. Science and theology are in this together, whether they like it or not.

Science is also shaped, as already suggested, by its *belief* that "the world . . . is orderly and open to human reason." Neither belief nor purpose, which are both foundational to science, are "facts" that can be subject to the methods of science itself (experiment, observation, mathematical definition); they are simply its presuppositions. Scientific programs inevitably have to invoke ideas and values of which the scientific method knows nothing.[33] This is not a criticism of science, but merely a description of its character and limits. We cannot get rid of belief, purpose, or value any more than we can completely sever the objective from the subjective; these two aspects of our intelligence are interdependent. Human existence is endemically about "science" (objective facts) just as it is endemically about "religion" (purpose and meaning). Though scientific method is distinctive and must be respected, its context among other branches of knowledge (philosophy, art, and so on) must not be neglected. The same can properly be said of the methods of theological inquiry, including study of the Bible. Confining ourselves to a purely materialist view of existence is far too narrow, but so also would be a purely biblical or religious view. In the task of understanding and living human existence, we need both religion and science, the Bible and Darwinism. After all, from faith's perspective, genuine knowledge from whatever source ultimately derives from God.

The Bible and Science as Partners in Understanding Reality

In spite of my disagreements with Dawkins and Dennett, the questions they raise are important for believers to contemplate. And although many fundamentalist believers look back on the Enlightenment, and its assertion of reason over faith, as a disaster, it really was not. The Enlightenment produced not only science and its emphasis on reason and concrete reality but it was also instrumental in bringing about modern

33. Langdon Gilkey, *Religion and the Scientific Future: Reflections on Myth, Science, and Theology* (New York: Harper & Row, 1970), 48–50.

democracy, individual human rights, and religious freedom, not to mention electricity and iPods. To be sure, the Enlightenment and science (just like religion) have had their downfalls, but they are nevertheless the achievements that have shaped the modern world, and that have made possible our new explorations of the universe, including ourselves and our religious heritage. The Enlightenment's chastisement, so to speak, of the excesses of religious dogmatism, was a much-needed step in Western history. Whether we like it or not, we are all children of the Enlightenment. To repudiate the Enlightenment would be to repudiate religious toleration, individual human rights, democracy, and electricity. Evolution is also simply an aspect of modern science, a product of the Enlightenment; it is not a worldwide atheistic conspiracy, as some creationists would have us believe. The atheistic *philosophy* that people like Dawkins, Dennett, and Rue derive from Darwinism is deeply questionable, but the science is assured, and should be respected.

More than that, science provides immense insights into the reality of the universe and of human nature, and should be studied by anyone who wishes to understand God's creation. But, equally, the Bible, and the vast religious heritage that it represents, is also a beautiful and deep resource for understanding ourselves and the mysteries of existence. Human knowing, in its fullness, is not purely objective, though to be sure, knowledge and truth are "out there" beyond our control, awaiting our investigation. But neither is knowing purely subjective, as though we had no capacity, by critical discernment and method, to reach out beyond our particular views and biases and attain some measure of understanding. Reality is neither an object we can definitively measure nor is it a mindless chaos that utterly escapes us. We are a part of the reality we seek to understand.

The major argument of this book is that both science and faith—the latter viewed primarily through the Bible—have essential roles to play in our quest for meaning, for a deeper entering into the value and purpose of human existence. Science is not the only lens through which to view the world, and precisely the same is to be said of the Bible and faith. From faith's perspective, science no less than faith derives from God, and therefore it is a thoroughly religious notion that science and faith alike are ways of knowing God. One and the same psalm tells us that "the heavens [nature] proclaim the glory of God" *and* that God's ways are to be known in "the Law" of Sinai (Ps 19)—the stuff both of science and of religion.

The more the modern world gains in material prosperity, the more it needs its spiritual traditions. Fundamentalists are not wrong to protest against the loss of transcendence and of spiritual value that arises from a purely naturalist understanding of the universe and of life. On the other hand, naturalists are not wrong to insist on the value of scientific knowledge and to decry attitudes that demonize science and try to define reality in the terms of a narrow religiosity. Many scholars (though by no means all) have broken free from seeing the science-theology dialogue in terms of conflict, but in the wider society, often encouraged by the mass media, the conflict model remains dominant. Contrary to such a view, Pope John Paul II said,

> Science develops best when its concepts and conclusions are integrated into the broader human culture and its concerns for ultimate meaning and value. . . . *Science can purify religion from error and superstition; religion can purify science from idolatry and false absolutes*. Each can draw [the other] into a wider world, a world in which each can flourish.[34]

This book is largely guided by this view that science and religion give witness to human genius and heroism and need to be studied for the different types of knowledge they provide. On occasion, however, both need to have their wings clipped and, as the pope suggests, in that regard they can be mutually corrective.

Let me be clear what I mean by this. Both disciplines have their specific methods and objectives, and both must be left free to pursue knowledge in their own way without interference. But from both sides errors arise. The pope admits frankly that religion sometimes gives rise to "error and superstition"; as noted above, religion has often been guilty of cruel violence and bigotry. The arrival of modern science on the human stage is far more recent, but it also has been allied with the worst excesses of humanity, including devastating pollution of the earth and horrific warfare. It seems to be endemic to humans to abuse all of their gifts and talents for their selfish purposes. But we must not throw up our hands in despair, and accept hatred and destruction as the inevitable fate of humanity. We have the resources to discover and to fight our faults, and perhaps the first fault to be faced on *both* sides is arrogance.

34. Quoted in George V. Coyne, "Evolution and the Human Person: The Pope in Dialogue," *Science and Theology: The New Consonance*, ed. Ted Peters (Boulder, CO: Westview Press, 1998), 157, emphasis added.

Overcoming Arrogance

Arrogance is still abundantly on display in religion. This is not an accusation against individual religious believers, so much as against whole religious traditions that imagine that they embody "the truth" to which all others must in some way submit. The fundamentalist tradition, especially as exemplified in creationism, is surely arrogant in imagining that it alone has the correct perspective on the Bible, a perspective that supposedly enables it to dismiss as false, and even as evil, major scientific conclusions in the fields of geology and biology. Fundamentalists sometimes suggest that their way of interpreting the Bible is the ancient and original way, but that is simply not true. As I will show in chapter 3 ("God"), the ancients regarded the "literal" sense of the text as of least importance; its true meaning was to be discovered in its symbolic senses (the allegorical, moral, and anagogical senses).

Saint Augustine's (354–430 CE) work on *The Literal Meaning of Genesis* (actually only Genesis 1–3) in no way resembles what creationists make of the Genesis creation stories. The six days, for him, were not twenty-four-hour periods, but simply a convenient teaching device for describing what God in fact did in an instant.[35] Fundamentalism only began in the late nineteenth century in reaction against science and modern biblical study that was accepting of science.[36] Individual fundamentalists are usually deeply sincere, and fundamentalism has important points to bring to the table, but the tradition, especially in its very recent incarnation of creationism, has led many believers astray.

Between the extremes of fundamentalism on the one side, and scientific materialists advocating naturalism on the other, there is a middle group to consider here. Religious liberals are guilty of arrogance when they imagine that their more "scientific" way of investigating the Bible gives them authority to dismiss ancient texts and traditions as either outdated or as mere human inventions. All readers of the Bible must begin with a stance of humility. At its best, biblical scholarship learns not only from "scientific" and historical investigation but also from the faith-perspectives

35. St. Augustine, *The Literal Meaning of Genesis*, vol. I, trans. and annotated by John Hammond Taylor (New York: Newman Press, 1982), 9, 19–20 (for figurative and other senses), and 133–35, 141–42.

36. For discussion of the rise of fundamentalism, see Roy A. Harrisville and Walter Sundberg, *The Bible in Modern Culture: Baruch Spinoza to Brevard Childs* (Grand Rapids, MI: Wm. B. Eerdmans, 1995, 2002), 195–216; and Robert Hasting Nichols, "Fundamentalism in the Presbyterian Church," *The Journal of Religion* 5:1 (January 1925).

of the ancient writers, communities, and texts. There is no worthwhile interpretation of the Bible that does not bring to the task a deep regard for the nature and aims of the texts, and at the same time a deep appreciation for the faith in God that was so alive in the biblical writers.

Arrogance also arises in science because of human ignorance and prejudice. Science in itself is simply a method, as well as a series of discoveries, theories, and well-tried conclusions; it has been enormously successful, and for that we can only be grateful. But arrogance arises because humans, sometimes ignorantly, sometimes greedily, forge ahead in producing whatever they want regardless of the consequences for other humans and for nature at large. Western Europe's Enlightenment, its science and rationalism, did not only, or even immediately, lead to those blessings of the Enlightenment (democracy, individual human rights) that I mentioned earlier. Science and its technology led to the industrial revolution and simultaneously to an alignment with the military and to the most horrendous wars the world has ever known. The knowledge produced by the rise of modern science did not lead unswervingly to the recognition that "all men are created equal"; indeed, even the framers of that proposition excluded native peoples, slaves, and women from it.[37] Furthermore, fascination with science sometimes leads people to imagine, as noted more than once, that science alone represents true knowledge; this is the source of the "idolatry and false absolutes" against which Pope John Paul II warned. Dawkins and Dennett are undoubtedly sincere in their beliefs, but they surely draw upon themselves the charge of arrogance when they insist that science demonstrates the truth of *their* view that the universe derives from "blind, pitiless indifference" and so on, even though most scientists draw no such conclusions.

Mariano Artigas (1938–2006), physicist, philosopher, and Catholic priest, lamented that one of the costs of scientific progress has been a questioning of the value of human beings. After an analysis of scientific method in relation to broader theories of human knowledge, he concludes with this protest:

37. As John Caputo says in *Philosophy and Theology*, 37–38, the Enlightenment ideals of democracy and equality devolved, in fact, into notions of white European supremacy with disastrous consequences for non-Europeans around the globe. The discoverers of "reason" convinced themselves that they were its masters and therefore were the masters of the whole earth! A cure for such notions of white European superiority has been provided by Jared Diamond, *The Third Chimpanzee: The Evolution and Future of the Human Animal* (New York: HarperCollins, 1992), 235–48; and *Guns, Germs and Steel: The Fates of Human Societies* (New York: W. W. Norton, 1999).

> Perhaps . . . we should learn to look at empirical science, and even more at the human being who does it, with more respect. . . . an enormous disproportion [exists] between our achievements in empirical science and our understanding of them. . . . Perhaps we should learn to admire more what we are, and to dismiss as nonsense theories that attempt to measure human beings by comparing us with some of our particular achievements, and even replacing us with them.[38]

Science is one of our *achievements*; it has no power to preside over humans in judgment and to define them in terms of its categories. One of the great dangers in the rise and success of science, and the consequent disparaging of faith in naturalism, has been the notion that humans are ultimately "nothing but" animals, that spirituality and free will are illusions. Science itself does not require any such conclusion, but the philosophy that life arises simply from "a blind, uncaring shuffle through Chaos" leads perilously in that direction.

Conclusion

Science demonstrates our desire and capacity for truth. It is a natural ally of theology in showing that we have within us a power of transcendence, an ability to rise above our material origins and to contemplate also our spiritual nature. The Bible is at home with the material origins and nature of human beings; God created *ʿadam* ("humanity") from *ʿadamah* ("ground" or "dirt")—dust we are, to dust we shall return (Gen 3:19). As science also shows, that is a part of the story, but it is not the whole story.[39] The full story, as told in the Bible, is that we are dust that has been created by the eternal beauty and Spirit that we call God.

I am not suggesting here any facile amalgamation of science and theology that makes either one dependent on the other. They have very differing methods and objectives that must be respected. On the other hand, both ultimately gaze upon the same reality, the same universe, and seek to know existence in its depth and mystery. Furthermore, the one who desires to know is simply the human subject, which in its heart is both "theologian" and "scientist." In the search for ultimate truth,

38. Mariano Artigas, *The Mind of the Universe: Understanding Science and Religion* (Philadelphia: Templeton Foundation, 2000), 207–21, here 221.

39. This argument is well made by Stephen M. Barr, *Modern Physics and Ancient Faith* (Notre Dame: University of Notre Dame Press, 2003), 19–32.

therefore, both the Bible and science have their place. Most people have a fairly robust idea of what science is and what it does; the same, however, cannot be said of most people with respect to the Bible. Our next chapter, therefore, will deal with the question, what is the Bible, and what might we learn from it?

CHAPTER
2

THE BIBLE

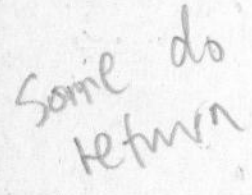

Just as from the heavens the rain and snow come down
And do not return there till they have watered the earth,
making it fertile and fruitful,
Giving seed to [the one] who sows and bread to [the one] who eats,
So shall my word be that goes forth from my mouth;
It shall not return to me void, but shall do my will,
achieving the end for which I sent it.

—Isaiah 55:10-11, NAB

For the word of God is living and active . . .

—Hebrews 4:12, RSV

Introduction

In this chapter, the focus falls on discovering what the Bible is all about on its own terms. Its main question is, how is the Bible to be interpreted? Fundamentalists and creationists regard the Bible as the source of truth about creation to the exclusion of physics and biology. They want nothing to do with methods of interpretation that take science seriously, since they cannot believe that science might be a way to know God. Extremists on the other side of the spectrum regard the Bible with contempt, since they cannot accept that biblical faith enables knowledge of ultimate reality. They regard science alone as the source of knowledge, and the only interpretation of the Bible they are interested in is that which reduces it to absurdity.

With just a little study, however, most people easily see that on its own terms the Bible is not in conflict with science, and that its theological perspectives have been preserved and studied over thousands of years for very good reason. In this chapter, I will provide some historical background to the Bible and the beginnings of modern biblical study. In doing so, I will espouse many different methods of interpretation that scholars have developed, though there will not be space to describe them in any detail. Chapter 5 will also focus on the Bible, devoting more space to questions of method and to some specific scriptural texts and themes. Second, in this chapter, I will emphasize that texts must be interpreted in light of the historical contexts that gave rise to them. In the absence of considering the culture, history, and language of a text, responsible interpretation is almost impossible. Finally, I will highlight the faith perspectives of the biblical communities and writers. The texts only exist because of faith, and indeed the faith behind the texts is the reason they have value for us today.

A large part of this chapter will defend the view that a historical-critical approach to interpretation of the Bible easily coheres with also taking the Bible seriously at the level of faith. Not everyone is convinced of this. Historical criticism (think "historical *analysis*") got started in the late seventeenth century with a largely polemical intent. The hope was that applying scientific and rational analysis to the Bible might persuade people not to use it as a weapon against one another. As we will see, that hope was not fulfilled in its time, though it has borne fruit in the centuries since. In any event, many see such analysis as a threat to the Bible, since it emphasizes more the human than the divine character of the texts. In itself this view of historical criticism is correct, but as I shall emphasize, study of the Bible's humanity does not compromise its divine character—no more than study of our own humanity compromises the belief that we are created in the divine image. God is present to us because of our humanity, not in spite of it; so also the Bible can be seen as inspired in and through its human language and perspectives.

Carefully employed, historical criticism enables a deeper appreciation of the theology in the texts. It helps us recognize the type of knowledge that the Bible conveys in its figurative language, rich symbolism, and dramatic narrative. It therefore easily demonstrates that the Bible's narratives of creation are not science in any sense—and more positively, that they have something to add to our knowing of creation that science cannot offer.

The Problem of Content

The Bible is not just one thing. Jews, for instance, from whose ancient tradition the Bible had its first origins, call the Bible the TANAKH[1] and the books that they include within it are the same as the books that comprise the Old Testament in Protestant Bibles. Catholics also have an Old Testament, of course, but they include books that Jews and Protestants do not regard as Sacred Scripture (e.g., Sirach, Wisdom of Solomon, and 1–2 Maccabees). Just in terms of the Bible's contents, therefore, we already have three Bibles: (1) the TANAKH of Judaism; (2) the Protestant Bible, which adds the New Testament to the books of the Jewish Bible; and (3) the Catholic Bible, which agrees with Protestants about the New Testament, but also adds further Old Testament books. If we were to add the Orthodox churches to our discussion, the issue would be even more complex. The story behind this multiplication of Bibles can be told fairly briefly.

TANAKH is a word formed from an acronym, TaNaK, in which the "T" stands for *Torah* (Instruction or Law), the "N" for *Nevi'im* (the Prophets), and the "K" for *Kethuvim* (the Writings).[2] Which books belonged within "the Law and the Prophets" was fairly fixed by the time of Jesus, but the books of that third section, "the Writings," are either unmentioned when the New Testament enumerates what is to be found in the Scriptures (e.g., Luke 24:27; Rom 3:21) or they are represented only by mention of "the Psalms," its first book (Luke 24:44; Acts 1:20). In other words, the canon (sacred listing) of Scriptures was only about two-thirds fixed by the time of Jesus.

During the third century BCE in Alexandria, Egypt, the Hebrew texts of the Old Testament were translated into Greek; the translation is known as the Septuagint. The Alexandrian canon included books like Sirach, Judith, and the Wisdom of Solomon, the latter originally written in Greek (but not, of course, by Solomon). Christianity was born into a world dominated by Greek; all of the New Testament was written in Greek and, not surprisingly, the version of the Old Testament that they used the

1. There are different spellings of this word; TANAKH is the spelling of the Jewish Publication Society.

2. The Torah comprises five books (Genesis–Deuteronomy). Prophets is subdivided into (1) Former prophets (six books; Joshua–Kings) and (2) Latter prophets (fifteen books; Isaiah–Malachi). Writings comprises thirteen books (Psalms–2 Chronicles), including Daniel (which Christians place among the prophets) and Chronicles, Ezra, Nehemiah, and Esther (which Christians place after Kings), and other books that Christians place earlier.

most was the Septuagint. The Bible of the earliest Christians, therefore, was the Septuagint collection. It did not include the books of the New Testament—they were not written yet—but it did include various books, which the Jews ultimately decided were not Sacred Scripture.

The further, very important, part of the story takes us deeper into Church history, especially to Jerome in the late fourth century, and to the Reformation and the Council of Trent in the sixteenth. The earliest Christians mostly relied on the Septuagint, but of course they soon began to regard Paul's letters and, slightly later, the gospels as also inspired Scripture. When 2 Timothy 3:16 speaks about "all scripture" being "inspired," the writer has in mind the Torah, the Prophets, some further texts from the Writings, and, in all probability, some of the letters of Paul. By the fourth century, the canon of the New Testament was fairly stable (letters, gospels and all), though disputes about some books—for example, Jude and Revelation—continued for centuries. The canon of the Old Testament, however, was not as settled, because great biblical scholars of the third and fourth centuries, like Origen, Athanasius, and Jerome, did not think that the Church should include books that, by that time, the Jews excluded. Jerome was perhaps the most influential of these scholars; he was the one who gave us the Latin translation (the Vulgate) scholars still use today. He made a concerted effort to convince Christians to regard as Scripture only the books approved by the Jews. He did not, however, win the day; Christians continued to use books like Judith, 1–2 Maccabees, and the additions to Esther and Daniel, though there were many who doubted their value. And that, more or less, was how things remained until the sixteenth century and the Reformation, led by Martin Luther.

One of the great battle cries of Luther and the other reformers was *scriptura sola*, "by the Bible alone" (was Christian doctrine to be determined). That focus on the Bible raised urgently the question, what is the Bible? The question was especially urgent with respect to divisive issues like prayers for the dead and purgatory, which were among the opening disputes. Luther, understandably, did not like 2 Maccabees 12:39-45, which tells the story of Judas Maccabaeus and his companions praying for their comrades who had been killed in battle. These dead comrades, it was discovered, had been wearing "sacred tokens of the idols of Jamnia" and it was concluded "that this was the reason these men had fallen." Judas urged the people to keep themselves from such sins, but also "took up a collection . . . and sent it to Jerusalem to provide for a sin offering" (2 Macc 12:40, 43, NRSV).

Most interesting is the conclusion provided by the writer of 2 Maccabees for why Judas did a good thing: he was "expecting that those who had fallen would rise again," and therefore he prayed for the dead "so that they might be delivered from their sin" (2 Macc 12:44, 45, NRSV). Such a text played into the hands of those who in Luther's time collected money to pay for indulgences, a practice that had been a source of corruption for many years, and that Luther rejected in his famous Ninety-five Theses. Luther, therefore, followed the great fourth-century theologians and others in insisting that Christians must only accept the books that were approved by the Jews. The Council of Trent (1546), not surprisingly, reacted by officially declaring the disputed texts to be fully a part of the Bible.[3] Since the sixteenth century, therefore, Christians in the churches of the West have had two different Bibles to add to the TANAKH of the Jews. In terms of content, the Bible is not just one thing.

What this history demonstrates is that the Bible, by whatever canon, is a collection of originally separate texts. These texts were not in their origins necessarily destined to be included in what believing communities of a later time called "the Bible." Indeed, as we have seen, the Jewish canon comprised a selection from among numerous texts, some of which were only included after a great deal of questioning. The Song of Songs (or Song of Solomon), for instance, was only included after considerable debate, and books like Sirach (Ecclesiasticus), Judith, and 1 Maccabees were for some period candidates for inclusion, but were ultimately excluded. An analogous selection process took place within Christianity with regard to New Testament texts. Some early New Testament manuscripts included additional texts—apocryphal books—as though they were Scripture on a par with Matthew and Romans. The book of Revelation, on the other hand, was a disputed book well past the fourth century. For both Jews and Christians, the most decisive criterion ultimately was whether a text was recognized and used by communities of faith in their worship and teaching. And that was largely determined by the character of the texts themselves and how they were interpreted.

The Problem of Interpretation

Content is only a part of the story. Far more complex, and ultimately far more important, is that the Bible is a different thing for different

3. The disputed texts are Tobit, Judith, Wisdom of Solomon, Ecclesiasticus (Sirach), Baruch (including "the letter of Jeremiah"), 1 and 2 Maccabees, and additional chapters in Esther and Daniel.

groups and individuals with regard to interpretation. Already, the story of content illustrates how, depending on context and presuppositions, and with the best of intentions, people approach the Bible in different ways and arrive at very different conclusions about what the Bible teaches. The more that interpretation enters the picture, the more complex it is to say what the Bible is. The Bible for Luther was different from the Bible for the pope not only, or even primarily, because of the differences of content but also because of the context within which each approached the task of interpretation.

The pope presupposed not only the traditions and doctrines of the Church but also his own authority to define what qualified as authentic doctrine. Luther, by contrast, rejected any notion of the pope's authority over the Bible; the Bible, he insisted—somewhat anticipating Baruch "Benedict"[4] Spinoza—must be interpreted in its own terms, from within its own texts. The Bible is the measure against which traditions and doctrines are to be measured, not vice versa. Today, Catholic scholars know well that Luther was right about many things, and Lutheran scholars that he was not right about everything. The important point, for our purposes, is that even if Luther and the pope had been in complete agreement on the *content* of the Bible, large disagreements would have still remained with respect to *interpretation*.

Notice, in fact, how content (*what* one reads) and interpretation (*how* one reads) are closely related. One illustration of this is Luther's rejection of 2 Maccabees, which had to do with his interpretation of Paul's letter to the Romans. The latter teaches the true gospel, in Luther's teaching, since it proclaims that sinners are "justified" (reconciled with God) by God's "grace" (divine gift) and by "faith" (surrender to grace), not by human "works" (Rom 3:20-28; Gal 2:15-21). For Luther, this is what the entirety of the Bible is really all about, and one does not have to be Lutheran to appreciate the genius of his insight. That story of Judas and the dead soldiers in 2 Maccabees 12, however, implies that reconciliation with God can somehow be effected by "sin offerings" paid for with money. This went right to the heart of his dispute with Rome about the selling of indulgences. For Luther, the contradiction between "justification by faith" and the story in 2 Maccabees was too much. He, therefore, reopened the ancient dispute about what books truly belonged in the Scriptures and

4. "Baruch" in Hebrew means "blessed"; after he was expelled from the Jewish synagogue of Amsterdam (more on this below), he changed his name to "Benedict," which is Latin for "blessed."

settled it in line with his interpretation of what essentially the Scriptures teach. *What* one reads and *how* one reads are mutually influential. The canon, the listing of sacred books, is important, but so also is the question of what one thinks the Bible represents, what ultimately it is about. In fact, that question—what the Bible is fundamentally about—is *the* crucial issue.

Avoiding Extreme Views about the Bible

Richard Dawkins

If the Bible is to be of help in the science-theology dialogue and its search for a deep understanding of human existence, then two opposing extremes have to be avoided. One extreme is represented most vividly by Richard Dawkins in *The God Delusion*. Though he would be happy to see the Bible remain on school curricula for its value as background to studies in literature, he otherwise sees the Bible and its teachings as pernicious, and those who take it seriously as misguided at best.[5] The error in Dawkins's interpretation of the Bible is not that he exposes its harsh and cruel texts, and the many limitations of its moral and legal prescriptions, since even the most cursory reading of the Bible has to face such texts, and theology has to think very seriously about them. If one focuses, as Dawkins does, on selected texts, then one can indeed portray the God of the Old Testament as "a petty, unjust, unforgiving control-freak" and so on.[6] He could have added "drunken soldier" (Ps 78:65) and a number of other interesting epithets.

5. Richard Dawkins, *The God Delusion* (Boston: Houghton Mifflin, 2006), 340–44.

6. *God Delusion*, 31, quoted in chapter 1 above. The quote comes at the beginning of a chapter in which Dawkins aims to convince us that "the 'God hypothesis' is a *scientific* hypothesis about the universe" (2, emphasis added). This in itself demonstrates a lack of understanding about the distinction between philosophy and theology, on the one hand, and science, on the other. The simplistic character of his argument becomes clear, for instance, when he writes: "But if science cannot answer some ultimate question, what makes anybody think that religion can?" (56). Dawkins seems to think "answers" can come in only one form. The nature of religious discourse (theology) is completely different from that of science; what counts as an "answer" in science is often only the beginning of the question in philosophy and theology. The latter simply do not deal with "answers" in anything like the manner of science. To use an analogy employed by John Haught, *God and the New Atheism: A Critical Response to Dawkins, Harris and Hitchens* (Louisville: Westminster John Knox, 2008), 84: the ink and paper of this page are subject to the analysis of science, the words are subject to the analysis of English grammar, the meaning has to do with the author's intention and—to every author's peril—with what readers derive from the words based

The problem is that to stop, as Dawkins does, at those texts as though they did not have a wider context, and as though there are not numerous other texts that offer very different portraits, demonstrates vividly the depth of his bias. A similarly one-sided description of science would focus on industrial pollution, global warming, deforestation, the industrial poisoning of thousands of people at Bhopal (India) in 1984, the dropping of atomic bombs on Hiroshima and Nagasaki in 1945, WMDs of all sorts, and any number of other acts, accidents, and artifacts of the scientific era, and then conclude that science is the curse of humankind. Any such description and rejection of science would, of course, be just as narrow and unbalanced as Dawkins's description and rejection of the Bible.

Any reasonable description and use of the Bible has to take seriously what it is about on its own terms. There is no text, anywhere in the Bible, that wants to convince its readers that God is to be thought of or worshiped as a "bloodthirsty ethnic cleanser." One of the texts from which one might derive such a notion is Deuteronomy 7:1-5:

> When the LORD[7] your God brings you into the land that you are about to enter and occupy, and he clears away many nations before you— . . . seven nations mightier and more numerous than you—and when the LORD your God gives them over to you and you defeat them, then you must utterly destroy them. Make no covenant with them and show them no mercy. Do not intermarry with them, giving your daughters to their sons or taking their daughters for your sons, for that would turn away your children from following me, to serve other gods. Then the anger of the LORD would be kindled against you, and he would destroy you quickly. But this is how you must deal with them: break down their altars, smash their pillars, hew down their sacred poles, and burn their idols with fire. (NRSV)

---

on their experience and convictions. Now, which of those three levels "explains" (provides the "answer") for the page? Obviously, all three. And note that it would be easy to add further levels. Why can words convey meaning? What is "meaning"? Dawkins wants us to stop at the levels where things can be measured, but there is no competition between the "science" of this page (universe) and its deeper "meanings."

7. Capitalized LORD in the RSV, NRSV, NAB, and other translations stands for the sacred name YHWH (pron. Yahweh), the name revealed to Moses at the burning bush (Exod 3:14). YHWH is the sacred name that is not to be taken in vain (Exod 20:7); it contrasts with the generic name "God" (*Elohim* in Hebrew).

If one reads that text in its context—the most basic requirement of interpretation—it is easy to see that its intent is to stress God's love for, and protection of, Israel:

> For you are a people sacred to the LORD, your God; he has chosen you from all the nations on the face of the earth to be a people peculiarly his own. It was not because you are the largest of all nations that the LORD set his heart on you and chose you, for you are really the smallest of all nations. It was because the LORD loved you and because of his fidelity to the oath he had sworn to your fathers, that he brought you out with his strong hand from the place of slavery, and ransomed you from the hand of Pharaoh, king of Egypt. (Deut 7:6-8, NAB)

To be sure, any full interpretation of such a text must also wrestle with the issue of its portrayal of God in relation to the other nations, and must honestly admit that ancient Israel, like other tribes and nations before and since, did on occasion practice genocide (e.g., Josh 6:21). That is a part of the critical, theological task of biblical interpretation, and it inevitably raises important questions about the Bible as "the Word of God in human language." Ancient Israel, like ancient Christians, imaged God in accordance with their own ideas, desires, and fears.

Of course, Dawkins is correct that humans use religion to justify their aggression; what he fails to consider is that humans use any ideology in warfare. Hitler, Stalin, the Khmer Rouge, and the perpetrators of genocide in Bosnia-Herzegovina and Rwanda were more reflective of atheist than of religious ideologies. Soviet and Chinese repression of religion (to name obvious examples) had everything to do with official state atheism. Sam Harris argues that when nonreligious people commit horrible violence, they do so because they are not "especially rational," but when religious people do so, it is due to religion.[8] Such an argument only demonstrates the depth of his prejudice against religion. The sad reality is that humans employ their ideologies (religious and otherwise) to justify their wars, and their best science and technology to carry it out. If we attempted to eliminate from society all of the things that people use and abuse for evil purposes, religion would not be the only candidate for elimination.

8. Sam Harris, *Letter to a Christian Nation* (New York: Vintage Books, 2008), 40–41. Harris even tries to convince us, based on one of Hitler's speeches (!), that Hitler was more Christian than atheist.

Religion indeed deserves all of the criticism that it brings on itself by the evils perpetrated in its name, but there is more than enough evidence to show that even if religion disappeared, wars and violence would not disappear with it. At their worst, humans use and abuse whatever gifts they have for their self-serving ends. That only makes all the more urgent the task of attending carefully to both science and religion in the crucial task of trying to understand human beings. Dawkins's and Harris's rejection of the Bible and religion is very much like the fundamentalist rejection of evolution; it is born of an outright refusal to study in depth the thing being rejected.

Biblical Fundamentalism

The other extreme to be avoided, if the Bible is to be of value in the science-theology dialogue, is an insistence on fundamentalist interpretation. Just like Dawkins, fundamentalists have important points to make that must be attended to. Fundamentalism has its origins *not* in the ancient church, as some imagine, but in the late nineteenth century, as Christian scholarship in the United States reacted against the new scholarship of science, particularly Darwinism, on the one hand, and of historical criticism, on the other. Darwinism and historical criticism became linked at a very early point, since more liberal scholars, who accepted the historical-critical method as applied to the Bible, also tended to accept Darwinism. In their account of the 1873 conference of the Evangelical Alliance, Roy Harrisville and Walter Sundberg remark that "most evangelical leaders" at the conference "believed that the science of evolution, like the science of biblical criticism, reduced all events to mundane causality."[9] This belief epitomizes the confusion between science and biblical theology that continues to plague the science-theology dialogue to the present time.

However appropriate and well-intentioned the protest against reducing "all events to mundane causality" was, the fundamentalist solution produces far more problems than it solves. If historical criticism has sometimes gone too far with its endless analyzing and atomizing of the biblical text, fundamentalism has equally gone too far with its central claim of biblical "inerrancy." As expressed at the 1910 Presbyterian General Assembly, the doctrine claimed:

9. Roy A. Harrisville and Walter Sundberg, *The Bible in Modern Culture: Baruch Spinoza to Brevard Childs* (Grand Rapids, MI: Wm. B. Eerdmans, 1995, 2002), 197.

> It is an essential doctrine of the Word of God and our Standards, that the Holy Spirit did so inspire, guide and move the writers of Holy Scriptures as to keep them from error.[10]

A more recent statement expresses the same claim in purely positive terms. In its statement of "The Baptist Faith and Message," the Southern Baptist Convention in 2000 places its teaching about "the Bible" *before* "God" and "God the Son" (Jesus) and claims that the Bible

> is a *perfect* treasure of divine instruction. It has God for its author, salvation for its end, and truth, *without any mixture of error*, for its matter. Therefore, all Scripture is *totally true and trustworthy*.[11]

First, it is theologically strange, to say the least, to place the creedal statement about "the Bible" ahead of the statements on God and Jesus. It is no doubt guided by the Reformation principle of "Scripture alone" and by the American Baptist tradition as it reacted against (scientific) "naturalism" in the 1920s. The thinking seems to be that the Bible is "*the supreme standard* by which *all* human conduct, creeds, and religious opinions should be tried."[12] But such thinking, as I will emphasize below, demands far more of the Bible than the Bible claims or can provide. Second, such a statement about the Bible implicitly requires believers to accept, for example, that its many texts permitting and legislating slavery (e.g., Exod 21; Eph 6) are "true and trustworthy." Attempts to circumvent this difficulty by claiming that the texts in question are to be understood symbolically, that slavery in biblical times was gentle or other such explanations, are evasive and disingenuous at best. Other, even more difficult, texts portray God as commanding Israel to slaughter its enemies—men, women, and children alike (e.g., Deut 7:1-5; 1 Sam 15:1). Once one begins also to consider the more mundane, but nevertheless numerous, instances of other types of "errors" and contradictions in the Scriptures, then claims of the Bible being "*totally* true and trustworthy" and "*the* standard" for "*all* human conduct, creeds, and religious opinions" quickly become less and less convincing.

10. Robert Hasting Nichols, "Fundamentalism in the Presbyterian Church," *The Journal of Religion* 5:1 (January 1925): 18.

11. The statement is easily available online at the Southern Baptist Convention web site, accessed October 16, 2010, http://www.sbc.net/bfm/bfm2000.asp#i, emphasis added.

12. See previous note.

The same has to be said of fundamentalism as was said in response to the extreme views of Richard Dawkins: any reasonable description and use of the Bible has to take seriously what it is all about on its own terms. In 1923, after the General Assembly of the Presbyterian Church reaffirmed the inerrancy doctrine of 1910, 150 ministers, who *rejected* the doctrine, signed "An Affirmation Designed to Safeguard the Unity and Liberty of the Presbyterian Church." Hundreds of others, many of them conservatives, wishing "that the Church have room for ideas differing from their own," also subsequently signed the affirmation. Its statement regarding inerrancy was (and is) beyond reproach:

> *There is no assertion in the Scriptures that their writers were kept "from error."* The Confession of Faith [of the Presbyterian Church] does not make this assertion; and it is significant that *this assertion is not to be found* in the Apostles' Creed or the Nicene Creed or in any of the great Reformation confessions.[13]

As this statement demonstrates, fundamentalists claim more for the Bible than the Bible claims for itself. The Bible never claims to be "perfect" or "totally true and trustworthy" for the simple reason that "the Bible" as such never existed in the time of its originators! As already indicated, "the Bible" only came into existence very slowly, from "Torah" and "Prophets" to "Writings" and "New Testament" over many centuries. When its authors considered what "the Word of God" is, they did not point to themselves and their writings, but they pointed *away* from themselves, to creation (Gen 1–2; Pss 8 and 19) and to God's actions in history (Ps 78; Isa 55:10-13). When Hebrews 4:12 says that "the word of God is living and active," it is not referring to the Bible, but to the "word of God" that is infinitely greater than any text, and that can only be discerned by faith. When Jeremiah's scroll, containing "all the words" that God had spoken to him to that point, was burned by King Jehoiakim (Jer 36), "the word of God" was *not* destroyed. Indeed, if all the Bibles in the entire world were destroyed, the "word of God" would still be "living and active." It is a serious theological error to think otherwise.[14]

13. Nichols, "Fundamentalism in the Presbyterian Church," 30–31, emphasis added.

14. Those familiar with Gerhard Maier, *The End of the Historical-Critical Method*, trans. E. W. Leverenz and R. F. Norden (Eugene, OR: Wipf & Stock, 1977), may wonder what I make of his central assertion that "the Bible itself gives no key with which to distinguish between the Word of God and Scripture" (16). He is correct; there is no clear criterion. The task of articulating the Word (the gospel) is broadly theological, not just biblical, but in any

I was once leading a forum on the death penalty. There were fifty or sixty participants—some more liberal, others more fundamentalist—and the discussion was very lively, with some arguing in favor of capital punishment and others against. I was trying to make the point that we cannot simply be guided by the Bible, since the Bible prescribes the death penalty not only for murder (Gen 9:6) but also for adultery (Lev 20:10), working on the Sabbath (Num 15:32-36), taking the Lord's name in vain (Lev 24:10-23), disrespecting parents (Lev 20:9; Deut 21:18-21), and any number of other offenses. "God gave us the Bible," I said, "but God also gave us brains and expects us to use them both." My (comparatively) liberal attitude toward the Bible severely irritated one young man, who finally stood up and waved his Bible vigorously in the air, while shouting, "This is God! This is God! This is God!" That identification of the Bible with God, and with God's precise message for all humanity—as though God, and what God has to say to the world, were confined to the pages of the Bible—is probably the single most serious error that biblical fundamentalists make.

Those who accept such a notion will not be able to accept what I say about the Bible in these pages. The Bible is *not* God, and when we describe the Bible as "the *word* of God," we need to immediately add the qualification, "the word of God *in the languages of people*." Dawkins and fundamentalists alike make the serious error of insisting that the Bible is to be interpreted according to the surface meaning of its words. If there are texts that *portray* God as violent and vengeful, then Dawkins insists that religion's God *is* violent and vengeful, and therefore both God and the Bible are to be rejected. If Genesis 1 *portrays* God as creating the universe in six days, then fundamentalists insist that God made it in *precisely* that time frame and evolution is to be rejected. What is needed on both sides is a great deal more respect for, and study of, the Bible on the one hand, evolution on the other. With regard to the Bible, both sides need to consider far more carefully what is involved in the task of biblical interpretation.

Interpreting the Bible: The Problem of Method

The first thing that is needed in the interpretation of any text, but most especially the Bible, is a good dose of humility. At the very least,

---

event it is not a matter of eliminating texts of Scripture as though they had nothing to do with revelation, but simply of insisting that when inquiry is made as to "what the Spirit is saying," it is not enough to hand over the Bible as though it were the full answer! It is always a matter of what the Bible can contribute, and how it relates to all of the other sources and ways in which we discern the word of God—everything from poetry to hard science.

this means that the interpreter must first be an attentive reader or, one might say, listener; full understanding is not easy to attain. If you were to write an article for the newspaper about some important topic, you would be deeply offended—and justifiably so—if someone were to interpret your words in a manner contrary to your meaning. The advantage you would have is that you could correct the misinterpretation by a further article or even perhaps by personally confronting the one who either misunderstood or deliberately distorted your words. The biblical writers, of course, have no such advantage, because of the vast distance of time, not to mention the distances of culture and language. Modern interpreters of the Bible, therefore, must attend to the ancient writers with considerable care and humility, as one might listen, say, to representatives of a distant and different culture. Such listening has to begin with taking the speakers seriously in their own terms, no matter how strange they may seem.

That way of introducing the task of interpreting the Bible already raises a host of questions, not to say *objections*, which interpreters of all sorts have been raising for many decades. Some interpreters, especially, though not only, represented by fundamentalists, would point out that the Bible has "*God* for its author," and therefore all talk of "the ancient writers" immediately biases the discussion in the wrong direction. Even more than humility, they might stress the need for faith. Others, particularly historians of biblical interpretation, would remind me, quite rightly, that people have been interpreting the texts for as long as there have been texts, in other words, for millennia. There are now layers upon layers of interpretation, and unless a reader has somehow been hermetically sealed away from the Western world, interpretation is bound to be deeply influenced by the "meanings" already discovered. Catholics find "Catholicism" in the Bible, Lutherans "Lutheranism," and so on. Still others, especially the postmodernists, would appropriately ask, among other things, What is the *meaning* of meaning? "Meaning" is hardly ever something that is simply extracted *from* a text; it inevitably also includes, and is sometimes utterly dominated by, the meaning one *wishes to find* in it. In any case, there is no such thing as "*the* meaning" of something; meaning is determined not merely by the texts but by the interpreters, especially those who are in power.

These issues, and more besides, are all important within hermeneutics (the art and science of interpretation); it would take more than just another book to address them all. I will cut to the chase with a somewhat wide-ranging discussion of the historical-critical method, which developed during the Enlightenment (late seventeenth–eighteenth centuries) and has largely dominated interpretation ever since. Almost any discussion of the Bible nowadays has to take the historical-critical method into account, and it is necessary at this early point to explain my use of it. This is especially necessary since in recent decades the method has increasingly been criticized, and even abandoned, by many scholars.Nevertheless, historical criticism continues to be the backbone of modern biblical studies, and any attempt to say what the Bible is or to take it seriously on its own terms cannot avoid engagement with it. Even as careful an interpreter as Pope Benedict XVI, in his recent book on *Jesus of Nazareth*, insists that the historical-critical method is "indispensable" for study of the gospels and of Jesus, although—reflecting the same hesitation as other scholars—he also sounds several precautionary notes.[15]

The Historical-Critical Method: Benedict Spinoza

"Historical-critical method" is an umbrella term, covering numerous methods. All of them presuppose the human origins and character of the Bible, and investigate the texts as literature *almost like any other body of literature.* I have to write "*almost* like . . ." because the method has never fully extricated itself from seeing the Bible as special, and from agonizing over the question of how the Bible's human aspects cohere with faith's conviction that it is divinely inspired. Even the efforts of the most skeptical scholars, those determined to knock the Bible from its pedestal, testify to the unique role the Bible has played, and continues to play, within Judaism and Christianity and within Western culture of which those religions are such an important part. Most scholars of the historical-critical method, however, have been—at least in their own minds—far more supporters of faith than opponents. Whether they succeeded or not, their intention has nearly always been to understand the Bible more fully, and thereby to enable it to speak more directly and persuasively.

The method was born, in part, out of the Enlightenment's conviction that the Bible was being misused, and needed to be rescued from centuries of dogmatic and pious accretions. The origins of this conviction lay in the Renaissance and particularly the Reformation. As mentioned earlier, Luther wanted to rescue the Bible from the pope and the clergy. Luther did not, however, focus on the Bible's human character; its di-

15. Joseph Ratzinger, Pope Benedict XVI, *Jesus of Nazareth: From the Baptism in the Jordan to the Transfiguration*, trans. Adrian J. Walker (New York: Doubleday, 2007), xv–xxiii, here xv.

vine inspiration was no less important for him than for the pope. Making the Bible's human aspects central to the issue of how to interpret it began with Benedict Spinoza (1632–77) in his *Theological-Political Treatise* (1670).[16] Other scholars, like Thomas Hobbes (1588–1679), an English philosopher, and Richard Simon (1638–1712), a French Catholic priest, also made contributions, but it was Spinoza who most fully developed a method and philosophical reasoning for it.

Because of religious persecution of Jews, Spinoza's family had moved from Spain to Amsterdam, where Spinoza was born. As a child he was educated in the Hebrew Scriptures and tradition, but as a young man he increasingly turned to the study of philosophy, and even to Latin and study of the New Testament. Eventually, his differences with his ancestral tradition caused him, at the age of twenty-three, to be excommunicated from the Jewish community. The precise reasons for this are not known, but it is clear that Spinoza dedicated his life, at some cost to himself, to philosophy in the pursuit of truth. In some quarters, Spinoza is given rather bad press, but there can be no doubt that he was a man not only of great intellect but also of considerable integrity.

Spinoza wanted, above all, to defuse the Bible as a weapon of religious violence and persecution. "The basis and foundation of all Scripture" can be summarized, he said, in a few simple doctrines that revolve around God who is "supremely just and merciful" and who requires obedience. This obedience "consists solely in justice and charity, or love towards one's neighbour":[17]

> Scripture itself tells us quite clearly over and over again ["in both testaments"] what every man should do in order to serve God, declaring that the entire Law consists in this alone, to love one's neighbour . . . Therefore this commandment is the one and only guiding principle for the entire common faith of mankind, and through this commandment alone should be determined all the tenets of faith that every man is in duty bound to accept.[18]

If Spinoza's readers had focused on these aspects of his teaching, perhaps he and his work would have been better received. But the focus fell, not

16. Baruch Spinoza, *Theological-Political Treatise* (Gebhardt Edition), 2nd ed., trans. S. Shirley (Indianapolis: Hackett Publishing, 2001).

17. Spinoza, *Theological-Political Treatise*, 91, 162.

18. Spinoza, *Theological-Political Treatise*, 159.

surprisingly, on the method he proposed and on what his method suggested about the nature of the Bible.

"All knowledge of the Bible," he insisted, "is to be sought *from the Bible alone*" and from "a historical study" of it. Such study requires knowledge of the biblical languages, especially Hebrew, and of

> the circumstances relevant to all the extant books of the prophets, giving the life, character and pursuits of the author of every book, detailing who he was, on what occasion and at what time and for whom and in what language he wrote. Again, [historical study] should relate what happened to each book, how it was first received, into whose hands it fell, how many variant versions there were, by whose decision it was received into the canon, and, finally, how all the books, now universally regarded as sacred, were united into a single whole.[19]

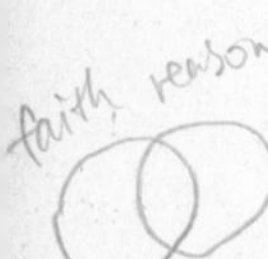

Spinoza was convinced that Scripture's purpose was simply to inculcate love of God and neighbor; in other words, "Scripture teaches only piety, not philosophy."[20] He, therefore, denied to the Bible and theology the realm of objective truth; the latter was exclusively the domain of reason and philosophy.[21] In theological terms, his view of faith was far too narrow; consistent with the Enlightenment critique of religion, he viewed faith as separate from reason, an idea that is properly criticized in modern philosophy.[22] For Spinoza, however, the nature of biblical language made such a conclusion unavoidable; it is full of contradictions and

> speaks of God and events in terms far from correct, its aim being not to convince on rational grounds [the domain of philosophy] but to appeal to and engage men's fantasy and imagination.[23]

19. Spinoza, *Theological-Political Treatise*, 87–90.

20. Spinoza, *Theological-Political Treatise*, 165, 153.

21. Spinoza, *Theological-Political Treatise*, 169, 155. Spinoza believed that true (objective) knowledge of God derives exclusively from philosophy, not theology. On the other hand, since he so closely identified "God" with "Nature" and since humans are part of nature, humans have a direct intuitive knowledge of God (10). Indeed, reason is "the greatest of all gifts and light divine" (167).

22. For example, John D. Caputo, "Open Theology—Or What Comes After Secularism?," *Bulletin of the Council of Societies for the Study of Religion* 37:2 (April 2008): 45–46. For a fuller discussion, see his *Philosophy and Theology*.

23. Spinoza, *Theological-Political Treatise*, 168, 180.

Since divine revelation only intended to inculcate obedience, what the prophets and evangelists experienced, and wrote down, was imaginative and metaphorical; it had nothing to do with truths about nature or God's "absolute essence."[24] Spinoza thereby rejected the historical, and philosophical, accuracy of the Bible, its "truth" in that sense. Study of the Bible largely came down to study of "the nature and properties of the language"[25] in which it was written, and all of those matters about historical circumstances, authors' intentions, variant versions, and so on that are enumerated in the above quote.

Spinoza was guided in his thinking by the emerging scientific method; he was also guided by his desire to show that the Bible ought not to be a source of "so much quarreling and such bitter feuding."[26] But the latter was largely forgotten. It was what his rational and historical analysis suggested about the nature of the Bible, which was remembered both by those who denounced his work as "blasphemous" and "diabolical"[27] and by those who pursued it in their own studies. These scholars, as already said, have mostly been believers in a way that Spinoza was not, and they labored—with considerable success—to use historical-criticism for deeper understanding of the Bible. Numerous modern translations and the many aids for biblical study—dictionaries, concordances, commentaries beyond counting—that are easily available today all attest to the explosion of research that Spinoza sparked. And, truth be told, Spinoza's idea that the Bible should inspire love rather than violence and warfare has, at least for the most part, slowly been heeded.

It is also the case, however, that if scholars have labored to put Spinoza's method of biblical interpretation into practice, they have also labored under the pressure of its central claims. If proper understanding requires historical and linguistic analysis, if the miracles were not divine interventions into human affairs,[28] if the Bible's assertions are subject to the critique of human reason, and if who and what God is cannot be known from biblical texts, then has not "the Bible" been utterly destroyed? How can a method of interpretation that makes understanding dependent on history, and subservient to knowledge derived from science and philosophy, possibly help anyone to read the Bible with faith, and derive truth from it?

24. Spinoza, *Theological-Political Treatise*, 155.
25. Spinoza, *Theological-Political Treatise*, 88.
26. Spinoza, *Theological-Political Treatise*, 86.
27. Spinoza, *Theological-Political Treatise*, vii.
28. Spinoza, *Theological-Political Treatise*, chap. 6.

In their critical history of the method, Roy Harrisville and Walter Sundberg reflect these and further concerns. They quote Gerhard Maier, who believes that the method should be completely abandoned:

> The most important objection is that historical criticism over against a possible divine revelation presents an inconclusive and false counterpart which basically maintains human arbitrariness and its standards in opposition to the demands of revelation. Therefore, because this method is not suited to the subject, in fact even opposes its obvious tendency, we must reject it.[29]

The heart of Maier's objection is that the Bible has a central role in faith as "the witness of divine revelation" and, faced with divine revelation, it is not for scholars (or anyone else) to place what God has to say on trial, so to speak, cross-examine it and pronounce judgment on it by the standards of "human arbitrariness." The persuasiveness of Maier's protest derives from the simple question, does the Bible comprise divine revelation or not? All who reverence biblical faith (Jewish and Christian alike) easily get the point of the protest. And yet Maier's radical solution—the abandoning of the method—has not persuaded most scholars. It goes beyond what Harrisville and Sundberg believe is necessary, and has not persuaded careful interpreters like Benedict XVI.

A further, much more substantive, challenge to the value of the historical-critical method has been articulated recently by James Kugel in his 2007 book *How to Read the Bible*.[30] Kugel, an orthodox Jew and former Harvard professor, knows the method well, and he is the leading expert on the more ancient approaches that the method has largely replaced since the Enlightenment, and that he now believes interpreters need to rediscover. There is much of Kugel's book with which I agree, but I am convinced that his rejection of historical criticism goes too far. The point of closest agreement, I believe, is Kugel's "Very Idea of the Bible," that ultimately the Scriptures are all about "standing up close" and being "God's familiar servants."[31] The greatest disagreement has to do with his conviction that "what Scripture means" primarily has to do with "what the ancient interpreters have always held it to mean."[32] As I see it, if we

29. *The End of the Historical-Critical Method*, 25, quoted in Harrisville and Sundberg, *Bible in Modern Culture*, 60.

30. James L. Kugel, *How to Read the Bible: A Guide to Scripture Then and Now* (New York: Free Press, 2007).

31. Kugel, *How to Read the Bible*, 682, 685.

32. Kugel, *How to Read the Bible*, 681.

want to know what the Bible is, and if it is to be a guide in the science-theology dialogue, then we must attend at least as carefully to Spinoza and his successors—though not to all of them or all of their ideas—as to "the ancient interpreters." Discussion of Kugel's "Very Idea of the Bible" will help to clarify the strengths and weaknesses of the historical-critical method, its value for relating science with faith, and why religious faith has to be foundational in biblical interpretation.

The "Four Assumptions" of the Ancient Interpreters and "The Very Idea of the Bible" (James Kugel)

Kugel's strongest statement against historical criticism, it seems to me—speaking as one, like Kugel, who values and believes in the Bible—is when he says that with the historical-critical method, "learning *from* the Bible gradually turned to learning *about* it."[33] This is largely correct, in my view, but a simple, initial response is that surely we can better learn from it, if we know more about it; in other words, the one dynamic does not exclude the other. Kugel, however, sees the method as "quite irreconcilable"[34] with the mode of interpretation of the ancient interpreters. At that point, I simply disagree. However, before getting into a detailed response to Kugel, a fuller description of some of his major ideas is in order, beginning with the paragraph from which the quotation above derives:

> With the emphasis on reading the Bible in human terms and in its historical context also came a subtle shift in tone. As modern Biblical scholarship gained momentum, studying the Bible itself was joined with, and eventually overshadowed by, studying the historical reality behind the text (including how the text itself came to be). In the process, learning *from* the Bible gradually turned to learning *about* it. Such a shift might seem slight at first, but ultimately it changed a great deal. The person who seeks to learn *from* the Bible is smaller than the text; he crouches at its feet, waiting for its instruction or insights. Learning *about* the text generates the opposite posture. The text moves from subject to object; it no longer speaks but is spoken about, analyzed, and acted upon. The insights are now all the reader's, not the text's, and anyone can see the results. This difference in tone, as

33. Kugel, *How to Read the Bible*, 666, emphasis in the original.
34. Kugel, *How to Read the Bible*, 687.

> much as any specific insight or theory, is what has created the great gap between the Bible of ancient interpreters and that of modern scholars.[35]

The "ancient interpreters" who, in Kugel's view, provide the best model for biblical interpretation "flourished from around 300 BCE to 200 CE or so."[36] They were mostly anonymous scholars who wrote some texts (like Sirach, Jubilees, and the Dead Sea Scrolls commentaries) but whose contributions are now mostly known in their gathering of the biblical texts and, especially, in the method of interpretation that they fostered. Their work was deeply formative of ancient Judaism and, via Judaism, of ancient Christianity. What the ancient believers, Jews and Christians alike, canonized, says Kugel, was "not only the text but their own peculiar way of reading and interpreting it."[37]

The initial impetus for their work was the great tragedy of the exile in Babylon (c. 597–538 BCE) following the defeat of Judah by the Babylonians and the destruction of Jerusalem and the temple in 586 BCE. During and following the exile, Jews gathered and edited their sacred texts and began to wrestle with the questions of how life as God's chosen people was to continue in the very different circumstances of being ruled, even in their own land, by foreigners. They looked for the answers in their ancient texts. Jewish scholars, therefore, not only copied, preserved, and edited the texts, but they also began to derive from them how God wanted them to live in their new circumstances. This process brought about a dramatic change in how the texts were understood:

> It is difficult to overstate the importance of this change. From now on, the books in Israel's sacred library would have a new role: these books may have been written long ago, but they were not just about things that happened in the past. Carefully analyzed, the words of these ancient texts might reveal a message about how people ought to arrange their affairs now and in the future.[38]

The change was profound with respect both to thinking about the texts and to thinking about God; from now on, the *texts*, more than history and nature, were the key to understanding God.

35. Kugel, *How to Read the Bible*, 666.
36. Kugel, *How to Read the Bible*, xii.
37. Kugel, *How to Read the Bible*, 679.
38. Kugel, *How to Read the Bible*, 10.

If one surveys "the vast body of ancient interpretations, we can gain a rather clear picture," says Kugel, "of what their authors were assuming about the biblical text."[39] There were, says Kugel, "Four Assumptions" that seem to have been the guiding principles of interpretation. "No one ever sat down and formulated" them,[40] but they clearly were operative for many centuries among both Jewish and Christian scholars. Even after scholars had devised further methods of interpretation, these assumptions largely remained as guiding principles and, in fact, Kugel properly says, "to a remarkable degree, they continue to color the way people read the Bible right down to the present day."[41] It is these assumptions and the underlying mode of interpretation they embody that transformed the collection of Israel's ancient texts into "the Bible."

First, "the Bible was a fundamentally cryptic text"; its true meaning was not necessarily obvious, and often required considerable imagination, ingenuity, and knowledge of other parts of Scripture to work out. The importance of this first assumption becomes clearer in the other three. Second, "the Bible was a book of lessons directed to readers in their own day." To be sure, it spoke of past persons and events, but its descriptions, language, laws, and imagery were all "intended for people . . . in the interpreters' own time."[42] As Paul wrote to the Corinthians regarding punishments Israel received in their desert wanderings, "these things happened to them as a lesson, but they were *written down for our instruction*" (1 Cor 10:11). It is easy to see how the application of this assumption—working out the present meaning from the ancient incident or law—required the first assumption. Third, the ancient interpreters "assumed that the Bible contained no contradictions or mistakes . . . [It] is an utterly consistent, seamless, perfect book." If one text *seemed* to be inconsistent with or contradictory of another, then it was simply a matter of looking deeper and finding the true, divinely purposed, meaning (first assumption, again). Finally, it was assumed "that the entire Bible is essentially a divinely given text, a book in which God speaks directly or through His prophets." Even the psalms, though they were prayers

39. Kugel, *How to Read the Bible*, 14. In an earlier book, *The Bible As It Was* (Cambridge, MA: Belknap Press of Harvard University, 1997), Kugel describes many of the major "exegetical [interpretive] motifs" of the ancient interpreters, and provides there a fuller description of "The World of the Ancient Biblical Interpreters" (1–49) than is provided in the more recent volume.

40. Kugel, *How to Read the Bible*, 14.

41. Kugel, *How to Read the Bible*, 16.

42. Kugel, *How to Read the Bible*, 14, 15.

addressed *to* God, "were written under divine inspiration . . . or even directly dictated to David, their traditional author."[43]

The advantage of such interpretation was that it saved the texts from their historical strangeness and made them immediately applicable, once sufficient ingenuity was applied, to contemporary living. It also enabled the deceits and other faults of biblical heroes to be explained as nothing of the kind. Thus, for example, in the famous story of Abraham and Isaac (Gen 22:1-13), "God tested Abraham" because (as in the book of Job) God was answering a challenge from Satan about human faith. God, of course, always knew that Abraham would be faithful—why else would God have chosen him?—but the test vindicated God's wisdom. Further, Abraham did not deceive Isaac, because in Genesis 22:8 what he says to his son, according to the interpreters, is, "God Himself will provide. The lamb for the burnt offering *is my son*."[44] Everyone agrees that the latter verse actually reads, "God Himself will provide the lamb for the burnt offering, my son," but that, of course, suggests deceit on Abraham's part, and such views of the great patriarch were problematic; a solution had to be found. Similar ingenuity was practiced by Jewish and Christian interpreters for centuries. For those who might see circumcision, for example, as strange or barbaric, Philo, a great Jewish philosopher (c. 15 BCE–50 CE), explained that its true meaning had to do with, among other things, "the excision of the pleasures which delude the mind."[45] Saint Paul, a near contemporary, came up with an analogous spiritual interpretation in his debate with Jewish Christians in Rome (Rom 2:27-29). If the gospels appeared to contradict one another, Tatian (c. 120–73), in his *Diatessaron*, exemplified one of the ways in which interpreters harmonized them. The interpretations were ingenious, and often very beautiful, but they rarely attended to the original intentions of the storytellers or the contexts of the writers.

With only a little thought, one can see that, as Kugel says, the four assumptions all remain operative today in one way or another. When some modern fundamentalists, for instance, insist that the book of Revelation and other texts (e.g., Daniel) are all about events of the modern period, demonstrating that "these are the last days," they essentially affirm—whether consciously or not—these four assumptions. But even more lib-

43. Kugel, *How to Read the Bible*, 15–16.

44. Kugel, *How to Read the Bible*, 12–13, emphasis added.

45. Philo, "The Special Laws," I:9, *The Works of Philo: Complete and Unabridged*, trans. C. D. Yonge (Peabody, MA: Hendrickson, 1993), 534.

eral scholars, who would utterly disagree with such an interpretation of Daniel and Revelation, mostly affirm the second and fourth assumptions (that the Bible has present relevance, and is divinely inspired). In fact, as will soon be clear, I am among the "more liberal scholars," though—as was true for the ancient interpreters, and remains true for scholars of all stripes today—my understanding of the assumptions is nuanced by my particular traditions and beliefs.

Kugel, of course, is *not* a fundamentalist, though he is vividly aware of the connections between the assumptions of the ancient interpreters and modern fundamentalism. He is, as noted already, a scholar of high standing, "who has spent most of his life studying and teaching modern biblical scholarship."[46] He has become convinced, however, that it is "irreconcilable" with what he sees as the irreplaceable guidance of the ancient interpreters and their "definitive reinterpretations"[47] of the biblical texts. The reason for this is not that he rejects the conclusions of the historical-critical method, as do fundamentalists. In fact, he knows that modern biblical scholarship has produced "spectacular results" and throughout his book he provides a detailed sampling of them from throughout the Old Testament, including the "Documentary Hypothesis" on the authorship of the Pentateuch (the first five books: Gen–Deut).[48]

The roots of the hypothesis go back to Hobbes, Spinoza, and Simon, all of whom speculated that Moses may not have been the (only) author of the Pentateuch. What developed by the nineteenth century was the notion, most fully elaborated by Julius Wellhausen (1844–1918), that the Pentateuch comprises four major sources, all of them deriving from long after the time of Moses. As Kugel says, "Some elements of Wellhausen's approach have been modified over time," but its "basic idea . . . has nonetheless survived."[49] According to this well-tested hypothesis, these sources (named Jahwist, Elohist, Deuteronomist, and Priestly) not only have different perspectives on God, and on events, characters, and laws of the narrative, but on these things and others they also sometimes flatly contradict one another.[50] Kugel's point is not at all to deny the accuracy of such observations; his point is that such observations are

46. Kugel, *How to Read the Bible*, 672–74 (re: fundamentalism) and 45.

47. Kugel, *How to Read the Bible*, 681.

48. Kugel, *How to Read the Bible*, xii and 41–42.

49. Kugel, *How to Read the Bible*, 42.

50. Kugel, *How to Read the Bible*, 39, 298–316.

> not all there is to the Bible. Knowing about the discoveries of modern scholars may certainly cause many people (as it has me) to think about Scripture in a somewhat different way. But what Scripture is, and how it is to be read, *cannot ultimately be separated from* still larger questions, questions about *our very way of thinking about God*, and about *ourselves in relation to Him*.[51]

This is the crucial point: how are we to relate our thinking about God with our thinking about Scripture? What does faith have to do with biblical interpretation? The ancient interpreters successfully wedded their faith in God's ongoing fidelity to Israel—even in the midst of exile, slavery, and domination by foreign powers—to their manner of interpreting their ancient texts. History had turned against them; they could no longer point to military victories and land conquest as evidence of God's presence and care, but their books remained a rich resource for recognizing the hand of God amidst the pains and vicissitudes of history. "It was in these crucial centuries," says Kugel, "that the great literary heritage of the past was truly becoming Scripture." The Jews and, soon enough, the Christians also, became "people of the book." But what "the book" was, what it had been for centuries prior to Spinoza and modern biblical scholarship, was not simply a collection of texts; "what made [these texts] the Bible," says Kugel, "was their definitive reinterpretation, along the lines of the Four Assumptions of the ancient interpreters."[52]

The "definitive reinterpretation" transformed the ancient texts; they were no longer merely the record of past persons and events—the laws of Sinai, the record of the prophets' oracles, the prayers of David, or the musings of Solomon—but now they were

> a great, multifarious corpus of divinely given instruction . . . to tell people what God wanted them to know and believe *and do*, to tell them how to be God's familiar servants.[53]

What made the Bible *the Bible* was precisely this link between the texts and God's *here and now* presence and guidance in the lives of believers. Of course, to make this work, there had to be, and there was, a sense

51. Kugel, *How to Read the Bible*, 46, emphasis added.
52. Kugel, *How to Read the Bible*, 671, 681.
53. Kugel, *How to Read the Bible*, 684.

of considerable freedom over against the obvious meaning of the texts; "the words" of the Bible "were evidently not sacrosanct":

> On the contrary, . . . their apparent meaning was frequently modified or supplemented by ancient interpreters—sometimes expanded or limited in scope, very often concretized through specific applications or homey examples, sometimes (as with "an eye for an eye") actually overthrown.

Such freedom was possible, and was not contradictory of faith in the texts' divine provenance, because "even more important, *more powerful, than the words of the text* themselves" was "*the very idea of Scripture at its essence*," that is, the "standing up close" and "being God's familiar servants" that Scripture enabled. "The very idea of Scripture," Kugel concludes, "was at its origin an expression of *a certain way of apprehending God*."[54] However, with the Reformation's focus on the Bible alone, and the detaching of the Bible from ancient tradition, the way was paved for Spinoza and his successors to focus exclusively on the Bible's human characteristics. Once that process got started, then increasingly it became a matter of "learning about" the Bible rather than "from" it, and as opposed to reverent listening, analysis and criticism became dominant. At that point, the Bible, for Kugel, is no longer the Bible.

There are many who will be sympathetic with his protest against the historical-critical method, and with his description of the Bible as "a way of apprehending God." I am certainly among the sympathizers, but I remain convinced that the method is indispensable, not least because of the most fundamental belief that the texts enshrine: if we wish to know God, we must look to history and nature, and therefore, in our context, also science. From Scripture's perspective, failure to find God within human experience is a sign of obduracy and disobedience (e.g., Ps 78; Rom 1:18-23); texts derive their value from people's experience with God, that is, from faith *and* history. From the perspective of the texts, the texts alone are not enough.

A Response to Kugel: Historical Criticism *and* Faith

Kugel overstates the case when he caricatures the historical-critical method as saying that "Scripture can be understood only in the context

54. Kugel, *How to Read the Bible*, 684–85, emphasis added.

of its own time."[55] The "only" in that sentence portrays the method far too narrowly. To be sure, its *primary focus* is the ancient context and an attempt to approximate the original intention of the texts, but several factors, including lack of ancient evidence, the vagueness of what "original intention" means, and, most especially, *faith commitments*, push its practitioners beyond those questions. The practice of historical criticism with which I am concerned here has everything to do with religious faith. A strong, representative exemplar of what I mean is Gerhard von Rad (1901–71), whose voluminous work on the Old Testament has had deep influence on generations of scholars. Von Rad followed in the tradition of Wellhausen and other influential interpreters, and like them had a genuine theological interest in the Scriptures. In his *Old Testament Theology*,[56] in which he consistently presupposes and employs historical criticism, von Rad is clear that "the Subject Matter of a Theology of the Old Testament" has to be "Israel's own explicit assertions about Jahweh." Theologians, he says, must "deal directly" with such "evidence."[57]

His writing illustrates how theology both wrestles with the challenges posed by historical analysis and is also immensely enriched by it. Theology has to deal simultaneously with both history (as discovered by scholarship) and faith:

> Two pictures of Israel's history lie before us, that of modern critical scholarship and that which the faith of Israel constructed—and for the present we must reconcile ourselves to both of them. It would be stupid to dispute the right of the one or the other to exist. It would be superfluous to emphasise that each is the product of very different intellectual activities. The one is rational and "objective" . . . the other . . . is confessional and personally involved.[58]

The *differences* between the "two pictures" present us with difficult challenges, but *both* must be held in view, since "the kerygmatic [faith-proclaiming] picture," no less than the historical, derives from ancient Israel "and has not been invented."[59] A genuine analysis, therefore, must take

55. Kugel, *How to Read the Bible*, 32.

56. Gerhard von Rad, *Old Testament Theology: Volume I: The Theology of Israel's Historical Traditions*, trans. D. M. G. Stalker (New York: Harper & Row, 1962).

57. Von Rad, *Old Testament Theology*, 105.

58. Von Rad, *Old Testament Theology*, 107.

59. Von Rad, *Old Testament Theology*, 108.

seriously Israel's testimonies to God's unswerving care for Israel. Such faith in God was thoroughly historical, in the sense that it was not an abstract idea, but was always tied to what Israel believed *God had done in history and would continue to do*. We can see this faith operative in the "historical poetry" of the texts; they are "historical" in that they tell the story of foundational people and events, but they are "poetry" in that they express the "significance," including the *present* significance, of the "historical facts."[60]

> Poetry alone enabled a people to express experiences met with in the course of their history in such a way as to make the past become absolutely present . . . the later story-tellers blatantly make capital of experiences which, although they are invariably brought in on the basis of the ancient event in question, still reach forward into the story-teller's own day.[61]

Notice here how historical criticism takes the texts seriously in their own terms and thus uncovers the ongoing challenge of their faith-claims (recall assumption two).

Von Rad criticizes earlier scholarship that had "divorced Israel's confessional utterances from the divine acts in history which they so passionately embrace." Such "study of the Old Testament [had] disengaged itself more and more from theology" and had focused on "Israel's history as a history of ideas," presenting it "from the standpoint of a spiritual evolution." But disembodied ideas (and texts) are not what biblical faith (Jewish or Christian) is all about; "what Israel herself regarded as the proper subject-matter of her faith" was "the revelation in word and deed of Jahweh in history."[62] In other words historical criticism brings readers back again and again to what the Bible is ultimately all about, the experience and confession of God's presence in the midst of the actual experiences in history of biblical communities and writers. Pope Benedict XVI makes the point well:

> It is of the very essence of biblical faith to be about real historical events . . . God's actual entry into real history. If we push this history aside, Christian faith as such disappears and is recast as

60. Von Rad, *Old Testament Theology*, 111–12.
61. Von Rad, *Old Testament Theology*, 109, 110.
62. Von Rad, *Old Testament Theology*, 112, 113, 114.

> some other religion. So if history, if facticity in this sense, is an essential dimension of Christian faith, then faith must expose itself to the historical method—indeed, faith itself demands this.[63]

A major problem, therefore, with making the ancient interpreters the primary criterion of how to interpret the Bible is their neglect of the historical character of the texts, dealing with them as though they are "cryptic" (assumption one) and "perfect" (assumption three). They are nothing of the kind, and one does not have to be a biblical scholar to know that. Kugel is quite correct, as I see it, to affirm "Scripture at its essence" as having to do with "standing up close" and "being God's familiar servants." Assumptions two and four (the texts' present relevance and their divine inspiration) are fully consistent with that, but abstracting the texts from what historical criticism reveals about them—their historical particularity—threatens to divest the texts of their humanity and of their linking faith with history. Kugel is in danger of this when he says:

> What Scripture means is not what today's ingenious scholars can discover about its original meaning (and *certainly not about the events and persons it describes*), but what the ancient interpreters have always held it to mean.[64]

But how can the Bible *not* be about Sarah and Abraham, Miriam and Moses, David, Amos, Huldah, Jeremiah, Baruch, Mary, Matthew, Prisca, Paul, and so on? How can it not be about "the flesh" of the "Word made flesh" (John 1:14)? How can the Bible not be about the Bible's creators as they were, *in their own historical contexts*? Surely their lives, beliefs, and doubts; their journeys and migrations, battles, slavery, exile, persecution; and their sometimes joyous, sometimes agonized, relationship with God have to be an essential component of what the Bible is all about. Or, to put the question differently, how can it be about them *primarily* as refracted through the lens of the ancient interpreters without *also* getting at the historical nitty-gritty of their original contexts? What the ancient interpreters have to offer is no doubt of great value, but—to mirror what Kugel says of the historical-critical method—they are "not all there is to the Bible."

With their clever, but often abstruse, meanings the ancient interpreters shield us too much from the humanity of the Bible's events, char-

63. *Jesus of Nazareth*, xv.

64. Kugel, *How to Read the Bible*, 681, emphasis added.

acters, and texts, but those human aspects of the Scriptures are no less important than its divine inspiration, nor are they separate from it. In fact, precisely *what the Bible is*, is the confession of the presence of God in the very midst of human stupidity, doubts, fears, sinfulness—in other words, many of the things that the ancient interpreters did not like and for which they found a "solution." Those human realities of the Bible are surely essential to our ability today to identify with, and own, the faith that it embodies. They are also essential clues to how we might discover God's presence in the midst of our own fears and foolishness. There is no other way to experience the divinity of the Bible than through its humanity. There is no lesson more pervasive in the Bible than that God is "with us" in *all* circumstances.[65] This is true in the realm of the Bible's spiritual influence and teaching; it is also of crucial importance with respect to the role the Bible can play as we learn the discoveries of science and face up to the challenges they comprise.

Learning from the Bible and Science:
The Assumptions behind the Combination

Behind the "Four Assumptions," there are even more basic assumptions: most especially that God is the ground of all existence, that God loves humanity, and that people can "apprehend God" and what God wants of them. But there is also the assumption that human apprehension of God is contingent and imperfect; human beings sometimes get it wrong! Inspiration does not guarantee perfect people or a perfect text. The freedom of the interpreters over against the texts presupposes that God's guidance in the *present* is not simply equivalent to what the *ancient* texts said. Even the ancient interpreters had to use not only the Bible but also their intelligence—some considerable interpretive ingenuity!—to enable the texts to "speak" in the context of their concerns and questions. Kugel illustrates the truth of this with respect to Judaism's consistent privileging of the "Oral Torah" (enshrined in the Mishnah, Tosefta, Talmuds, and so on) over against the Bible itself:

> The written Torah [the Bible] may say "an eye for an eye," but what these words mean is what the Oral Torah says they mean, namely, monetary compensation for any such injury . . . The

65. "With us" does *not* mean approval of all we stand for and do; it has more to do with Rom 5:6-8, that God loves us "even while we are sinners."

> written Torah may say that Jacob went to his father "deceitfully," but the Oral Torah explains that he really didn't lie. And so on and so forth for every apparent problem, every inconsistency and contradiction or infelicity in the written text.[66]

The same process of interpretation and reinterpretation has characterized Christianity. The text is never simply *the text* devoid of the particular circumstances, needs, and hopes of individuals and communities. Hence, there is no mode of interpretation that of itself is completely satisfactory.

Interpretation, therefore, can never rely on only one method, whether that of the ancient interpreters, historical criticism, or any of the dozens of other methods that have sprouted like mushrooms in recent decades. In fact, the questions of what the act of interpretation is, what "meaning" is, what we are trying to accomplish when we interpret a biblical text and so many others, are far from easy to answer.[67] The attempts to address these questions range across numerous disciplines, extending far beyond the field of biblical studies, and far beyond the individual methods of historical criticism. Philosophy, psychology, and neuroscience are just some of the disciplines engaged with the issues of what mind is, what knowledge is, how we know what we "know," and—here theology has to engage with those disciplines—what is involved when we say, "We believe in God" or "God so loved the world."

Amidst the plethora of disciplines and methods, however, the historical-critical method remains essential, because it is, on the one hand, born of the Enlightenment and thus has a foot, so to speak, in the camp of science and its insistence on reason and method, but it also effectively functions within theology, discerning faith and spirituality within their historical contexts. Part of the genius of the method is its capacity to turn its critical eye back on *itself*, which is why, for instance, it has fostered so many other approaches, some of which are highly critical of the method, and yet cannot escape their debt to it. But more than that, historical criticism—as von Rad illustrates—enables careful readers to examine biblical texts through two, somewhat contrasting but equally

66. Kugel, *How to Read the Bible*, 680.

67. An important discussion of many of these issues is provided by Sandra Schneiders, *The Revelatory Text: Interpreting the New Testament as Sacred Scripture* (Collegeville, MN: Liturgical Press, 1999); see also Jeannine K. Brown, *Scripture as Communication: Introducing Biblical Hermeneutics* (Grand Rapids, MI: Baker Academic, 2007); and Avery Dulles, *Models of Revelation* (New York: Orbis Books, 1983, 1992), esp. 193–210.

important, lenses, one historical, the other spiritual.[68] The historical lens is obviously essential; seeking to understand the texts without benefit of history would be like trying to understand Shakespeare devoid of knowledge of sixteenth-century England. But the texts are also spiritual, in the sense that both in their origins and in what they became (e.g., in the hands of the ancient interpreters) they comprise divine inspiration. As such, for people of faith, they have an eternal value that no amount of human analysis can either diminish or improve.[69]

Of course, the historical-critical method cannot demonstrate the truth of this last claim; that is purely a matter of faith, but the method also *cannot evade the claim*. To the contrary, the method lays it bare and brings it vividly to the foreground, even as it also exposes its historical contingency. No one can read Exodus, for example, and ignore Israel's confession that it was God who rescued them from slavery. That is why historical criticism is fully compatible with a faithful reading of the Bible, and why we cannot follow Kugel in his pessimistic assessment of it. In the end, the method only *serves* "the Very Idea of the Bible," the process of "standing up close" and being "God's familiar servants." It does so by its simple requirement that the texts are to be taken seriously on their own terms, historical and spiritual. It also does so by being a bridge, a kind of intermediary between science, which has no capacity either to detect or to evaluate divine presence, and biblical faith that forcefully witnesses to that presence. As a method born of science, it is able to examine the origins and purposes of biblical texts and relate the believers' "reason for hope" (1 Pet 3:15) to their concrete, historical realities. As a method that can enable reaching into the Bible's theological heart, it can uncover how the ancients experienced God, how they faced the contradictions

68. To anticipate a point I will argue at greater length later, what I am saying here about examining the Bible through two lenses also needs to be applied to our examination of reality in broader terms.

69. At this point, some might observe, or even object, that the same claim is implicit in the literature of numerous other religions—do they, therefore, deserve the same respect? A full discussion is far beyond the scope of this book, but I would say that they absolutely deserve "respect," but whether one accords them the "same" respect has to do with personal faith and how much attention one actually gives them. I might say they deserve the same respect, but if I do not read them, such a statement is meaningless. Further, acknowledging that the literature of other religions is also sacred surely *strengthens*, rather than weakens, the case for the inspiration of the Bible; God is "the God of the Gentiles" as well as the Jews (Rom 3:29), and the same God who "delivered Israel from Egypt" also rescued "the Philistines from Caphtor and the Arameans from Kir" (Amos 9:7). That "God is with us" applies to all creation.

to faith and continued to hope in God even in circumstances that might seem to allow only despair.

Historical criticism cannot, in scientific terms, prove the truthfulness of faith, but it can demonstrate that faith is not without "reason" and that it has nothing to do with checking one's intelligence at the door of worship. In that sense the method can be an ally of faith, but never a substitute for it. For skeptics, it can demonstrate that biblical faith is self-critical and knows well the ambiguities that faith faces in a modern, as it also did in an ancient, context. At the same time, it shows that faith enables a deeper experience of reality, beyond the materialism of the modern worldview to a view that owns and reckons with *all* of the knowledge with which we have been endowed by both science and religious faith. It is historical criticism that enables us to place the Bible and evolution (science) *together*, both functioning without compromise or apology in the development of a worldview that is far richer than either one alone can enable.

We cannot, therefore, return to the ancient interpreters. Kugel himself admits that the method has achieved a great deal, and he is "not saying that this evolution ought now to be reversed."[70] Neither would such a reversal be either desirable or possible. Trying to get back to a time before Spinoza and the insights of historical criticism would be like trying to deny the Copernican revolution or Darwinism. On the other hand, reliance on reason *alone* has not always proven to be wise, and the treasure of faith that the ancient interpreters handed on can hardly be abandoned. What we need to hold onto is their stance of faith, their sense that we must "stand up close" and apprehend the ways of God. We have to do that, however, as people of our own world, with all of its science and technology, its tarnished history and contending philosophies. We cannot recreate the world of two thousand years ago.

Today, we must learn to put our faith together with our science. We cannot accept the fundamentalist (creationist) stance that wants to rule out elements of science (e.g., evolution). Nor can we accept the science-dominated, naturalist stance that regards faith and Sacred Scriptures as, at best, museum pieces that have no further value. God gave us both brains and Bibles and expects us to employ both. Science and religion should be partners, the truth of one being supported by the other, but in the real world, the partnership is complicated by ideologies and stereotypes on both sides. The latter require that on occasion, as Pope John

70. Kugel, *How to Read the Bible*, 687.

Paul II said, science and religion have to "purify" one another of their excesses. If the Bible is to be a part of that enterprise, the first and third assumptions of the ancient interpreters are no longer adequate; in fact, they are part of the problem. Presuming that the Bible is "cryptic" and "perfect" plays right into the hands of the creationists and fundamentalists who insist that only they truly understand the Bible, while those who read it critically are faithless. Such a stance eliminates biblical faith from any dialogue with science, puts faith and reason in opposing camps, and perpetuates the schizophrenia of science and religion as, at best, separate realms of knowledge that have nothing to do with one another. In the presence of the latter, no wonder society is divided among right-wing evangelicals, left-wing agnostics, and large groups in the middle who are confused or just alienated by the dispute.

We need to consider again our foundations, the assumptions that guide the reading of our religious and our scientific heritage. Every worldview—of whatever sort—has its assumptions, and if we are to understand what we are doing, we need to consider them carefully. The following seven assumptions, in my view, have to be operative in any attempt to put biblical faith alongside a modern scientific view of the world. They are, of course, as subject to critique as any other assumptions, whether those of the ancient interpreters or of fundamentalists. Others might wish to modify or delete some of these, or perhaps add new assumptions. These have the strength, I believe, of taking seriously on their own terms what we have received both from faith and from science, and thus enable genuine dialogue, and even integration, between them.

1. *All knowledge ultimately derives from God*, whether the "knowledge" of revelation and faith in which theology specializes or the more concrete knowledge of the sciences. Both faith and science are divine gifts and, though it is not easy to discover, there is a unity to all knowledge. Reason is foundational for both theology and science.

2. *All humans are created "in God's image and likeness"* (Gen 1:26-27) and their stunning gifts and capacities (art, philosophy, science, and religion) are indications of how humans reflect and image the Creator, the ground of all existence. Human evolution is fully consistent with this assumption.

3. *The inspiration of the Bible* (Kugel's assumption four) *began with the people*, centuries before the writing of the texts, and it had to do not only with the great persons (Sarah, Abraham, Moses, and

Miriam) and writers (Amos, Isaiah, Paul, and Matthew) but also with the communities of ancient Israel, Judaism, and Christianity. Long *before* the book, what God created was a *people*, and the book (like the Sabbath) exists "for people," not vice versa (Mark 2:27).

4. *The most fundamental biblical claim that "God is with us," as attested throughout both testaments, applies also to people today* (Kugel's assumption two). Specifically, the inspiration of the Bible extends not only to its ancient originators but also to its modern readers, especially in the context of faith. This does not make our reading perfect, any more than the texts are perfect (next assumption), but it does enable us to discern—especially when we pool the inspiration—how God "speaks" through the Scriptures today.

5. *Regarding inspiration, people are primary; the inspiration of the texts is derived and secondary*, and in fact can only be discovered by faith and careful discernment. The texts are reflective not only of God's guidance but also of human emotions, longings, anger, and despair. There are ideas and values in the Bible that ultimately, in themselves, have to be rejected.

6. *The Bible is unique because of the uniqueness of Israel and of Jesus*. It is linked through tradition and inspiration to the foundational people and events of Israel, Judaism, and Christianity. In one sense, it is just like any other body of literature, but at the level of faith it is God's word in the language of humans and therefore has a unique capacity to mediate understanding of God's care for humanity.

7. *The "original meaning," insofar as it can be discovered, is valuable in and of itself, but it is by no means the sum of all meaning*. The ancient interpreters, the rabbis, the fathers of the Church, the insights of science, and centuries of interpretation before and since the Enlightenment all contribute to what the Bible *means*, but ultimately the determination of meaning must have to do with *how the ancient text, taken seriously on its own terms, functions today in the context of believers' obligation to discover and embody the love of God in the world.*

The Bible in the Context of the Science-Theology Dialogue

Creationists notwithstanding, the Bible cannot inform or change science, but the God of the Bible is *also* and *no less* the God of science. To be sure, science and Scripture are vastly different in how they view the world, but there is only one world, and science does not originate from some "elsewhere," different from the Bible and theology. Both theology and science are human disciplines that respond—though in very different ways—to the desire to understand existence, and it is a thoroughly biblical notion that revelation (the word of God) reaches humans not only through prophetic visions but also through history and nature. Everything comes from the hands of the Creator, all the stuff of faith and reason, all the stuff of theology and science.

It follows from this that all human capacities reflect God's creativity, just as does the entirety of creation. The belief that humans "image" God is not contradicted by the scientific observation that humans evolved and are closely related genetically to the other primates. Humans have unique capacities that enable them to know and relate with God, but all creation "proclaims the glory of God"; all creation is spiritual. From human awe, questioning and reasoning derive the experiences that lead to faith, art, philosophy, theology, and science. These are all different *methods* for apprehending and expressing reality, but in a very real sense, they all have the same origin and the same purpose—humanity reaching out to apprehend its encompassing mystery. Inspiration and revelation (the *how* and *what* of divine communication) have to do, in part, with God's presence suffusing the entire universe at every moment. But they also have to do with *particular* moments and places of history; certainly this is the case for biblical faith. God is not *merely* a pervasive presence, and biblical faith is not *merely* a vague notion of a divine creation. In both testaments, "the Word became flesh [in particular times and places] and pitched a tent among us" (John 1:14).[71]

In response to God's historical revelations, ancient Israel and then ancient Judaism and Christianity first *lived*, and then *wrote down*, the stories, questions, laws, and prayers of their life with God. The Bible only became "the Bible" quite late in that history. Its inspiration is at least as ancient as Abraham and Sarah and at least as recent as this morning. My assumptions three–five all deal with inspiration, believing that it is a broader and deeper reality than authors penning their texts from divine dictation. The inspiration had to begin *before* the writing of the texts, otherwise Abraham and Sarah were not inspired, and it has to continue *after* their composition, otherwise we affirm that God is less "with us" than with the ancients, and such a view would be utterly contrary to

71. The Greek verb *eskenosen*, usually translated "dwelt" or "lived," is related to the word meaning "tent" or "dwelling."

what the Bible is all about (e.g., Deut 5:1-4; Matt 28:20). The undeniable humanity of the texts mirrors our own humanity, just as our belief in their divine origin reminds and challenges us to believe in our own. Pointing to their contradictions and errors no more denies their divine origin than confessing our own faults denies ours.

In coming to terms with interpretation, it is an absolutely bedrock principle, in my view, never to forget that *the people come before the book*. This is such an obvious assumption that it is usually forgotten, but it is clear that there was Judaism long before the TANAKH, and there was Christianity long before the New Testament. The "book" exists because of, and for, the people, not vice versa. The Southern Baptist notion that the Bible determines what we can say about God and Jesus has everything exactly *backwards*! God and Jesus are infinitely more than the Bible. Of course, how we interpret the Bible will deeply influence how we think of God; that is why Kugel's "Very Idea of the Bible" as "standing up close" is so important. But we cannot allow the Bible or, for that matter, any creed or theology to be utterly determinative of our view of God; if we do, then Richard Dawkins's rejection of God on the basis of rejecting biblical images of divine violence ends up as quite sensible. It is not sensible, however, because both in the Bible and in the wider revelation, God infinitely transcends the "ways" and "thoughts" of human beings (Isa 55:10). If we wish to know God and the ways of God with humanity (the stuff of theology), then our "text," so to speak, has to derive from as much of human experience as possible. That certainly includes the Bible, but it has to be the Bible in the fullness of its ancient contexts (the stuff of the historical-critical method) as well as centuries of its interpretation (the ancient interpreters, Mishnah, Church fathers) and all the other stuff of human knowledge, including history, philosophy, and science.

There is a famous proverb to the effect that "when the wise one points at the moon, the fool only sees a finger." The glory of the Bible is that it represents numerous centuries of pointing to the presence of God. It represents its first originators (from Abraham to the John of Revelation), centuries of composition and editing, and centuries of compilation and interpretation, but in its entirety as well as in its individual texts, it ultimately points *away from itself* to the transcendent God of all creation. "God alone" (Deut 6:4) is the ultimate object of biblical faith. Scriptures, creeds, and theologies—even the best of them—are no more than fingers pointing at the moon. All we can learn from science is another finger pointing in the same direction.

Depictions of God as cruel are present in the Bible because ancient Israel, Jews, and Christians put them there; they have about them all the limitations of human perceptions of God, and the disadvantages of being full of vengefulness toward enemies. The Bible has less the character of a well-organized thesis than a raucous town-hall debate; it contains numerous inconsistencies and contradictions. It also harbors unacceptable ideas about slavery, women, and the death penalty. Such admissions bring us to Kugel's question: "Where is the word of God" in a book that contains all these limitations?[72]

I cannot improve on what I take to be his answer to that question, at the very end of his book. He compares Scripture to the Temple Mount in Jerusalem, on which he and other religious Jews, unlike Christians and Muslims, refuse to walk, "lest by accident their foot defile the place where once the Holy of Holies stood." No one knows that place, though anyone can hazard a guess. Similarly, we all have our own favorite Bible texts, the ones that, for us, articulate best what the Bible is all about. Most of us would find ourselves in agreement with Baruch Spinoza—of all people—who insisted that Scripture's heart has to do with the love of God for people and their obligation to love one another. In any event, Kugel ends with these words:

> The fleshing out of that primal commandment [to be God's "familiar servants"] takes place in Scripture and outside of Scripture, and it is *all one sacred precinct*; indeed the *divine presence suffuses every part of it*.[73]

"The word of God" in the Bible, in other words, is like the presence of God in creation; it "suffuses every part of it," even the parts we dislike. The negative parts are not there, of course, as commandment or model, but even they can play a role in reminding us both that God is with us in the most nitty-gritty details (e.g., see Deut 23:12-14!) and that those close to God still live and think in terms of their own cultures. If we instinctively recoil—as indeed we should—when Exodus and Ephesians presume the acceptability of slavery, and when Samuel and Matthew presuppose divine violence, it is largely because other parts of Scripture and what we have learned from beyond it have taught us a different view.

72. Kugel, *How to Read the Bible*, 316.

73. Kugel, *How to Read the Bible*, 689, emphasis added.

Dawkins notwithstanding, the Bible is not about violence and hatred; Spinoza was much closer to the truth.

Biblical faith is of immeasurable value to the modern world precisely because it represents a faith-filled view of human existence. No matter their own failures or the cruelties of history, ancient Israel—even centuries before the ancient interpreters—held on to the tradition of the covenant and God's faithfulness. Viewed in the breadth and depth of both history and faith, the Bible reveals human existence much as it is lived in any age, most especially as people struggle with how ancient faith can retain its vision in the midst of both the darkness and the competing, often glaring, lights of a wholly different time. For some, biblical faith ought now to be consigned, if not to the rubbish bins of history, at least to its museums; science and technology have come; faith is dead. That has largely been the battle cry of rationalism (reason *without* faith) at least since the nineteenth century, the age when atheism first gained broad popularity. But, to paraphrase John Caputo, "a funny thing happened on the way to [faith's] funeral."

Reliance on reason alone quickly became reliance on ourselves, those we regard as the most "reason-able." The great European countries of the Enlightenment, and their young sibling, the USA, "placed the crown of reason on white male European heads" with disastrous consequences for the native peoples of the Americas, Asia, Africa, and Australia.[74] Just when reason and its young protégé, science, were gaining their stride, they were employed in the most horrendous genocides and wars. The fault, of course, was not with reason or science as such, but with an overly narrow view of what reason is and how it is to be employed. It also lay, of course, with an overly narrow view of humanity. What has been realized more and more is that just as the Enlightenment was correct to clip the wings of the Bible and religion, and thus to put an end to dogmatism and religious violence, so also reason has an equal capacity for arrogance, does not have all the answers, and needs itself to be subject to careful discernment, a discernment that necessarily involves the perspective of faith. "Reason" and "faith" need each other. Far from burying faith, what this postmodern world seems to be crying out for is to rediscover faith and how it relates to all of our other knowledge.

John Caputo suggests that the border between faith and reason is far fuzzier than the modern world has realized. Both represent a "seeing as," in that reason also

74. Caputo, *Philosophy and Theology*, 35, 38.

> involves an ongoing faith and trust in its ensemble of assumptions and presuppositions, which functions like a set of anticipatory fore-structures that enable us to make our way around—a lab or an archive, a poem or an ancient language, an economic system or a foreign culture.[75]

Both reason and faith enable us to reach out and understand our encompassing reality more deeply. In the coming chapters I want to follow this theme of faith *and* reason, the Bible *and* science, emphasizing always that, for all their differences, they are neither utterly separate from, nor in competition with, one another. There will always be those who emphasize or exclude one or the other. The key is to understand how they can be mutually corrective and enriching.

For those willing to give it a hearing, the Bible witnesses that God is concerned with history in all of its depth and mystery, its suffering and joy. It does not present us with a perfect view of God, but it does insist that humans have an origin and a purpose that are full of hope and promise. Its testimony is that through all of the horror and perplexity, the twists and turns of history, God's presence shines through and invites us to know ourselves as God's children, and the whole universe (or multiverse) as God's creation. Recent centuries, however, have distorted our understanding of, and even our capacity for faith in, God. We turn to that problem next.

75. *Philosophy and Theology*, 56.

CHAPTER 3

GOD

For my thoughts are not your thoughts,
nor are your ways my ways, says the Lord.
For as the heavens are higher than the earth,
so are my ways higher than your ways
and my thoughts than your thoughts.

—Isaiah 55:8-9, NRSV

The "Problem" of God

This chapter is about both the capacity to know God and the barriers to such knowledge that have come into existence with the rise of science. The thesis pursued here is that human beings can know God, and that both theology and science are aids to that end. Knowing God is a matter of faith, as well as it is a matter of reason. The reasons for faith in God are compelling, including from the side of science, as we shall see, but this does not mean that we can definitively prove God's existence.[1] Knowing God is a deeply paradoxical notion. According to an old theological saw, God is only revealed in hiddenness. God's concealment is the necessary price, so to speak, for creation's freedom. Knowing God is a different type of knowledge from our everyday knowing. God is not

1. I am aware that Anselm (11th c.) and Aquinas (13th c.) both offered what are regarded as formal proofs. Further, Paul (1st c.) regarded God as *theoretically* knowable through creation (Rom 1:19-20), and official Catholic teaching maintains that we can know God by the light of reason. Nevertheless, there are no "proofs" that can convince skeptics, and those devised by Anselm and Aquinas are as much in the character of meditation as logical demonstration, as suggested by John Caputo, *Philosophy and Theology* (Nashville: Abingdon, 2006), 14–16 (re: Anselm); and Karen Armstrong, *The Case for God* (New York: Alfred A. Knopf, 2009), 144–46 (re: Aquinas). Nevertheless, Aquinas's five "ways" of demonstrating God's existence perhaps did—contrary to his intention—contribute to making "God" subject to "Reason" (see Caputo, *Philosophy and Theology*, 19 and 21–34); more on this below.

subject to our examination or description, which means that we have to abandon images of God that are unsuited to their subject. Since all images, including scriptural images, are limited and limiting, this process is unending; when describing God, it is always a matter, as mystics have so often insisted, of "not this, not that."

On the positive side, we have to engage mystery as a deep and eternal reality. "Mystery" here does not mean a puzzle we have yet to solve. In this context, mystery is that which in principle is forever beyond human comprehension and control. Mystery is not a scientific issue, and is equally beyond the investigations of philosophy and theology. All the latter can do is affirm the presence of mystery and contemplate its implications and meaning. Scientists and theologians alike stand mute before the ultimate mystery of reality. That is why there are no adequate images of God, the source of all reality and all mystery. That is also why both in Scripture and theological tradition there is strong emphasis on God as beyond all knowing; "for as the heavens are higher than the earth, so are my ways higher than your ways and my thoughts than your thoughts."

The distance between that ancient thinking about God and the type of thinking that has come to dominate the modern Western world is enormous. At the outset of her book, *The Case for God*, Karen Armstrong goes to great lengths to describe why this is such a problem:

> [People] look perplexed if you point out that it is inaccurate to call God the Supreme Being because God is not *a* being at all, and that we really don't understand what we mean when we say that [God] is "good," "wise," or "intelligent." People of faith admit in theory that God is utterly transcendent, but they seem sometimes to assume that *they* know exactly who "he" is and what he thinks, loves and expects. We tend to tame and domesticate God's "otherness." . . .
>
> There is also a tendency to assume that, even though we now live in a totally transformed world and have an entirely different worldview, people have always thought about God in exactly the same way as we do today.[2]

But that is not the case at all. Though the modern world is amazingly sophisticated in its technology and nuanced understanding of the physical universe, much modern thinking about God, over against that of cen-

2. *The Case for God* (New York: Alfred A. Knopf, 2009), ix–x.

turies ago, is stunningly crude and "trivial"; we have made God "too small,"[3] so small, in fact, it is easy to see why atheism is so popular. For us, God has become an intellectual puzzle, an issue to be debated, whether in universities or over beers at the local pub, but in any event an issue, a problem that we have to "prove" or "disprove." The ancient world would be amazed at our naïveté in the face of Eternal Mystery. For the ancients, God could properly be envisaged only with the deepest contemplation and the most profound symbolism.

To illustrate what I mean, permit me to spend some time on what one of the great religious thinkers of the ancient world, Origen of Alexandria (185–254 CE), had to say about one of the Bible's most intriguing texts. Origen is important for our purposes because he was such a comprehensive thinker. To a degree that is not easy for modern minds to appreciate, he took for granted that the eternal mystery of God accounts for all things, and that therefore all things, including the very best learning of his time, pointed to, and had to be considered in, the search for God. My contention is that whereas much modern thinking about God is naïve and trivial, Origen's was vast and deep. I will indicate reasons why we must be critical of Origen in some respects, but in the first instance, we can only deepen our understanding if we spend some time contemplating reality through his eyes.

Origen: The Highest "Branch of Learning"

Consider Origen's commentary on the Song of Songs. The Song is unique within the biblical canon; it comprises in its entirety erotic love poetry. It *never* mentions God, commandments, great events or persons of Israel's history; it is all about romantic and erotic longing. In the event you are not very familiar with the book, here is a brief sampling of verses:[4]

B Let him kiss me with kisses of his mouth!
More delightful is your love than wine!
Your name spoken is a spreading perfume—

3. See the reflections on this theme of Elizabeth A. Johnson, *Quest for the Living God: Mapping Frontiers in the Theology of God* (New York: Continuum, 2007), 14–17, here 16.

4. The translation is from the New American Bible. B, D, and G represent the characters who speak in the drama (however, no clear story line can be detected). B = bride or young woman; D = her companions ("daughters of Jerusalem"); G = groom or young man.

that is why the maidens love you.
Draw me!—
D We will follow you eagerly!
B Bring me, O king, to your chambers.
D With you we rejoice and exult,
we extol your love; it is beyond wine:
how rightly you are loved! (1:2-4, NAB)

G How beautiful you are, how pleasing,
my love, my delight!
Your very figure is like a palm tree,
your breasts are like clusters.
I said: I will climb the palm tree,
I will take hold of its branches.
Now let your breasts be like clusters of the vine. (7:7-9, NAB)

Origen begins by discussing the nature of the book itself, and insists from the outset—as did the Jewish Rabbis before him—that what it is really all about is the longing of the human soul for God. He describes it as "a marriage-song, . . . a drama," composed by Solomon as the third book of the trilogy that includes the books of Proverbs and Ecclesiastes (Qoheleth). Solomon's wisdom in these books was foundational, claims Origen, for "the branches of learning" found in Greek philosophy. Origen was mistaken in that regard, but he shows here his high regard for the best scholarship of his time, which divided learning into three areas: "Ethics, Physics and Enoptics," what we might call the moral, physical, and spiritual aspects of reality. A fourth area was "Logic," but Origen agreed with those who said that this "rational" branch of learning "requires not so much to be separated from the others as to be mingled and interwoven with them."[5]

Origen's divisions of the methods and "branches of learning" rely on his trust in the Christian canon, and on his multileveled understanding of reality. He presumes that the books of Solomon are arranged in their proper order and that therefore ethics comes first, since it "inculcates a seemly manner of life and gives a grounding in habits that incline to virtue." The modern mind is jarred a little that "the study called natural"

5. Origen, *The Song of Songs: Commentary and Homilies*, translated and annotated by R. P. Lawson (Westminster, MD: Newman Press, 1957), 21, 39 and 40.

(physics) comes second to the moral (ethics), and we might imagine that Origen himself should have seen the logic of the reverse order. However, for him, physics follows ethics not only because of the order of Solomon's books but also because physics has to do with "the nature of each single [physical] thing . . . so that nothing in life may be done which is contrary to nature, but everything is assigned to the uses for which the Creator brought it into being."[6]

In Origen's world, physics (science) requires ethics and, as soon as we are spurred into thinking about it, we quickly recognize the logic of his view. The pursuit of truth requires a passion for the truth, as well as dedication and willingness to sacrifice oneself in its cause.[7] This, in fact, is true of all genuine scholarship, which is why in the ancient world—as clearly exemplified, for instance, in Socrates—"philosophy" ("the love of wisdom") was about the pursuit of virtue; it did not primarily have to do with logic and rationalism. Indeed, at least until Blaise Pascal (1623–62) and Benedict Spinoza (1632–77), virtue was explicitly understood to be foundational to the pursuit of knowledge. The big difference today is not that scientists and other scholars are less virtuous, but that "physics" has been radically divided in the modern mind from "ethics"; they are made into separate "branches of knowledge," having nothing essentially to do with one another. So, although it remains true that science requires virtue, we pay no attention to the virtue (until someone cheats) and grant it no significance. That separation of science from ethics is symptomatic of our worldview and of our thinking about God—which brings us to Origen's third, and highest, "branch of learning."

"Enoptics" ("insight"), also termed the "inspective science," "is that by which we go beyond things seen and contemplate . . . things divine and heavenly, beholding them with the mind alone, for they are beyond the range of bodily sight."[8] For Origen, only this highest capacity of the human mind is adequate for understanding the Song of Songs; in fact, Solomon wrote the book precisely so as to teach this "science." On the surface, as Origen knew well enough, the Song employs "the stimulus of love's desire," describing the passionate longing of bride and groom for one another. He warns, however, against reading the book in such "a

6. Origen, *Song of Songs*, 40.

7. On this point, see Michael Polanyi, *Science, Faith and Society* (Chicago: University of Chicago Press, 1946, 1964), e.g., 63–73; and Langdon Gilkey, *Religion and the Scientific Future: Reflections on Myth, Science and Theology* (New York: Harper & Row, 1970), 47–50.

8. Origen, *Song of Songs*, 40.

vicious and carnal sense" and insists that only those should read it who come to it "purified," knowing "the difference between things corruptible and things incorruptible." Readers must advance through the lower levels of knowledge (ethics and physics) before attempting "mystical matters" and advancing "to the contemplation of the Godhead with pure and spiritual love."[9] The lower levels enable the knowing of God, but they are ultimately only prerequisite to the mystical and contemplative capacities of the mind.

Now consider the difference between Origen's contemplation of God, employing every branch of learning, and our confused debates about God, and between Origen's easy acceptance of erotic poetry as a way to speak of God and our infantile notions of God "as some kind of *chap*, however supersized."[10] The first reaction of the modern, critical mind is either to dismiss Origen as steeped in religious bias or, in a more patronizing tone, to smile at his naïve faith. It is a fact, however, that Origen was a towering intellect, who produced the most comprehensive and authoritative multi-language edition of the Old Testament text (the *Hexapla*), wrote numerous biblical commentaries, and, as already indicated, was well versed in Greek philosophy. He studied the sneering rejections of Christianity that were current among the philosophers of his day, and in his *Contra Celsum* answered one of the most sophisticated of them. Further, Origen was far from the mentality of modern biblical fundamentalism and its "creationist" interpretation of Genesis. His methods of interpretation were highly sophisticated and deeply symbolic; he would have scorned attempts to turn Genesis into "natural" science. As to the question of "bias," the answer is that of course Origen was biased. The shallowness of our thinking is on display when we imagine that *we* are *not*!

Symbolism and Contemplation of God

Our biases derive from the worldview we have inherited from the Enlightenment, and from the presumption (the bias) that modern knowledge, particularly science, dispenses with the realm of the metaphysical. The ease with which Origen interprets biblical texts as symbolic is very different from our way of thinking. Origen was well aware of the literal

9. Origen, *Song of Songs*, 24 and 44.

10. Johnson, *Quest for the Living God*, 14, quoting a review by Terry Eagleton of Richard Dawkins's *God Delusion* (2006); emphasis in the original.

sense of the Song of Songs, but it was its "inner meaning,"[11] its mystical sense, that was decisive, and that enabled "the contemplation of the Godhead." This was not unique to Origen. We saw in chapter 2, in our discussion of James Kugel's book and its examination of the ancient interpreters, that for them the world was suffused with the presence of God. It was not merely the texts of Scripture that revealed that presence; they could meaningfully interpret the texts with as much spiritual freedom as they did, because they experienced the entire world as symbolic of realities deeper than surface appearances.

We can see this worldview on full display in the symbols and parables of the Bible. Words were not mere pointers; they were conveyors of power. This was true, for instance, of names, and of blessings and curses, as when *ʿadam* named the animals (Gen 2:19), when Jacob's name was changed to "Israel" (Gen 32:29; 35:10), and when Balaam was prevented by God from cursing Israel, being compelled to utter only blessings (Num 22–24). In every case, the ancient mind easily understood that names and words, like the things to which they point, mean far more than is apparent in their mere literal (surface) intent or character. Since symbolism has largely become foreign to us, we cannot understand the explaining of things, for example, by the use of stories, but this was second nature for the ancients. When David seduced Bathsheba and had her husband Uriah killed, Nathan the prophet told him a story, a piece of fiction, about a rich man who owned large flocks of sheep but who stole, and slaughtered for his feast, the one little ewe lamb that a poor man kept as a pet. David pronounced the judgment that such a man "deserves to die," and then immediately recognized the intent of Nathan's parable when the prophet replied, "*You* are the man" (2 Sam 11–12)! Truth was conveyed in the fiction far beyond the recitation of mere facts. Stories, parables, proverbs—even allegories (as in Ezekiel)—were normal teaching devices of the ancient world. For us, such devices have been reduced to the level of children's fairy tales. But it was adults whom Jesus was teaching when he "taught them in parables" (e.g., Mark 4:2).

Our word "parable" (from Greek *parabole*) translates the Hebrew term *mashal*, which, in the Old Testament, means far more than just "parable." It refers to all sorts of figurative and symbolic speech by which the ancients would point to invisible or abstract realities by reference to more concrete things. Jesus' "parables" include more than stories; he also used images, like mustard seed (Mark 4:31-32), lightning (Luke 10:18),

11. Origen, *Song of Songs*, 59.

and even references to real events (13:1, 4); all of them were "parables." To understand the parables, we need to understand not only the specific points they make but also their power as symbols. Symbols do more than point to a reality; when they truly work, they also convey reality; they are like Valentine's Day flowers that effectively embody and convey love.

As symbols, parables presuppose that the world itself is a parable: the heavens proclaim the glory of God . . . (Ps 19); consider the grass, how it grows . . . (Luke 12:27). Jesus regularly spoke in parables, and also, so to speak, acted them. The prophets of Israel had conveyed their preaching not only in words but also in symbolic actions, as when Isaiah walked around naked (Isa 20) or Jeremiah smashed the clay pot (Jer 19). Jesus also performed signs that, like his words, were representations of "the kingdom of God": the choice of Twelve (Matt 19:28; Luke 22:30), eating with sinners (Mark 2:15-17), and riding into Jerusalem on a donkey (Matt 21:1-10).[12] Like the word-parables, these action-parables depended on the view that "there is nothing in all creation" that is outside of "the love of God" (cf. Rom 8:35-39) or that is not, in some sense, meaningful as a spiritual lesson. Parables, prophetic signs, stories, and blessings worked, because for the ancients the whole world was suffused with the presence of God. For Origen, as for the ancients in general, contemplation of the Godhead required for its fullness the highest capacities of the human mind; the literal, physical level was simply inadequate.

The Song, for Origen, was the climax of the six great songs that Israel had sung, from the song at the sea (Exod 14–15) to the song of David (1 Chr 16:8)—the seventh and greatest being the Song of Songs (hence its name).[13] It was the climactic song—the "holy of holies"[14] within the Scriptures—because it represented the arrival of the bridegroom himself (God/Jesus) to his bride (the Church/the Soul). Prior to his arrival, the groom had already conferred "betrothal gifts": for the Church, "the volumes of the Law and the Prophets," and for the soul, "natural law,

12. We also have to reckon with the "signs" of the miracles, particularly exorcisms and healings, not to mention the nature miracles (walking on water, multiplying of bread and fish). Obviously the historicity (did they happen?) of these sign-events is no small question, and I am not presuming that all of them are historical—quite to the contrary. On the other hand, neither can they all summarily be dismissed. I will discuss miracles in chapter 5.

13. Origen, *Song of Songs*, 46–50. The six songs are Exod 14:31–15:1; Num 21:17-18; Deut 32:1-43; Judg 5:1-31; 2 Sam 22:1-51 (see also Ps 18); and 1 Chr 16:8-36. We would expect him to have included Hannah's song in 1 Sam 2:1-10, but he does not. In his first homily on the Song, he substitutes the Song of the Vineyard (Isa 5:1-7) for the sixth song (267).

14. Origen, *Song of Songs*, 266.

and reason and free will." Wonderful though these gifts were, however, what the bride longs for is the beloved himself, "the kisses of his mouth" (1:2): "The plural, 'kisses,' is used," says Origen, "in order that we may understand that the lighting up of every obscure meaning is a kiss of the Word of God bestowed on the perfected soul."[15] For Origen, the greatest gift and highest capacity of the human mind is the recognition and contemplation of the presence and love of God.

Beyond ethics, physics, and logic is the intimate contemplation of the Godhead, a mystical communion that is the source and summit of all knowing. What we today might call rationality and analysis were, for Origen, the literal or natural level; he acknowledged such "branches of learning" and made use of them, but they cannot by themselves reach to the fullness of knowledge or tell us what the world is really all about. They cannot convey ultimate meaning. Literal thinking, divorced from a sense of transcendence, reduces God to a problem or to childish images like "the big man in the sky." If we wish to "contemplate the Godhead," we have to engage the highest capacities of what it means to be human, and attaining to that level, as the ancients insisted, requires not only the literal and natural but also the level of the mystical and symbolic. Any notion that, in the endeavor to know God, science (reason) and theology (faith) would be separated or (worse yet) be in competition would have seemed to Origen strange in the extreme.[16]

The Loss of Symbolism

None of this is to suggest that we can or should return to Origen's worldview, much less that we should attempt to revive his methods of interpreting the Bible. As discussed in chapter 2, we cannot return to the assumptions of the ancient interpreters, pretending that we do not know

15. Origen, *Song of Songs*, the last two quotes are both from page 61.

16. Some might object that I am portraying the relationship between faith and reason in the ancient world in a far too idyllic manner. After all, from Tertullian (c. 200 CE) to Augustine (400 CE) and on into the Middle Ages (e.g., the Paris condemnations of 1270 and 1277), "philosophy" was often berated and sidelined by "theology," especially if it was thought to be challenging Christian faith. I am aware of all of this, but it is a fact that it was always what were perceived to be abuses and misunderstandings of sound "reason" that were condemned; reason and philosophy as such, including "natural philosophy," could never be excluded from theological thought—quite to the contrary. For balanced examinations of these issues, see David C. Lindberg, *The Beginnings of Western Science*, 2nd ed. (Chicago: University of Chicago Press, 2007), esp. 203–15 and 225–53; and Caputo, *Philosophy and Theology*.

the fallible process of the Scriptures' composition or that science has not radically altered our understanding of the universe. To the contrary, the explosive expansion of knowledge that characterizes the modern world is, in itself, a cause for gratitude. When *we* read the Song of Songs, we can and should steer clear of Origen's bias against sex, and contemplate more than he could the significance of erotic poetry as a metaphor, a symbol, of the love of God. Sex is affirmed in the Song as good in itself, beyond any requirements of procreation. Would that Christianity over the centuries had taken the Song seriously at that level and avoided its many regrettable ideas about sex and marriage!

In other words, we can and should be aware of Origen's limitations and learn to get past them, as also we should study the Bible from a modern historical-critical perspective in order to gain a deeper grasp of its original meanings. On the other hand, we would impoverish ourselves if we did not also learn from him—as from the ancient interpreters in general—and even more important, come to terms with our own biases. Our blindness to symbolism and to multileveled explanations of reality is no less a narrowing of vision than any biases we might detect and regret in the ancients.

For nearly all of human history, symbolism and transcendence have been essential elements of human thinking; they were not marginal to the process of thought, but they were at its center. As Peter Harrison has shown, a multileveled, symbolic worldview was dominant right into the time of the Protestant Reformation. However, once Luther and his heirs insisted on "Scripture alone" as the source of Christian doctrine, consequences followed that were far beyond either their desires or their ability to predict. Luther detached the interpretation of the Bible not only from the papacy but also from the entire tradition of interpretation that had prevailed for close to a thousand years. In 1513, just four years before his publication of the Ninety-five Theses that led to his break with Rome, Luther famously provided his students with a text of the Psalms "which was free of the glosses and commentaries of the Fathers and Doctors" of church tradition. In short order, what became dominant in Protestant interpretation was the literal sense, also referred to as the "grammatical" or "historical" sense, and what they rejected were the allegorical and symbolic interpretations that had prevailed for centuries.[17]

17. Peter Harrison, *The Bible, Protestantism, and the Rise of Natural Science* (New York: Cambridge University Press, 1998), 93 and 108–9. See also his book *The Fall of Adam and the Rise of Natural Science* (New York: Cambridge University Press, 2007).

Such a change was already seismic. One only has to consider the social and religious upheavals attendant on Rome's reaction to Luther's protests of papal corruption. The further, far-reaching consequence that concerns us here was that

> the assertion of the primacy of literal reading . . . entailed a new, non-symbolic conception of the nature of things . . . As an inevitable consequence of this way of reading texts, nature would lose its meaning, and the vacuum created by this loss of intelligibility was gradually to be occupied by alternative accounts of the significance of natural things—those explanations which we regard as scientific.[18]

At least from the time of Saint Augustine (354–430), the figurative interpretation of Scripture had largely directed the interpretation of nature, but with the rise of the Reformers' "literal" sense, the question of how to interpret reality beyond the Bible had to be revisited. The change did not happen all at once, and it certainly was not an item on the Reformers' agenda, but the chain of events set in motion by the loss of symbolic reading was long and consequential: "Iconoclasm with respect to images directly parallels literalism with respect to texts."[19] This was only the beginning, but it truly was the beginning of the end for the Western world's appreciation of the power of parables, and of nature as an image of the glory of God. From now on, what increasingly prevailed was a view of reality in terms simply of physical stuff and physical laws.

A Science-Dominated World

The story develops further in the Enlightenment, the eighteenth-century assertion of reason over traditional faith. Galileo (1564–1642) is an interesting transitional figure. Though he was silenced by the Vatican in 1633, he retained a lively sense of the religious value of the Bible and by no means lost his Catholic faith. Nevertheless, like the Reformers, his ideas had consequences far beyond what he might have desired. Arguably, his greatest impact was not his teaching the heliocentric universe but rather his scientific method, which focused simply on "matter in motion," and relegated human subjective experience to the periphery

18. Harrison, *Bible, Protestantism*, 114.
19. Harrison, *Bible, Protestantism*, 116.

of reality.[20] Galileo did not intend it, but this marks the beginnings of modern scientific materialism (naturalism), which long after his time has become a rallying cry of atheism. His view was carried forward by Descartes (1596–1650), also a faithful Catholic, who made rational analysis alone the guide to understanding reality:

> As a mathematician and a physicist, . . . Descartes said that, much as we love the odors and colors and feels of physical objects, as strictly rational beings we have to give them up and concede that the only thing that is "really out there," "objectively" (this was an entirely new way to talk) is mass and velocity, while such pleasant things as blue or sweet are strictly subjective or private sensations.[21]

Descartes seems to have been sincerely religious, but he was no Origen; genius though he was, the depth of his thought ended with discovering certainty about the nature of the physical world and with trusting in rationality alone for knowing reality, including God. The upshot of his method over time has been a narrowing of our view of reality, since—following Galileo—he made the "objective" alone, as defined by rational analysis, the measure of all existence. In the process, human subjectivity and its perceptions of reality as suffused with meaning and purpose have been sidelined.

Descartes's thinking about God was particularly devastating. He was a sincere believer; indeed, as Karen Armstrong says, God was "necessary" to Descartes, "because without God he had no confidence in the reality of the external world" or in the mind's capacity to perceive it accurately.[22] For Descartes, God was still the origin of all things, including of the mind's capacity for reason. The problem was that he tried to prove

20. See William R. Shea and Mariano Artigas, *Galileo in Rome: The Rise and Fall of a Troublesome Genius* (New York: Oxford University Press, 2003), 118–19, quoting from Galileo's *The Assayer* (1623): "I think that tastes, odors, colors and so forth are no more than mere names so far as pertains to the [human] subject wherein they seem to reside, and that they only exist in the body that seems to perceive them. Thus, if living creatures were removed, all these qualities would vanish and be annihilated." On this "mechanistic" view as foundational to the rise of modern science, see Lindberg, *Beginnings of Western Science*, 364–65.

21. Caputo, *Philosophy and Theology*, 26. John Locke (1632–1704), the British philosopher and statesman, also follows this distinction in Book II (e.g., chap. 8:9–10) of his *Essay Concerning Human Understanding* (1690). The idea has ancient roots in the Greek atomists, such as Democritus (c. 460–370 BCE). On the latter, see Lindberg, *Beginnings of Western Science*, 29–31.

22. Armstrong, *Case for God*, 196, with reference to Descartes, *Meditations*, 6.80.

God's existence by principles derived purely from reason, and in the process he subjected God to reason's scrutiny, as though it is for humans to decide whether God can be permitted into the realm of existence. As John Caputo says it:

> From a theological point of view, no matter how high you heap your praise of God, if that praise is based upon measuring God by the tests written and administered by reason, you are debasing God.[23]

The contrast with Origen and the ancients could not be more dramatic. Whereas, for them, "physics" was an invitation to deeper levels of knowledge and meaning, for the heirs of Galileo and Descartes, physics became the only true knowledge. Whereas, for Origen, God was the beginning and end of all things, and of all contemplation, for the scholars of the Enlightenment, God became one object of inquiry among others. Whereas the world had been suffused with the presence of God, so that all things were symbols, and potential parables, bespeaking the deeper mystery that undergirds physical reality, the unexamined presumption of the world since the Enlightenment is that reality begins and ends with the physical.[24] Origen's bias led him to see numerous levels of reality; our bias causes us to collapse all things to one level.

The Trivializing of God and Humanity

Truth be told, of course, the fault for the collapse does not lie only—or even primarily—with Galileo, Descartes, and the Enlightenment. The early modern scientists were all, in differing ways, sincere believers and hoped, through their science, to provide more certain knowledge of God.

23. Caputo, *Philosophy and Theology*, 28. See also Armstrong, *Case for God*: "There was no awe in Descartes' theology: indeed, he believed it was the task of science to dispel wonder. In the future people should look, for example, at the clouds, 'in such a way that we will no longer have occasion to wonder at anything that can be seen of them, or anything that descends from them'" (197, quoting Descartes, *Les Météores*); and Alister McGrath, *The Twilight of Atheism: The Rise and Fall of Disbelief in the Modern World* (New York: Doubleday, 2004), 31, says, "To his critics, Descartes merely managed to show that, by his own criteria, God's existence seemed rather unlikely."

24. Among the many authors who have written on this theme in recent years are Stephen M. Barr, *Modern Physics and Ancient Faith* (Notre Dame: University of Notre Dame Press, 2003), 1–29; John Haught, *Is Nature Enough? Meaning and Truth in the Age of Science* (New York: Cambridge University Press, 2006); and John Hick, *The Fifth Dimension: An Exploration of the Spiritual Realm* (Oxford: Oneworld, 2004), 13–24.

The charter of England's Royal Society (1660), for example, "instructed its fellows to direct their studies 'to the glory of God and the benefit of the human race.'"[25] The theology of the scientists was simplistic in that, as we shall see presently, they did not truly understand theology's sources and methods; they were unwitting contributors to the rise of modern atheism. The blame for the "debasing" of God lies mostly with the churches and theologians. First, in the aftermath of the Reformation, Europe descended into religious divisions and persecutions, including horrendous violence and wars. Descartes developed his "new philosophy" (his scientific method) in the midst of the Thirty Years' War (1618–48) in the hope that certainty of knowledge might bring the warring factions of Europe together. Descartes's near contemporary, Benedict Spinoza (1632–77), wrote the *Theological-Political Treatise*, as we saw in chapter 2, with a similar hope: that historical knowledge of the Bible would defuse it as a weapon of violence and persecution. Both were sadly disappointed. Religious vision collapsed, in other words, because far too often Christianity was associated with bigoted dogmatism, and was under the control of those who were bent on pursuit of political power; its mystical and contemplative character was lost in the carnage of violence.[26]

A second reason for the collapse was that, as Christian factionalism increasingly called religious truth into question, the new philosophy (science) more and more rose to prominence as a new source of certainty, so that even some theologians began to look to science to prove the truth of the Bible and God's existence. That scientists would look to physical demonstrations as a superior way of knowing God was somewhat problematic; that theologians would be seduced by such thinking was disastrous.[27] Ideally, they should have embraced the methods and discoveries of science, but also insisted on the particular genius of religious insight that is dissatisfied with the surface levels of understanding and pushes on always to grasp the deeper meaning of existence. At the very least they should have insisted that reason, free will, and logic are divine gifts

25. See Ian Barbour, *Religion and Science: Historical and Contemporary Issues* (New York: HarperCollins, 1997), 19.

26. McGrath (*Twilight of Atheism*, e.g., 24–36) shows how the corruption of the Catholic Church (as well as the failures of theology—see next note) opened the door for the allure of atheism.

27. Armstrong (*Case for God*, 197) recounts that Descartes dedicated his *Meditations* to the theologians of the Sorbonne and told them that science "*rather than theological argument*" (Descartes's words) was the way to understand "questions respecting God and the soul," "and the theologians were all too happy to agree"!

("gifts of the Bridegroom") that enable knowledge of God, and that God is the Giver of reason, not a problem for reason's analysis. As is common in the modern world, however, many theologians were swept away by science's success, and began to look to the new philosophy as a way to prove God's existence and the truths of the Bible.[28] Religion itself, after all, by the seventeenth and eighteenth centuries, was severely discredited; it was all too easy to look to science to provide the answers when traditional authorities had failed so badly. The theologians' mistake was not, of course, in their affirmation of science, but in their complicity in the process of making science alone the way to understand existence.

Once Isaac Newton (1642–1727) published his *Mathematical Principles of Natural Philosophy* (1687), which united in a great synthesis the discoveries and calculations of Galileo, Johannes Kepler (German astronomer, 1571–1630), and Descartes, it seemed that science had succeeded in describing completely the workings of the world. Newton himself was always deeply religious and saw the laws in terms of God's action in the universe, but again science was being invoked as though it were needed to shore up God's reality. It was a short step from such a view to imaging God as a clock maker, who had built the mechanism and then stepped back to allow the world to tick its own course through time, guided only by its laws of motion. This was the God of Deism (seventeenth–eighteenth centuries), the cold God of the philosophers, which still, at least subconsciously, haunts modern thinking about God. That step led in turn quite quickly to the views of Pierre Laplace (1749–1827), French physicist and great admirer of Newton, who imaged the universe as so purely determined by its own laws that if a great mind could know both the laws and the motions of particles of matter, then it could calculate all events of both the past and the future. Asked, therefore, by Napoleon Bonaparte about "the Author" of the universe, Laplace could only reply, "I have no need of that hypothesis."

28. As Avery Dulles points out in *The Craft of Theology: From Symbol to System, New Expanded Edition* (New York: Crossroads, 1992), 4–5, it was a matter of theologians trying "to fight against criticism with its own weapons" as though by the use of historical criticism and "syllogistic logic" they could prove the historical accuracy of the Scriptures, and present the gospel miracles as "evidential signs." The attempt failed completely. William Paley's *Natural Theology* (1802) was a much earlier, at first influential, but also failed, attempt to "prove" God by natural observation and scientific reasoning. A modern edition of the latter is available: William Paley, Matthew Eddy, David M. Knight, *Natural Theology: or, Evidence of the Existence and Attributes of the Deity, Collected from the Appearances of Nature* (New York: Oxford University Press, 2006).

Not surprisingly, although Laplace himself was not hostile to religion, he is often seen as a major landmark signaling the transition from a sacred understanding of the universe to a view dominated almost purely by science.[29] How far we have come from the worldview of the Bible and of Origen! What most marks the difference is not whether God remains as part of our thinking, but *how we think* of God. The ancients saw all things—nature, history, humanity—in terms of God. By comparison, we have debased God, making "him" one thing among other things; God for us is a problem, a mere point of debate or, worse yet, the "big man in the sky."[30] That has come about as we have increasingly lost any sense of symbolism as a key to knowing the multileveled character of reality. It has been fostered as we have collapsed all of reality, and all types of knowledge, to the one level of "physics," and have divorced God from science to the point that we sometimes speak as though science were some sort of rival to God. "Can God survive in an age of science?" asks the media; from a theological perspective, the very question is utter nonsense!

Not only is the question nonsense but it also bespeaks how, in losing a sense of the sacred in nature, we have divided ourselves from the sacred. As many thinkers have noted, the science-dominated worldview has led to a narrower and devalued sense of human beings. By this, I am not referring to the notion that, from Copernicus through to Darwin and Freud, humans (supposedly) have been shown to be unimportant; none of those revolutions of themselves necessarily involves any such thinking.[31] What I mean is that, as we have relegated God to the periphery and lost any notion of ourselves as embodied souls and children of God, we have more and more come to define humans simply in terms of physics and chemistry, as though we were "nothing but" so much

29. See Armstrong, *Case for God*, 227; Barbour, *Religion and Science*, 35; and Barr, *Modern Physics*, 171.

30. The fuller story is not merely the "debasing" of God but the aggressive assertion of atheism, and its rise as "the established religion of modernity" (McGrath, *Twilight of Atheism*, 221).

31. On this, see Ted Peters and Martinez Hewlett, *Theological and Scientific Commentary on Darwin's Origin of Species* (Nashville: Abingdon Press, 2008), chap. 6, esp. 115–17; and the critique of Barr, *Modern Physics*, e.g., 20–29. For example, some imagine that because biology shows humans to be animals, humans have been lowered in status, but actually evolution shows that we are far more complex than any other species. Further, the Bible described humans as animals (e.g., Gen 2:7 with 2:19; Eccl 3:18-20) long before biology, but nevertheless regards them as "little less than the angels" (Ps 8:6).

physical stuff.[32] Even free will and purpose have been called into question as though such quintessential human capacities were mere illusions. I said enough about the issue of purpose in chapter 1. Regarding free will, suffice it to say for now that the complete denial of free will is an exercise in self-contradiction, since in that case we could never even deny free will's existence, or affirm it, for that matter! Indeed, we could not meaningfully make *any* assertion; we would be no more than chattering computer programs, saying only what colliding atoms would force from our mouths! Unless we have some genuine capacity for discernment and decision, some power of transcendence, then not only our knowledge but even our humanity is called into question.[33] This is an important matter that will receive fuller treatment in the next chapter.

The fact that such debates arise today indicates how, having trivialized God, we have also belittled ourselves. It is ironic to discover, in an age when the expansion of knowledge is so impressive, that we have been so lacking in wisdom. It is also ironic, at a time when so much of theology has either ignored or sometimes opposed the rise of science, that religious insight should receive new impetus from the realm of science. When scientific method was first applied to the Bible to produce modern biblical scholarship, some believed that theology was losing its way and denying its own essence, and to some degree those criticisms were appropriate. In the end, however, historical criticism has been a great gift to theology and biblical understanding. Similarly today theology is only enriched when it fully embraces the new knowledge provided by science, particularly cosmology and biological evolution. As it does so, of course, theology must not repeat the mistakes of earlier generations and attempt to establish religious truth on the discoveries of science. Theology derives not from physical proofs but from the realm of faith; it

32. For example, Ursula Goodenough (*The Sacred Depths of Nature* [New York: Oxford University Press, 1998], 46–47) says: "All of us, and scientists are no exception, are vulnerable to the existential shudder that leaves us wishing that the foundations of life were something other than just so much biochemistry and biophysics. . . . But the workings of life are not mysterious at all. They are obvious, explainable and thermodynamically inevitable. And relentlessly mechanical. And bluntly deterministic. My body is some 10 trillion cells. Period. My thoughts are a lot of electricity flowing along a lot of membrane. My emotions are the result of neurotransmitters squirting on my brain cells. I look in the mirror and see the mortality and I find myself fearful, yearning for less knowledge, yearning to believe that I have a soul that will go to heaven and soar with the angels."

33. I will discuss these issues more fully in the coming chapter on humanity. For a thorough defense of free will against its denials by naturalism, see Barr, *Modern Physics*, 175–219.

begins and ends with the gifts of God. Science is one of those gifts, and theology cannot fulfill its task by ignoring it.

Theology and Science: Sources of Knowing

I have maintained that modern thinking—more or less from the time of Galileo and Descartes—has become narrow over against the symbolic, multileveled worldview that preceded the Enlightenment. This is not a criticism of the scientific method as developed by the early modern scientists and as further refined with the rise of technology. Galileo, Kepler, and Newton immeasurably expanded our view of the universe, and in the mid-nineteenth century Charles Darwin's *Origin of Species* (1859) vastly improved our understanding of human beings in relation to nature. Geology and cosmology expanded our understanding with their discoveries of the ages of the earth and the universe, and from astrophysics we now know that humans are quite literally "starstuff."[34] In other words, with respect to the *physical* universe science has been amazingly successful, opening our eyes to vistas of reality that Origen could never have imagined. The narrowing has come from our fixation on science as though it were the only source of knowledge, the only solution for all of our ills.

This narrowing of thought has also come from scientists, philosophers, and theologians alike who have allowed the sidelining of human subjectivity—and, with it, human perceptions of God—to go unchallenged. So enthralled was the nineteenth century by scientific discoveries, the Newtonian universe, and the machinery of the industrial revolution that in the minds of many the complete collapse of a religious worldview was imminent. "God is dead," proclaimed Friedrich Nietzsche, and by the early twentieth century the intellectual world chimed along. However, as John Caputo remarks wryly, "A funny thing happened on the way to the funeral,"[35] except that what happened was not very funny, and it had been happening for centuries.

Armed with their knowledge and technology, Europeans had already been busy colonizing the world and, convinced of their own superiority, slaughtering the people they encountered, whether in Africa, Asia, Australia, or the Americas. In that regard the lofty ideals of the Enlightenment (freedom, self-determination, tolerance, and democracy) did

34. Carl Sagan, *Cosmos* (New York: Ballantine Books, 1980), 190.
35. Caputo, *Philosophy and Theology*, 34–35.

not slow them down in the least. And, whereas faith and religion had been thrust aside, discredited by dogmatism and religious violence, one might have hoped that the assertion of reason and the rise of science would have produced a more enlightened approach to conflicts. In fact, however, Europeans demonstrated the same old human propensity to use whatever weapons and motivations lay to hand to slaughter their enemies. The wars of the twentieth century—devoid of religious motivation—were far more violent than the religious wars following the Reformation. The discovery "on the way to the funeral" was that the substitution of reason for faith was no cure for the endemic disease of human evil.[36] The more subtle, but also essential, discovery was that reason and faith are not so different after all; they are, in fact, intimately related to one another.

Human subjectivity (mind, awareness, intelligence) is the source of reason *and* faith, science *and* theology. And, whether we like it or not, reason and faith are inseparably involved in the task of knowing and understanding. Discussions of the relation between reason and faith, however, are plagued by the problem of defining the terms. Extremists in the debate use definitions that vilify the one or the other as though either "reason" simply amounted to human arrogance against God or "faith" was no more than child abuse, "an evil precisely because it requires no justification and brooks no argument."[37] All such definitions make sensible discussion impossible. Origen would be horrified not just at the narrowness of our thinking but at our strange dichotomizing of these two intimately related "gifts of the Bridegroom."

Reason and faith are aspects of what it is to be a human being, and unless our minds are severely impaired, we all regularly employ both. Reason has to do with our efforts—through exploration and questioning—to discover the real truth about the world. I have to say "*real* truth," because we are all aware of our capacity to be deceived or indeed to deceive ourselves. This is why all true communities of learning invite criticism; the "historical-*critical* method" is well named in that regard. Both science and theology utterly depend on reason's inquiring and critical capacities; the differences between them do not have to do with

36. On this theme, see the reflections of McGrath, *Twilight of Atheism*, 183–89.

37. Dawkins, *God Delusion*, 308 and 311 onwards. Dawkins's lack of understanding about faith is symptomatic of his refusal to examine religion as it actually exists for most people, in most places, most of the time. He focuses purely on the negative and takes that as the essence.

the extent to which they employ reason but with their differing starting points—the one in the realm of immediate physical reality, and the other in the realm of ultimate reality and divine revelation.

Science has the obvious advantage of being able to pin down, so to speak, the objects of its inquiry, and to make its results publicly accessible and testable. In that sense, science is more objective. But no less than philosophy and theology, science derives from human subjectivity, as we can easily see from the extent to which choices, values, and ethics are involved—though often unacknowledged—in every step of the scientific process.[38] Michael Polanyi (1891–1976, scientist and philosopher) makes this point forcefully. In a lengthy investigation of science's role in society, he describes the crucial role of tradition and community within science. These are the source of "the premises of science," to which scientists "subscribe . . . by an act of devotion." In the absence of such devotion, there can be no integrity in science. Polanyi goes on to call the tradition, which undergirds science "a spiritual reality which stands over [scientists] and compels their allegiance."[39] This is an aspect of science we rarely consider, and yet it is crucial. It is a characteristic it properly shares with all true scholarship, including theology.

For its part, theology is often berated for being subjective and, for sure, its obvious disadvantage is its inability to pin down the objects of its inquiry and render them measurable and observable. Theology's subjectivity, however, does *not* have to do with "belief without evidence." To the contrary, it has to do with affirming the truth and value of what is beyond calculation or measure, not only God, but also all of those aspects of the human subject that surpass easy observation—the things we can only express in metaphor, poetry, and symbol. The evidence a theologian examines is the human experience of God articulated in the texts, traditions, and worship of religious communities and in the theologian's own life.

Theology, to use a well-tried definition, is "faith seeking understanding." It employs reason to examine the experience of faith, the assertions of believers, and the doctrines and prayers of worshiping communities. "Do not despise the Spirit, . . . but *test everything*," warned

38. See Polanyi, *Science, Faith and Society*, esp. 54–62 and 70–84. Langdon Gilkey (*Religion and the Scientific Future*, 48–49) describes the "underlying eros to know," the passion to pursue knowledge, as a "religious dimension" in scientific inquiry. He does not mean by this that science, in some sense, proves the existence of God (62). His question (48), rather, is, Does the act of knowing "reveal a dimension of ultimacy in human experience"?

39. Polanyi, *Science, Faith and Society*, 54.

Paul (1 Thess 5:19-21), by which he meant that believers should never presume that their religious beliefs and experiences are beyond question. Theology employs reason very much in the manner of philosophy—assertions must be logical—except that unlike philosophy, theology takes as given that its ultimate goal, and reason's ultimate purpose, is the contemplation of God. The latter is what makes religious faith distinct, but science—like philosophy—also requires faith in a more general sense.

What is faith? In the realm of religion, faith is often equated with belief in the sense of particular beliefs, creeds, and doctrines, but that sense of the term is quite distinct from its fundamental meaning. At root, faith has to do with *trust*, and everyone has to exercise faith in this sense. Centuries of investigation—from the ancient Greeks to modern psychology—tell us that our ordinary perceptions of the world are often mistaken, and indeed modern science has confirmed this in dramatic ways. The spectra of light and sound, for instance, are many, many times wider than the narrow spans of our seeing and hearing. So narrow are our perceptions and so easily are we deluded that some philosophers—from Plato to Immanuel Kant—have been quite radical in their denials of our ability to be truly in touch with reality.[40] Nevertheless, theology and science *trust*—and this act of faith is foundational to all they do—both that the human mind is not *ultimately* deceived, and therefore can reach out and gain *some* meaningful grasp on reality, and second, that the reality out there is itself rational and orderly; its properties and laws can be detected and understood; there is such a thing as truth and it can be known. The difference, again, is that science's inquiries extend only to the realm of the physical, whereas theology presses on to engage the questions of ultimate meaning and the nature of God. Both, however, rest on faith in the rationality both of human minds and of their encompassing reality.

This means that, for all their differences of starting points and of method, science and theology can be seen to derive from the same source (human subjectivity) and to have a certain commonality of purpose. In a sense they merge at the point where we ask the questions that are most profoundly difficult and meaningful to human beings. Science's self-

40. See Bertrand Russell's account in *Problems of Philosophy* (New York: Oxford University Press, 1912, 1998), 1–24, and his staunch defense of the human capacity for knowledge and truth. Though Russell was strongly antireligious, his theory of knowledge (e.g., 52–57) and his robust sense of the human "Self" (esp. 92–93) strike me as strong allies of the view of humanity being developed here. More on this in the next chapter.

limitations to the domain of the physical mean that we can never look to it as the be-all and end-all of our questioning, but we now know—creationists and fundamentalists notwithstanding—that science has a unique and essential role, including as a brake on religion's "error and superstition."[41]

Our particular problem today is that we have lost our bearings with respect to God. Religion in general and Christianity in particular have not only been discredited due to their dogmatism and violence but they have also, to a large degree, lost their power to communicate the richness of their spiritual traditions. Religion, at least its public face, has been hijacked by suicide bombers and abusive clergy; less dramatic but no less tragic, it has yet to learn how to incorporate the best of its ancient wisdom with the new awareness gained from modern philosophy, history, and science. Truth be told, the task is far from easy and I make no claims to know the answers. I insist, however, that in the face of the profound and difficult questions of existence, we need all of the richness of both theology *and* science—there is no either-or at this point. Origen's assumptions—that all "branches of learning" taken together bring us to the contemplation of Eternal Mystery—prove to be fully accurate.

Science's Suggestions of God

Though religions have been abused and discredited, all of the things for which religion exists in the first place—meaning, purpose, and the sacred and moral aspects of life—remain of paramount importance in the lives of individuals and of society as a whole. Though Christian churches are not as full these days in comparison with a few decades ago, people's spiritual concerns remain high, and it is easy to predict that this will continue to be the case. Human beings are endemically spiritual in the sense that they are instinctively guided by commitments and values of a transcendent nature that they know to be true, but that ultimately lie beyond demonstration or measurement. I have already suggested that the practice of science requires ethics. Science, every bit as much as theology, can only remain true to itself if it is guided at every moment by ethical principles and indeed, as Michael Polanyi (1891–1976) has shown, by "metaphysical beliefs [that are] shared by members of the

41. Recall the words of John Paul II, quoted in chapter 1, to the effect that "Science can purify religion from error and superstition; religion can purify science from idolatry and false absolutes."

community."[42] This is true of science and theology because it is true even more fundamentally of human existence in general, which gravitates around values and relationships—family, friends, political and moral causes. True, we all also have basic material concerns for food, housing, and clothing, but a life consumed only by these needs we do not usually regard as a living of our humanity in its fullness. The fullness of human life we regard as involving far more than material stuff. It is not "physics" that guides our daily existence but transcendent and spiritual concerns.

It might be objected that commitment to spiritual values far too often seems to be singularly lacking; crime and corruption, greed and callousness seem to be the order of the day. This can hardly be denied, but what we experience in moral evil is not the absence of spiritual reality but an exercise of the perversion of spiritual power that is all the more destructive because it injures and kills not just physical bodies but the fiber of "metaphysical beliefs" on which our shared life depends. Evil of this sort has always been with the human race, as our history shows beyond question. Part of our modern dilemma in face of it is that whereas in the past there was a firm belief in spiritual reality and a sense that spiritual power could be brought to bear to defeat moral evil, today such belief is seriously weakened. To the extent that we ignore our spiritual character, and define ourselves and our encompassing reality in purely physical terms, we are utterly confused and lost in the face of evil, which strips us of all sense of goodness and hope. The only possible response, therefore, to the pervasive presence of evil is the reassertion of the power of human spirituality. We need to confront evil by affirming the truth that evil itself would only want us to deny that we are endemically spiritual and, our moral failings notwithstanding, we have a profound capacity for goodness—more than that, we are *capax Dei*, "able to know God."

42. Michael Polanyi, *Science, Faith and Society*, 70; Polanyi (scientist and philosopher) argues this point at great length in order to show what kind of society is needed for the flourishing of science (he did so in reaction to what he saw in Stalinist Russia and Nazi Germany). Most fundamentally, science requires a society that espouses freedom, is dedicated to the truth, and conducts its inquiries with fairness and tolerance. The only alternative for a society that is not "dedicated through its members to transcendent ideals" is "submission to a single center of unlimited secular power" (79). In other words, free societies that live by the "democratic spirit" (70) must be guided by the *consciences* of their members. "The denial of all spiritual reality" (78) is impossible; the only issue is what sort of spiritual reality we espouse. It is a matter of "dedication [to transcendent goodness] or servitude [to power less than ourselves]" (63–84).

Obviously, such a statement derives from faith; it has to do with the trust that reality is more than random materiality, that it has its ground in God, in whom "we live and move and have our being" (Acts 17:28).[43] Those words are original neither to Acts nor Paul; they are from the poetic tradition of Crete—they have a universal character, bespeaking the ancient and universal conviction that in its ultimate depth reality is sacred. In our modern context—this would never have been necessary in the ancient world—we have to stress that the affirmation of all reality as sacred is fully reasonable. The grounds for this claim have to do with whether or not we are willing to accept as evidence for it those aspects of human knowing that go beyond the level of physics. I do not mean that any and every belief has an equal claim to be regarded as true, but I am insisting that truth itself—though beyond our final grasp—does exist and that, by the allure of both reason and faith, it draws us toward itself; it is "knowable" even though it is not "demonstrable."[44] The truth "out there" is the source of philosophy, theology, and science; none of those things would exist without it! This is why belief in God is fully reasonable; it is not a matter of blind faith but of following *all* of the evidence. For now, the point to be stressed is that science also has a role in our knowing of God.

In pursuing this thought, let me stress that it is not a question of using science to try to prove God's existence; it does not seem to me that such a thing is possible. But in a context where so often science is seen by some as the opponent of religion, and even as disproving God's existence, it is worth noting the extent to which science can inspire a sense of religious awe, and even lead to some measure of religious faith.[45] Numerous scholars today, simply by their contemplation of scientific discovery,

43. This is from Acts' description of Paul's preaching to the philosophers in Athens. He was quoting from "one of [their] poets," perhaps Epimenides (6th c. BCE); the following quote—"For we too are his offspring"—is from "Aratus of Soli, a third-century B.C. poet from Cilicia [southern Turkey]" (NAB note).

44. See Polanyi, *Science, Faith and Society*, 82. On the theological significance of the objective character of truth, see John Haught, *Is Nature Enough?*, 32–54, esp. 37–39. On objective truth as an issue of epistemology from an atheist philosopher, see Bertrand Russell, *Problems of Philosophy*, e.g., 52–57. Russell (57) distinguishes "the world of being" (abstract universals) from "the world of existence" (things in time)—a metaphysics of considerable value for theology.

45. I stress *some measure*, since faith in its full religious sense has to do with far more than intellectual assent to the existence of God. Faith is a gift, which becomes a type of knowledge, and then commitment and devotion. In other words, faith has to do with *relationship and love*, not mere acknowledgment. This is what Paul Davies (*God and the New*

have come to regard "the laws of nature as thoughts of the Mind of God." That quotation is from Antony Flew, a philosopher and "notorious atheist" who in recent years "changed his mind" about God, and did so simply on the basis of the evidence provided by modern science. Flew is a fascinating illustration of how science can lead to a sense of God; he also reports on similar views of other philosophers and scientists.[46] It is beyond the scope of this book to examine those views extensively, though we might profitably dwell for a moment on observations that have caught the attention even of the skeptics.

For most of his academic life, Flew was sure that, in the debate about God, the unliftable burden of proof lay with believers. One of the things that changed his mind was the evidence of "DNA investigations," which have shown, "by the almost unbelievable complexity of the arrangements which are needed . . . , that intelligence must have been involved" in the origins of life. The notion that life arose purely by chance has sometimes been defended by "using the analogy of a multitude of monkeys" hammering randomly on a keyboard and eventually "writing a Shakespearean sonnet." Flew quotes at length from Gerald Schroeder's "refutation" of this claim.[47] The likelihood of random typing on a 26-letter keyboard producing a sonnet of 488 words[48] is "26 to the 488th power. Or, in other words, in base 10, 10 to the 690th."

Physics [New York: Simon & Schuster, 1983], ix) misses, in my view, when he suggests that "science offers a surer path to God than religion." Science is *necessary*; it is far from *sufficient*.

46. Antony Flew, *There Is a God: How the World's Most Notorious Atheist Changed His Mind* (New York: HarperOne, 2007), 96–112 (the quotation is on 97).

47. Richard Dawkins (*The Blind Watchmaker: Why the Evidence of Evolution Reveals a Universe without Design* [New York: W. W. Norton, 1986, 1996], 46–49 and 141–42) uses this idea but insists on "cumulative" rather than "random" selection, and so for the chaotic monkeys substitutes a computer program that works toward a target phrase ("Methinks it is like a weasel"—*Macbeth*, act III, scene 2). The strengths and weaknesses of his arguments depend entirely on the assumptions one brings to them. He assumes that *somehow* "cumulative selection could have been set up by the blind forces of nature" (49) and his book is largely one long argument in that direction, but of course, once he appeals to "blind forces," the randomly bashing monkeys are back in operation. He also assumes that "once life originates . . . it always advances to the point where its creatures evolve enough intelligence to speculate about their origins" (145–46). This assumes that the output (life, intelligence) *somehow* far exceeds the input ("blind forces" working *without* life or intelligence); such assumptions are massive, to say the least. In my view, the simpler, more reasonable, assumption is the Eternal Mind of God that both gives rise to the laws (of cosmology, biology, etc.) and uses them to draw creation forward into ever greater diversity and beauty.

48. This number, 488, comes from the number of letters in the sonnet "Shall I compare thee to a summer's day?" (Shakespeare, Sonnet 18).

> If you took the entire universe and converted it to computer chips—forget the monkeys—each one weighing a millionth of a gram and had each computer chip able to spin out 488 trials at, say, a million times a second . . . [producing] random letters, the number of trials you would get since the beginning of time would be 10 to the 90th trials. It would be off . . . by a factor of 10 to the 600th. You will never get a sonnet by chance. The universe would have to be 10 to the 600th times larger. Yet the world just thinks the monkeys can do it every time.[49]

The point, of course, is that life is staggering in its complexity, and the chances of it arising by chance from inanimate matter—life from non-life—are very remote, *unless* there are forces at work that steer the universe in that direction.[50] It must be conceded, of course, that someday scientists may discover the recipe for life and be able to duplicate it in the laboratory,[51] which is why theology must not fasten on to the amazing fact of the universe being biocentric as though it proved God's existence. It does not. Nevertheless, the realization dawning on many is that even for the conditions to exist to make life *possible*, long before evolution could begin its work, the forces that built the universe had to be just right, and they had to be so from the first moments of the big bang. This has been documented and commented upon by numerous scientists.

Martin Rees, astronomer royal of England, describes six forces or "numbers" that "constitute a recipe for a universe" that can produce life; "if any one of [these numbers]," says Rees, "were to be 'untuned,' there would be no stars and no life." He recognizes that this fact might point to "a benign creator," but he does not favor that option and resorts instead to the notion of a "multiverse," a sort of universe of universes.[52] In terms

49. Flew, *There Is a God*, 75–77.

50. As yet, no one knows whether life is unique to our planet (in the entire universe) or whether (the more common view) the universe is predisposed to life so that it will inevitably arise wherever the conditions allow. For a lengthy discussion, see Paul Davies, *The 5th Miracle: The Search for the Origin and Meaning of Life* (New York: Simon & Schuster, 1999), esp. 245–73. Which scenario is theologically more significant is also debatable.

51. On the other hand, the difference between "duplicating" and "creating" is to be noted. On "emergence" as a key characteristic of the universe that "explains" life arising from non-life, see "Emergence" in the next chapter.

52. Martin Rees, *Just Six Numbers: The Deep Forces that Shape the Universe* (Lymington, UK: Basic Books, 2000), 4 and 164–71. Rees reports, for example, that "nothing as complex as humankind could have emerged if N were much less than 1,000,000,000,000,000,000, 000,000,000,000,000,000" (35). "N" is the number by which gravity is weaker than electric

of explaining, however, why the laws of nature have their amazing life-friendly properties, the multiverse concept is no solution, nor is it an alternative to "a benign creator," since one can certainly believe in God and in a multiverse at the same time. Indeed, in the thirteenth century already, theology defended the idea of God being able to create other universes against Aristotelian philosophy, which was inclined to deny it.[53] The point to be explained, as Paul Davies says, is why there is a link between the laws that create the universe (or multiverse) and the laws that create life, and further, why there are laws that create universes in the first place.[54] The "how" of the laws is amazing enough; it is the "that" of the laws, their very existence, that is utterly mysterious. "How" requires a recipe of some sort; "that" and "why" are suggestive of a Cook! "So multiverse or not," says Flew, "we still have to come to terms with the origin of the laws of nature. And the only viable explanation here is the divine Mind."[55] In fact, however, as Rees's interpretation shows, none of this *proves* that "the *only* viable explanation" is God; the most that science can do is *suggest*.

Its suggestions, nevertheless, are valuable, since in the context of openness to Eternal Mystery they can both challenge and enrich traditional ideas and images of God. It is a matter of "a theology of nature."[56] As opposed to the "natural theology" of the eighteenth and nineteenth centuries, which began with nature and science and tried to argue its way to God, a theology of nature begins where the Bible and Origen began, namely, with gratitude for the gifts of creation and a longing to know the Creator through nature and the knowledge we have attained of it. The gifts in question include the universe around us, but also, and no less important, the mysterious complexity of the human mind and soul, without which gratitude and knowledge are impossible. Theology here provides a wider context for interpretation of scientific discover-

---

forces (30–33), and is related to the fine delicacy of the force of the big bang. According to Paul Davies (*God and the New Physics*, 179), had the big bang "differed in strength at the outset by only one part in 10^{60}, the universe we now perceive would not exist."

53. Lindberg, *Beginnings of Western Science*, 247.

54. Paul Davies, *The Mind of God: The Scientific Basis for a Rational World* (New York: Touchstone Books, 1992), 215–22.

55. Flew, *There Is a God*, 121.

56. John Haught, *Christianity and Science: Toward a Theology of Nature* (New York: Orbis Books, 2007), e.g., 47–48. In *God After Darwin: A Theology of Evolution* (Boulder, CO: Westview Press, 2000), 117, Haught properly says: "current scientific information is remarkably consistent with faith's conviction that the physical universe had always held at least the *promise* of emerging into life . . . mind, and even spirituality."

ies and also examines how its own formulations might gain from those discoveries.

Having looked at what science suggests about creation, we can now look briefly at what the Bible says of creation and the Creator. In doing so, we must avoid concordism, the attempt to show that the Bible has already revealed whatever knowledge science has acquired.[57] The Bible derives from a culture that knew nothing of modern science, and it is no denial of inspiration to recognize that knowledge of physical reality is not the focus of the Scriptures. We must let the Bible be the Bible, and science be science, without squeezing either the one or the other into an artificial straitjacket. Jesus' parables are not history, and Genesis 1–2 is not science;[58] the Scriptures nevertheless have symbolic and theological truth to reveal for those willing to give them a hearing.

God of Creation and Hope

The more science discovers of the universe, the more it becomes reasonable, as Antony Flew shows, to believe in the divine Creator. However, we have come to this point of starting from unbelief and working our way toward belief with the help of physical clues, because of that long history that turned God into a problem we have to solve. As we now turn to the world of the Bible, we need to permit ourselves to enter again into the world of symbolism and multiple levels of reality, where God is not so much a problem as Eternal Mystery, the Ground of all being, and the Giver of all gifts. Such phrases somewhat represent

57. A common example is the way that the six days of creation (Gen 1) are sometimes correlated with the ages of the universe; there is no such correlation. Though I respect deeply the scholarship of Gerald Schroeder, I regret that his interpretation of the Bible is full of concordism, as when he tries to show, for instance, that the Bible knows of dinosaurs (*The Science of God: The Convergence of Scientific and Biblical Wisdom* [New York: Broadway Books, 1997], 191–94). The context shows that *hataninim hagedolim* (Gen 1:21) denotes "sea monsters"; translating the phrase as "great reptiles" and suggesting this denotes dinosaurs reads too much into the text.

58. Contrary to the arguments of John C. Whitcomb and Henry M. Morris, *The Genesis Flood: The Biblical Record and Its Scientific Implications* (Philadelphia: Presbyterian and Reformed Pub. Co., 1961). They argue, for instance, that "antediluvian climatology and meteorology" were "much different from the present" (121; see also 255–58 and 328), which requires us to think that God created the world one way but causes us to think of it in another, but in that case, no one's science—whether modern science or that of *Genesis Flood*—could be seen as reliable.

how the ancients thought of God, but the range of images of God in the Bible goes far beyond such phrases.

The better known images include Father, Husband, and Creator, but God is also thought of as Mother, Midwife, Lover, Rock, Eagle, Shepherd, Light, Warrior, Bear, and so on. Jesus used some of these images and added more: Sower, Baker woman, Mother Hen, Woman in search of a lost coin, and more besides.[59] The list looks strange to the modern mind; we do not know what to make of it. With the loss of symbolism, which in the Reformation went along with the smashing of images and the discarding of sacramental signs, came an impoverishing of religious imagination.[60] The focus on science as the only way to view the world further discouraged imagery, so that whereas for the ancients the world was full of signs of God, for the modern world God became intellectualized, a distant and cold designer, then a problem to be solved. It soon seemed to make sense to do without God altogether. But there is a problem: the expulsion of the sacred as constitutive of life also narrowed our thinking about ourselves. The list looks strange not only because we do not image God in those ways but also because we barely use our imaginations at all! We have settled for chemical and biological definitions of the world and ourselves. Perhaps it is time to give the biblical stories and images another look.

What unites the various images, and brings them together even with the depictions of God as violent and vengeful, was the experience and conviction that God is passionate about human affairs. The cold God of the philosophers was far removed, as Blaise Pascal experienced, from "the living God of Abraham, Isaac and Jacob."[61] The Bible mostly expresses God's passion in terms of Israel and the Church, but a number of texts—from creation to Revelation—emphasize that God's gaze is far wider than any chosen people, extending to the whole world. Amos,

59. Father (Deut 32:6; Luke 11:2), Husband (Hos 2), Creator (Job 38), Mother (Num 11:11-12), Midwife (Ps 22:10), Lover (Song of Songs), Rock (Ps 18:3), Eagle (Deut 32:11), Shepherd (Ezek 34), Light (Ps 27:1), Warrior (Ps 78:65-66), Bear (Hos 13:7-8; also lion and panther), Sower (Mark 4:3-8), Baker woman (Matt 13:33), Mother Hen (Luke 13:4), and Woman in search of a lost coin (Luke 15:8-10).

60. On the impoverishing of the religious imagination, see McGrath, *Twilight of Atheism*, 198–212.

61. Pascal (1623–62) had a "vision" that he described as "fire." It was so intense and transforming that he carried a "memorial" of it, a note sewn inside his jacket, recording the time and date: "Nov 23, 1654, from about half past ten in the evening until half past midnight." See Hans Kung, *Does God Exist? An Answer for Today* (New York: Doubleday, 1980), 42–92, esp. 57–58; and Keith Ward, *Pascal's Fire: Scientific Faith and Religious Understanding* (Oxford: Oneworld, 2006), vii, 197–98.

for instance, chastised Israel by emphasizing that God's wrath against Israel's enemies extended also to them (Amos 1–2), and that God's providence for Israel extended also to its enemies (Amos 9:7). And the entire point of the book of Jonah is not the "big fish," but the assertion that God's love includes those who know nothing of God.[62] Our focus, therefore, on the Bible in no way excludes recognizing other ways of knowing God that are found in the world's religions and elsewhere. In the amazing gifts of life, the beauty of the world and the sometimes agonized, sometimes ecstatic, meditations of their own minds, humans in all traditions and cultures have experienced the presence of an Eternal Giver.

The first eleven chapters of Genesis, beginning with creation, are unique in Scripture for their consistent focus on the story of the whole universe and all nations of the world. This universal story is told, of course, from the confined and parochial viewpoint of a small nation that knew nothing of the true vastness of the universe, its immense ages of time, or even of the other continents of the earth. This restricted geographical view makes all the more remarkable the theological reach of these chapters, which tell of the beginnings not in terms of Israel's place in the world but in a manner that might provide context for any culture.[63]

The first creation story (1:1–2:3; six days of creation) images God (named *Elohim*) in transcendent terms, as above and beyond the primeval chaos (formless void, dark abyss) from which God forms the universe.[64] Creation is a sovereign act by the power of the Word ("Let there be . . ."), an imposition of order by separation: light from darkness (day 1), waters above the sky from waters below it (day 2), and land from the watery chaos (day 3). On the next three days God decorates: night and day with sun, moon, and stars (day 4), the heavens and seas with birds and fish (day 5), and the land with its animals (day 6). The climax (along with the establishing of the Sabbath) comes with the creation of humanity (an entire population)[65] in God's "image and likeness . . . male and

62. This is clear if one simply reads to the climax of the book, God's question to Jonah: "Should I not have compassion on Nineveh . . . ?" (4:11).

63. Israel's particular story begins with the call of Abraham and Sarah in Gen 12, a tribal saga that, to be sure, ultimately issues again into universal themes, particularly with the classical prophets and the New Testament.

64. Gen 1–2, not unlike other creation myths, seems to presuppose that God created *cosmos* out of *chaos;* the first clear expression that God created the universe from nothing is found in 2 Macc 7:28; see also Heb 11:3.

65. It has caused enormous confusion over the centuries that the account of the creation of humans on day six has been conflated with the account in chapter 2 where an

female"—overtime work, so to speak, on the sixth day, corresponding to overtime on day three to "bring forth vegetation." That humans are created "in *Elohim's* image" contrasts with plants and animals, which are made "after their kind." Genesis 1 sees humans as part of creation, along with flowers, stars, and "creeping things," but also as distinctive within it, reflecting the image of the Creator.

The second creation story (2:4b-25) images God not as the cool executive of the first account but as a blue-collar worker, so to speak, who fashions clay and plants a garden with "his" own hands. Though different in several respects, the second account completely agrees with the first on the place of humanity between God and the rest of creation. It begins, somewhat strangely, with the creation of *ʿadam* ("humanity") before anything else. *ʿAdam* is cast in the guise of a single, representative figure, who at this point has no identity or even gender; it is simply "human," into which God breathes "the breath of life," so that "the *ʿadam* becomes a living being" (*nephesh chayah*, 2:7). That same phrase (*nephesh chayah*) will also soon describe the animals (2:19). Humanity's distinction is not in its physical being, but in its relation to God.

Creation again begins with a sort of chaos (featureless watery ground) from which God (now named *Yahweh*)[66] takes "dust [clay] from the ground [*ʿadamah*]" to form the *ʿadam*. It is this same *ʿadamah* from which God will create the animals. First, however, God "planted a garden" ("in Eden," an idyllic fertile region) as humanity's home, which *ʿadam* must "cultivate and care for." God then fashions the animals, because "it is not good for the *ʿadam* to be alone." None of them, however, proves to be "a suitable companion," which leads to God inducing "a deep sleep" and performing surgery so as to transform the *ʿadam* into *ʿish* (man) and simultaneously create woman (*ʿisshah*) from its side.[67] The climax

---

individual "human" (*ʿadam*) is created first and then placed in the garden. The Hebrew word *ʿadam* means "humanity." Gen 1, in other words, envisages the creation of men and women *at the same time in a large population*; Gen 2 speaks symbolically of an original (at first, sexless) individual.

66. "Y[J]ahweh" (see Exod 3:14, discussed below) is *the* sacred name for God, whereas *Elohim* is a generic name that could denote *any* god or gods. This difference of names is one of the notable differences between the two creation accounts. The others have to do with the order of events (e.g., humans created last, *ʿadam* created first), the literary style (rhythmic poetry, prosaic narrative), and the image of God (transcendent and organized, immanent and spontaneous). The first is ascribed to the "Priestly" tradition, the second to the "Jahwist."

67. Traditional interpretations of the creation accounts have presumed that they teach a God-ordained priority, both in time and importance, of men over women. Such inter-

of this account, therefore, is the creation of sex and marriage, the man and woman becoming "one flesh." Even more than in the first account, humans here know God, receiving the divine "breath" and a divine commandment ("Eat from any tree, except . . ."), but no less than in the first account, humans share their origin with the animals—both alike come from dirt (*ʿadamah*).

In all cultures, including the science-dominated West, humans experience themselves as placed precariously between their animal nature and their transcendent possibilities. Many creation myths reflect this tension, sometimes describing a time when animals and humans lived in harmony, with the bond being broken by some transgression or other event. Genesis may reflect such a notion,[68] but its primary focus falls on an original harmony of humans with *God*, when God "moved about in the garden in the cool of the evening" to converse with *ʿadam* (3:8). This harmony was shattered with the act of disobedience, which in turn brought about disruption among humans themselves and between humanity and the rest of creation (Gen 3). Genesis 4–11 then relates further myths explaining why humans became alienated from God and one another.

Human evolutionary history, of course, knows of no period of idyllic harmony among humans or between humans and the animal world; humans have been violent, and subject to violence, throughout their evolution. Furthermore, the nature of the texts themselves shows that the idea of original innocence, shattered by an "original sin," is not a historical narrative in the manner of Samuel and Kings. What, then, are we to make of the theme of humanity's alienation and evil, on the one hand, and yet of their knowing, on the other, the possibility of peace with God? It is a theme that is well established in the Bible, not to mention in other mythologies. The question to be asked is theological, not historical; we are not looking for the Garden of Eden or for some time period but for the theological meaning of the symbolic narrative.

There is a sense in which the entirety of the Scriptures, indeed the entirety of the human spiritual tradition, is a response to this problem

---

pretation exemplifies sexism far beyond the text of the Bible and profoundly distorts our understanding of Gen 1–2. I am following the lead here of Phyllis Trible (*God and the Rhetoric of Sexuality* [Philadelphia: Fortress Press, 1978]), who shows that male dominance is accounted for as arising from *sin*, not from creation (see esp. 72–143).

68. The food provided for humans in both accounts is simply fruit and vegetation; only in the aftermath of the flood is there explicit mention of animals as food (Gen 9:3). Whether, on the other hand, "dominion over . . . all the living things" (1:28) and the naming of animals (2:19) was seen as including the right to eat meat is difficult to say.

of alienation and evil. Genesis 1–11 points to the dilemma and offers the explanation that it originates with human arrogance and rebellion. Whereas God has placed humans in paradise and provided for their every need, humans want more; they seek to "be like gods," and end up destroying themselves and their world. But, with even more vigor, the conviction is also born that *ʿadam*, women and men, are not in the situation that corresponds to their true nature; they have an origin, as God's "image," and a destiny, defined by God's promise, which will ultimately achieve fulfillment. There is, in other words, a deep hope and longing for God and all that God represents in the human soul: justice, peace, communities of love, genuine knowledge, and truth. Augustine took the biblical theme of "longing for God" (e.g., Pss 42; 63; 84) and expressed it with a poignancy that has become well known:

> You [O God] have prompted humans that they should delight to praise you, for you have made us for yourself and restless is our heart until it comes to rest in you.[69]

The biblical story, from Abraham and Sarah onwards, is a story of God's promise to bring their descendants, and ultimately "all nations" (e.g., Gen 18:18), to "rest" in God. The promises of posterity, land, and blessing (12:1-9) were, in a sense, fulfilled in the great empire of David and Solomon (c. 1000–920 BCE), but though Israel looked back on that time as a golden age, what it longed for far exceeded any political entity. Indeed, from the very beginning, there was considerable skepticism that a king was even desirable, since exploitation and injustice were inevitable (1 Sam 8:6-18); "put no trust in princes" (Ps 146:3) was a watchword for many. David and Solomon, therefore, were not the fulfillment but simply another aspect of the promise (e.g., 2 Sam 7), another reason to hope and wait for God. Christians tend to think, of course, that the fulfillment came with Jesus, and the notion of fulfillment is to be found in the New Testament,[70] but Christianity has been quite mistaken when it has seen itself as the endpoint of the ancient promises to Israel. Indeed, that idea has had tragic consequences both for Christianity and its mission to preach the gospel, and for others, most especially the Jews. Jesus' preaching and promise focused on "the kingdom of God," but Christianity is definitively *not* that kingdom; it is merely one of its witnesses.

69. Saint Augustine, *Confessions*, 1:1.

70. E.g., Matt 12:17; 2 Cor 1:20; Gal 3:16; Heb 8–10.

Jesus is "fulfillment" for Christians as "God with Us" (*Immanuel*—Matt 1:23; 28:20). He embodies the ancient desire to heal the alienation between God and humans; he is "the Word made flesh" (John 1:14), "walking about in the garden" to seek conversation with humans. As Origen expressed it, beyond the gifts the bridegroom sends prior to the wedding, Jesus *is* the bridegroom who fulfills our longing for the kisses of God. Other religions find this communion with the divine in their own distinctive ways; the longing is universal, but no religion or philosophy is the perfect way to God. Jesus proclaimed "the kingdom of God," an articulation of what all the promises to Israel entailed, but which no human kingdom (or church) could ever deliver. Israel hoped for a kingdom where "compassion and truth will meet, where justice and peace will kiss" (Ps 85:10). Christians also, like all peoples in their own ways, pray for the coming of such a kingdom, just as Jesus himself prayed (Luke 11:2-4). Consistent with this, the New Testament and Christianity are radically oriented toward the future, as was the ancient Judaism into which Jesus was born. It always was, and always is, a matter of "waiting in hope."[71]

Conclusion: Rediscovering God

Augustine was right; what we wait and hope for is God. Paradoxically, we wait for God in the very presence of God; the whole universe is suffused with God's presence. But such faith is more difficult these days. From sometime in the eighteenth century through to at least the third quarter of the twentieth, a practical atheism (sometimes termed "agnosticism") prevailed, and its influence continues even among those who define themselves as believers. We go to church and profess faith on Sundays, but neither God nor faith has much to do with our Mondays through Saturdays; no wonder the churches are emptying! The religious imagination even of the believers has grown thin. And yet we remain restless, "believers" and "nonbelievers" alike. We know instinctively that we are not *just* animals; we have a sense of our own transcendence and have become impatient with the notion that we are chemical machines.

Alister McGrath is probably right that atheism has reached its "twilight." Our centuries-long experiment with atheism has failed; it has not produced the liberation and justice its propagators imagined. To the

71. Pss 27:14; 33:20-22; Isa 40:31—an important theme in Jewish Passover ritual and in Roman Catholic liturgy.

contrary, we know now in crushing detail what societies dominated by atheism are capable of; "as Dostoyevsky foresaw, the elimination of God led to new heights of moral brutality and political violence in Stalinism and Nazism."[72] This is not to say that atheists are necessarily less moral than people of faith; that is clearly not true, and it was not simply atheism that caused the horrors of those regimes. But a society that defines itself purely in terms of a materialist ideology—as though human life only had to do with the exertion of power regardless of transcendent values such as truth, compassion, and justice—deserves our condemnation, as Michael Polanyi says.[73] Atheism has failed, because its claim that if we could rid ourselves of the old traditional beliefs, we would be set free by our own knowledge and accomplishments has been proven false.[74] But though we are recoiling from atheism, we do not know how to find our way back to God or even whether we wish to bother.

We are like Adam and Eve cast out of the garden, stunned that we are so lost. We are powerful and prosperous, but utterly destitute, disoriented between our record of evil and violence and our capacity for God and goodness. We cannot turn the clock back to a time of innocence before the Enlightenment and the rise of science; truth be told, it was not an innocent time—it had its own violence and evil. We have gained immeasurably from the vast growth of knowledge in recent centuries. The problem is, we have become fascinated with our knowledge as though it were a substitute for, rather than a gift from, God.

Something began to die in the human spirit when we lost touch with the world as a sacrament, a symbol, of the presence and power of God. The declaration of the death of God was mistaken above all because it killed something in us. Once we dispense with transcendent reality, then we are ourselves diminished. The question of God has everything to do

72. McGrath, *Twilight of Atheism*, 235, and see 184 for the notion of atheism as a "failed experiment."

73. Polanyi, *Science, Faith and Society*, 81: "believing as I do in the reality of truth, justice, and charity, I am opposed to a theory which denies it and I condemn a society which carries this denial into practice." Polanyi was writing in 1946, and he was thinking of Stalinist Russia and Nazi Germany in the aftermath of the Second World War when the horrors of the Holocaust were being revealed, but before the full disclosure of the genocides of Stalinist Russia, whose victims numbered somewhere "between 85 million and 100 million"! On the latter, see McGrath, *Twilight of Atheism*, 233.

74. McGrath, *Twilight of Atheism*, 230–37. McGrath comments wryly: "Atheism was just as bad as any other religion"; after the revelation of the genocides of Stalinist Russia (last note), "no longer could anyone take the suggestion that atheism was the liberator of humanity with any seriousness" (235).

with the question of humanity. To rediscover God, we have to look again through the eyes of faith and reason, symbolism and imagination, at the spiritual animals we are. We need to take seriously the challenges posed by both the Bible and science, and we need to take into account all of the evidence, both what we can measure and observe as well as what escapes our calculation but that we "know" to be true. Why is it that we live in an "emergent universe"[75] that from its first moments is oriented toward life and mind? Why are we so oriented toward the future and purpose and yet can never completely say what our purpose is? What is life? Why, on the one hand, is it as frail as "dust," and yet, on the other, so utterly mysterious and precious? The questions go on and on, and they become all the more acute as we try to understand ourselves, both what and who we are.

This chapter has been about the contrast between the deep and rich ways of knowing God in the ancient world over against modern debasing of God, and my proposal is that we need to rediscover the beauty and richness of the ancient symbols and parables without in any way compromising the knowledge we have attained with the rise of science. I hope that what might also have emerged from this discussion is the sense that ancient faith and modern science have much in common, in that both arise from human subjectivity and both strive for greater understanding. As we will see in the coming chapter, they can also be partners in our wrestling with how to fulfill the human vocation to be just and loving. It is true, of course, that religion and science have been weapons we have used to perpetrate the most horrendous evils; both have been tainted with the original sins of arrogance, violence, and greed for power. But that fact only makes all the more urgent that we bring together ancient and modern wisdom in the quest for our humanity. That is the topic of the next chapter.

75. To be discussed in the next chapter; see Harold J. Morowitz, *The Emergence of Everything: How the World Became Complex* (New York: Oxford University Press, 2002).

CHAPTER
4

HUMANITY

Then God said, "Let us make human beings [ʿadam]
in our image, after our likeness" . . .
So God created humans in the divine image.

—Genesis 1:26-27[1]

What Is a Human Being?

At the heart of our discussion is the question, what is a human being? Humans are the best clue we have to the mystery of reality. We are properly stunned with amazement when we view the images of deep space from the Hubble telescope, and contemplate that our galaxy, which is a hundred thousand light-years across, and contains a hundred billion stars, is just one of perhaps as many as two hundred billion galaxies in the known universe! We are equally stunned when we consider that if we could build a single atom to the scale of a cathedral, the nucleus would be the size of a baseball in the center of the nave and the electrons would be moving in arcs described by the outer walls—all the rest would be "empty space"![2] However, no matter how stunning the universe is, whether at the macro or micro level, it is boring and pedestrian in comparison with the complexity of a human being! Stars and galaxies, protons and electrons are tricycles; the Cadillac is humanity.

1. As I will explain in more detail later, the Hebrew word *ʿadam* means "humanity," referring to "human beings" generally, "male and female." The "us" in "Let us make . . ." refers to the divine council around God's throne; God is addressing the angels, so to speak (see Pss 82:1; 89:7).

2. On the basic structure of atoms, see Paul Davies, *God and the New Physics* (New York: Simon & Schuster, 1983), 144–63, here 146.

It is conceivable that the universe contains creatures and civilizations far more complex than humanity and its achievements,[3] but for now humans are the most complex entity we know of that the universe has produced. As such, we are the best avenue for making sense of it. Scientific materialism, to be discussed at length below, maintains that science alone is the pathway to genuine knowledge. Without denying the importance of science, it ought to be obvious that humans themselves, not only as objects of analysis, but also as subjects who seek knowledge, are essential for understanding the nature of reality.

We are the originators of knowledge in the sense that we shape and use it. To be sure, our knowledge is limited, nevertheless we can analyze not only the world beyond us but also ourselves, and we can critically appraise whether such knowledge as we attain is accurate. There is no religion or metaphysical system, no scientific exploration or theory that has not originated with human minds. The very existence, therefore, of systems of knowledge—of whatever type—attests not only to the uniqueness of the human animal but also to the nature of the cosmos of which we are a part. Our sense of purpose, therefore, is not to be seen, as Dawkins would have it, as something we "have on the brain," as though it were a condition from which we need relief.[4] To the contrary, it is a gift that empowers us to hope in the promises of God.

This does not mean that humans are the goal of the universe, as though everything was created just for us. To the contrary, *homo sapiens* is a very recent species in a universe that conceivably will go on for billions of years after we are extinct. We are an infinitesimal part even just of our galaxy; it is presumptuous to imagine that it and the billions of

3. It is sometimes thought that the existence of intelligent life on other planets would constitute a challenge to religious faith, but this is not necessarily the case at all. The dignity of human beings as God's children would not be changed by their existence, nor would the status of Jesus or of any other figures of religious history. For a discussion of the issue, see Ted Peters and Martinez Hewlett, *Theological and Scientific Commentary on Darwin's Origin of Species* (Nashville: Abingdon Press, 2008), 115–35, esp. 132–34.

4. Richard Dawkins, *River Out of Eden: A Darwinian View of Life* (New York: Basic Books, 1995), 96. Dawkins says that asking, "Why is there something rather than nothing?" is a "vacuous existential question" (97), by which he sidesteps any questioning of his unproven presupposition that nature accounts for itself and that reality is "indifferent to all suffering, lacking all purpose" (96). This curtailing of discussion leads to a shrunken view of human beings in which the quest for understanding (its purpose!) is allowed no part or is simply reduced to a survival mechanism gone haywire. A problem for Dawkins is that his own quest for ultimate truth witnesses against him, since it suggests that the universe is far from "lacking all purpose."

other galaxies exist solely for our sakes. Of course, both Genesis creation stories—in different ways—see humans as the climax of creation and as endowed with unique power. It is easy to see, therefore, why medieval theology, before Copernicus and Galileo, concluded that the earth was the center of the universe and that humans were the center of everything. A wider and more critical reading, however, shows that the biblical writers were not convinced of the supreme importance of humankind. What the creation stories reflect is the experience of human uniqueness within the animal world, but they do not claim that humans are the reason for the universe. Psalm 8 speaks for most of Scripture in this regard:

> When I look at your heavens, the work of your fingers,
> the moon and the stars that you have established;
> what are human beings that you are mindful of them,
> mortals that you care for them?
> Yet you have made them a little lower than God,
> and crowned them with glory and honor.
> You have given them dominion over the works of your hands;
> you have put all things under their feet . . .[5]

For the psalmist, the mystery is why humans are of any importance, and why God has given them so much power. The texts gravitate between these two points: humans are small, but they have a special significance. The point about human smallness is made by God's speeches "out of the whirlwind" in Job 38–41: creation is not for the service of humans, does not work by their wisdom, and is not subject to their control; Job is properly reduced to awed silence. Even more emphatic is Ecclesiastes 3:19-20, which states baldly that "humans have no advantage over the beasts . . . both were made from the dust, and to the dust they both return"! The Bible, in other words, does not conform to the shallow theology that humans are "the center" of everything, nor is it vulnerable to the facile notion that science, with its discoveries of the origins of the earth and of humans, threatens faith.[6]

5. Ps 8:3-6, NRSV. "A little lower than God" is sometimes translated "a little lower than the angels." *Elohim* is variously translated—according to context—as "God," "gods," or "angels." In any event, the point remains clear: as in Genesis, humans are small within creation, and yet God endows them with a special dignity and power.

6. For example, Steven Weinberg, "Without God," *New York Review of Books* 55:14 (September 25, 2008): 73–76; and see again note 31 in the previous chapter.

In Scripture, the smallness of humans and their origin from dust, in common with animals, are well-established ideas. What, nevertheless, the Bible always affirms is God's intense love for humanity. From a theological perspective, that is the revelation that has to be set alongside all other knowledge. In this chapter, the other knowledge mostly to be considered is the human quest for knowledge, truth, and goodness.

Scientific Materialism

What are human beings? What is the significance of their knowledge and power? According to the views of scientific materialism (naturalism), there is no particular significance. The universe, in this view, "just is"; it is an accidental collocation of atoms; there is no meaning or purpose, and human knowing signifies nothing about the nature of reality. Knowledge has just somehow evolved as a survival mechanism, enabling the species to prosper. In the movie *Matrix*, "Smith," the representative of the impersonal artificial intelligence inadvertently created by science, calls human beings "a cancer"; "we," says Smith, "are the cure" that will wipe the earth clean of the human infection.

Similar unappealing views of human existence—purely materialist views that divest life of anything sacred—have become well established in recent years. Edward O. Wilson, the great biologist and strong advocate of scientific materialism, is aware of this. His thesis is precisely that "the intellect" was constructed simply "to promote the survival of human genes," but such an idea, he properly recognizes, leaves us with a dangerous dilemma, "the rapid dissolution of transcendental goals toward which societies [or individuals] can organize their energies."[7] He is quite correct, of course; once we espouse the notion that our quintessential human qualities (intellect, truth-seeking, moral questioning, and so on) are nothing more than the haphazard results of evolution, then "transcendental goals" and values are all reduced to meaningless nonsense. If our triumphs of reason and our egregious sins are nothing more than an impersonal process, then everything we think of as valuable and good is nothing of the kind. Indeed, on this view of things, there is no difference between good and evil, and the notion that there is, is simply a cultural "meme" (analogous to "the selfish gene") that has propagated itself and now gives us the illusion that our lives have value—in reality,

7. Edward O. Wilson, *On Human Nature* (Cambridge, MA: Harvard University Press, 1978), 2–3 and 4 respectively.

they do not.[8] We might try telling ourselves a "noble lie" that life has value and purpose, and we might hope that most people will continue to act as though it did,[9] but the dogma of scientific materialism assures us that the opposite is the case.

Notice how we have come to this point. The question of God has everything to do with the question of humanity. We have abandoned branches of learning that have to do with the contemplation of Eternal Mystery; we have turned away from seeing the universe as sacred and interpreting its beauty and depth as symbolic of even deeper reality. We have narrowed our understanding of knowledge as though it were reducible to physical science, and in the process we have come to define humans as though they were only so much chemistry and biology. Wilson raises something of a protest to this, striving to maintain that "this perception, which equates the method of reduction with the philosophy of diminution, is entirely in error." He nevertheless insists that "biology is the key to human nature" and explains every aspect of human existence in terms of biological evolution.[10] For his part, Dawkins highlights the human capacity for "true altruism" as "a note of qualified hope" in the midst of the pervasive and unavoidable influence of "the selfish gene," which "neither knows nor cares," but to whose "music" we "dance."[11] Such protests and rescue attempts are significant, as I shall presently emphasize, but if reality is as scientific materialism describes, then the vast majority of humans both of the past and the present have been living lives of utter self-delusion, and the prospect before us is only more of

8. On "memes," see Richard Dawkins, *The Selfish Gene*, 30th Anniversary Edition (New York: Oxford University Press, 1976, 2006), 189–201.

9. The idea of the "noble lie" comes from Loyal Rue, *By the Grace of Guile: The Role of Deception in Natural History and Human Affairs* (New York: Oxford University Press, 1994). It is a stunning thesis, to which I cannot possibly do justice here. Its barest outline is that the old myths (traditional religion) have been exposed as false; the reality is "nihilism," but the latter is "maladaptive" since it militates against "personal wholeness and social coherence." What we need, therefore, in place of the truth is a "noble lie," some myth we can espouse that will provide meaning and value. Rue seems to be utterly serious, though at times one imagines his tongue to be planted firmly in his cheek! See especially pages 3–5 and 274–86.

10. Wilson, *On Human Nature*, 13. Wilson argues his thesis further in *Consilience: The Unity of Knowledge* (New York: Vintage Books, 1998), in which he tries to show how the social sciences and humanities (including theology) would best be studied as subdisciplines of biology.

11. Dawkins, *Selfish Gene*, 200–201 (on "real altruism") and *River Out of Eden*, 133 (on DNA).

the same. It is difficult to see how such "reduction" amounts to anything other than "diminution."

Let me emphasize again that my argument is not at all with the science that Dawkins, Wilson, and others propound. Science must go as far as it can in its explanations, including with respect to the evolutionary origins of intellect and the religious spirit. It is shortsighted at best when people of faith try to forbid scientific investigation in these areas as though they were off-limits. The problem with scientific materialism is not with its science but with its claim that science provides the only tools for understanding human existence to the exclusion of all others. Far more reasonable is Origen's method of recognizing differing levels of knowledge, one level allowing for the next. "Physics" is not in competition with "ethics" or "enoptics" (divine contemplation), and all levels of understanding and expression must alike employ "logic" (critical reason).

John Haught provides a more contemporary illustration of this idea. Suppose a fire is burning, and the question is asked, why the fire? A possible explanation is the application of heat to wood that enables oxygen to combine with carbon and produce a flame. That physical explanation would in no way compete with purposeful explanations that the fire was lit to provide warmth or that the maker of the fire wanted to roast marshmallows, send a smoke signal, make charcoal, or whatever.[12] Materialist thinking imagines that because science has discovered the physical explanation for things, all other explanations are forbidden. This is analogous to discovering the recipe for a cake and concluding that therefore there is no such thing as a baker. "The evolutionary epic," which Wilson espouses,[13] is a wonderful explanation of the physical world, but the notion that it necessarily excludes all other explanations leads only to a narrowing of thought. By contrast, Haught insists:

> Reasonable theology . . . allows for many layers of explanation. It argues that divine action or divine creativity stands in relation to nature—to such occurrences as the emergence of the cosmos, life, mind, ethics and religion—analogously to the way in which "I want marshmallows" stands in relation to the chemistry of burning firewood.

12. John Haught, *Is Nature Enough? Meaning and Truth in the Age of Science* (New York: Cambridge University Press, 2006), 16.

13. *On Human Nature*, 201; see pages 10–11 for Wilson's insistence that religious explanations are not to be tolerated alongside those of science.

In addition to its collapsing of various levels and types of knowledge, further weaknesses of scientific materialism arise when its proponents argue that, once the transcendental values of traditional ways of thought have been exposed as meaningless, scientific materialism will step in as a substitute "mythology." According to Wilson, "scientific materialism is itself a [noble] mythology" and is "superior to religion" because it (he ought to say *science*) can successfully explain and control "the physical world." Further, it is "self-correcting" in its method and will ultimately explain everything, including "traditional religion by the mechanistic models of evolutionary biology." Wilson is also convinced that "only hard-won empirical knowledge of our biological nature will allow us to make optimum choices" for ethical behavior.[14]

The first of several problems here is the identifying of science with scientific materialism, as though science sanctioned that particular philosophy, which is nonsense; science deals with physical realities, not with philosophy or religion. Science no more favors scientific materialism than Christianity, atheism, or Buddhism. This first error leads to the second: turning scientific materialism into a religion that will give an account of "all subjects sacred and profane," including ethical choices. Wilson can even envisage a future when "knowledge of human heredity" will provide "the option of a democratically contrived eugenics."[15] Presumably this means that humans would decide at the ballot box which sorts of human traits, and humans, should be favored for propagation, and which disfavored.

This nightmare scenario illustrates graphically a third error that can arise when science is made into a mythology. In the mid-twentieth century, Herbert Spencer's (1820–1903) notion of "the survival of the fittest"[16] was mixed by the Nazis with the worst aspects of Friedrich Nietzsche's notion of the "master race," to justify genocides and holocaust.[17] Neither Wilson nor other scientific materialists would sanction

14. *On Human Nature*, 200–201 and 7 respectively. For Wilson's view that science (specifically biology) can provide ethical direction, see especially 6–7, 196 onwards, and note the chapter on "Altruism."

15. *On Human Nature*, 198.

16. On Herbert Spencer's philosophy and how it has been seriously misinterpreted as "coarse social Darwinism," see David Weinstein, "Herbert Spencer," *The Stanford Encyclopedia of Philosophy*, Summer 2009 Edition, ed. Edward N. Zalta, http://plato.stanford.edu/archives/sum2009/entries/spencer/.

17. On Nietzsche's philosophy, see Keith Ward, *God and the Philosophers* (Minneapolis: Fortress Press, 2009), 115–29; for the issue here, esp. 122–23.

such a path, but the notion that we can get ethics from science plays right into the hands of a philosophy that assesses the value of humans in material terms. Science provides important insights into human evolution and nature, and those insights should certainly be used by philosophy and theology for all they are worth. But nature as such (what is) can never tell us what ought to be (ethics). In the words of Paul Ehrlich, a scientist with no religious agenda, "there is nothing in . . . evolution that tells us *what* we should do. The attempt to establish an ethical 'ought' from a natural 'is' deserves its old title, 'the naturalistic fallacy.'"[18]

It is not a criticism of science to point to its limitations in this regard; it is simply a description. If we wish to understand the human mind and its moral and spiritual capacities, we must encourage science to go as far as it can in its investigations of the brain. But we cannot stop at the physical level, and leave unchallenged such ideas as that the mind is no more than the electrical actions of the brain, that consciousness is no more than a feathery transient phantasm, that free will barely exists if it exists at all, that the human self is more illusion than substance, and so on.[19] All such notions, which have become curiously popular in recent years, bespeak the belittling of human beings that can all too easily occur when we focus exclusively on the physical level of our reality. Science is

18. Paul Ehrlich, *Human Natures: Genes, Cultures, and the Human Prospect* (Washington, DC: Island Press, 2000), 309. Ehrlich is sympathetic with Wilson's attempt to do what Ehrlich thinks is probably impossible, and notes that Wilson has "modified this view somewhat over time," though he apparently clings to the idea that "neurobiology can help us understand ethical issues" (422, note 20). For myself, I do not doubt the importance of science in this area; my major point is that science cannot even completely explain itself or any other aspect of human knowing. Certainly it cannot account for the higher levels of moral and spiritual development. On "the naturalistic fallacy," see Peters and Hewlett, *Theological and Scientific Commentary*, 40–41; and James Rachels, *Created From Animals: The Moral Implications of Darwinism* (New York: Oxford University Press, 1990), 66–70. Rachels also (73–79) critiques quite strongly Wilson's sociobiological theory that genes and biology account for human behavior.

19. For such notions, see Edward O. Wilson, *Consilience*, the chapter on "Mind," esp. 120 (his denial of "an executive ego") and 130–32, where he describes free will as an "illusion," but then says that "confidence in free will is biologically adaptive," and finally says that "the mind *does* have free will." In *On Human Nature*, Wilson says that "altruistic perfection" (165) is impossible; "the genes hold culture on a leash." "Human behavior . . . is the circuitous technique by which human genetic material has been and will be kept intact. Morality," he thinks, "has no other demonstrable ultimate function" (167). For a thorough critique of *Consilience*, see Wendell Berry, *Life Is a Miracle: An Essay Against Modern Superstition* (Washington, DC: Counterpoint, 2000).

amazing, but as Merlin Donald, a psychologist (again, with no religious agenda), who rejects such "minimalist" notions, says:

> There are limits to science. Although it seems to evolve and expand endlessly, at any given moment it is finite, like space. We must respect that limit, wherever it may fall, in each generation, even though we may be impatient for a complete theory. At the moment we still do not know why there is a strong gravitational force or why certain macro-molecules come alive. For now we must accept that there just is and they just do. Brains that pulse with certain patterns of electrical activity are conscious. Why? They just are.[20]

A major reason that science will always have its limits, "in each generation," is that science limits itself purely to the physical level of explanation. It deliberately leaves out of consideration all of those aspects of knowing that we can neither measure nor prove, but that we know to be real—things like our sensations of beauty, convictions of morality, depths of relationships, experiences of the spirit, and so on. These were the things, as we saw in chapter 3, that science had to marginalize in order to explore the basic laws of nature. Galileo, Descartes, and Newton remained vibrant religious believers, because although they marginalized these aspects of human subjectivity for the sake of science, they nevertheless continued to accept their importance and reality. As the centuries have rolled by, however, that multilayered type of thinking—science deals with the physical, but the spiritual is the encompassing vital reality—has given way to monistic (one-level) thinking, and, without much thinking about it, we have all bought into the science-dominated monistic view.

It is no criticism of science to say that it can never provide "a complete theory" of the human reality. Stephen Hawking, the great physicist, has famously claimed that "if we do discover a complete theory [uniting all the fundamental laws of physics] . . . then we would truly know the mind of God." I do not believe he means that the theory itself would lead us to "the mind of God." That would be like imagining, if I may use the

20. Merlin Donald, *A Mind So Rare: The Evolution of Human Consciousness* (New York: W. W. Norton, 2001), 178. For Donald's refutation of "minimalist" views of consciousness, see especially xi–45; the balance of the book provides the evidence and argumentation for the refutation, particularly in terms of consciousness as the creator of culture and language, and as "always on watch" in "our drive" for truth (279).

cake metaphor again, that if we knew the recipe, we would know the mind of the baker, which we would not—any more than if we know how fire burns, we know the mind of the fire maker. What Hawking actually says is, that a complete theory might lead us to "take part in the discussion of *why* it is that we and the universe exist, and if we find the answer to *that* . . . then we would truly know the mind of God," and that idea is rather closer to the truth. But physics can take us only so far; the theory would answer the question, how? and might advance our discussion of, why? but for the latter more would be needed. "A complete theory" would require knowing not just the "equations" but why there is "fire in the equations" (to use Hawking's metaphor).[21] Ultimately what is needed is contemplation of God, and that is beyond the realm of science alone.

The Liberation of the Human Spirit

The differences between animals and humans should neither be exaggerated nor ignored. There are clear anticipations in the animal world of many of the qualities that we often think of as distinctively human. Certainly animals have amazing intelligence; they have capacities for problem solving, theory of mind, and rudimentary language. Numerous species care very tenderly for their young, and there are examples of compassion, especially among primates.[22] It is not surprising that this should be the case; we are indeed "created from animals." However, the discovery of the similarities has sometimes provoked the idea that humans are "nothing but animals," and that any differences are merely differences of degree, not of nature. The idea is commented on and lamented by Antony Flew, particularly in relation to two books by the zoologist Desmond Morris.[23] In relation to such evaluations, the famous biologist Ernst Mayr (1904–2005; again, with no religious motivation) said:

> When it was realized that apes had been man's ancestors, some authors went so far as to state "Man is nothing but an animal." However, this is not at all true. Man is indeed as unique, as different from all other animals, as had been traditionally claimed

21. Stephen Hawking, *A Brief History of Time* (New York: Bantam Books, 1988, 1996), 190–91, emphasis added.

22. James Rachels, *Created From Animals*, 149–52.

23. Flew, *There Is a God*, 79. The books by Desmond Morris are *The Naked Ape: A Zoologist's Study of the Human Animal* (New York: McGraw Hill, 1967); and The Human Zoo (New York: McGraw Hill, 1969).

> by theologians and philosophers. This is both our pride and our burden.[24]

Even differences of degree are sufficiently dramatic that they point to the essential difference of nature. Various primates, for example, create and use tools in the wild, especially to get at food sources (nuts, termites) that would otherwise be inaccessible. But the difference between choosing and refining rocks and twigs, on the one hand, and building cities, airplanes, and the Large Hadron Collider, on the other, is so massive that it demonstrates beyond question the utter uniqueness of the human animal. But even the difference of tool use is small when we consider the fine arts, philosophy, metaphysics, science, and theology; there are simply no precedents for these things in the animal world. As Edward Wilson says, "Religion is one of the categories of behavior undeniably unique to the human species,"[25] but also unique to humans are Beethoven's symphonies, Newton's *Principia Mathematica*, or, for that matter, the endless questions of a five year old. These accomplishments and more demonstrate that there is a deep essential difference between humans and animals, not merely a difference of degree.

What most sets humanity apart is its "*pure* desire to know . . . the truth, no matter what the cost."[26] Scientific naturalism might wish to respond that such desire is simply the extreme development in human evolution of animal curiosity exemplified in numerous mammals, from rats to chimpanzees. Curiosity, however, is not the issue. We are curious and desirous of many things that have nothing to do with truth, but simply with appetites and needs, as in our animal forebears. The Rubicon, which the human mind has crossed and which places us in a radically different relationship with ourselves and our encompassing reality, is "the pure desire" to know the truth, the ultimate truth, not merely about what we are but about who we are. It is that desire that lies at the source of our systems of knowledge, from the arts, philosophy, and theology to physics, chemistry, and biology; in that regard, these disciplines are all one and the same.

Because humans seek knowledge and truth, there is also a transcendent and ethical component in their endeavors. Animals deal only in facts: food sources, safety, finding a mate; purpose for them has to

24. Ernst Mayr, *What Evolution Is* (New York: Basic Books, 2001), 252.

25. *On Human Nature*, 175.

26. John Haught, *Is Nature Enough?*, 37, emphasis in the original.

do only with satisfying the facts. That is why for animals there is no morality as such. Not even the most intelligent of nonhuman primates, though intensely enculturated to human society (as in the case of the bonobo Kanzi), go beyond first-level reality to the invention of symbols, and the creation of narrative, much less to ethical speculation.[27] Paulo Freire (1921–97), the great philosopher of education, properly says that only humans are "historical beings." "In contrast to other animals who are unfinished, but not historical, people know themselves to be unfinished; they are aware of their incompletion." Accordingly, humans seek knowledge, and their seeking is "directed towards humanization—the people's historical vocation."[28]

In Freire's context—the plight of the poor in the favelas of 1960s Brazil—"humanization" meant liberation from oppression. It involved enabling uneducated peasants to attain "conscientization," an awareness of their oppression not only as external (extreme social disparity, structures of injustice) but also, and most especially, as internal. The oppressed had to recognize the extent to which they were "'hosts' of the oppressor" to avoid emulating the "oppressor consciousness" and themselves becoming oppressors. Only that intense level of awareness could enable what Freire saw as the goal of his educational plan, the true humanization of the whole society, oppressed and oppressors alike:

> It is only the oppressed who, by freeing themselves, can free their oppressors. The latter, as an oppressive class, can free neither others nor themselves. It is therefore essential that the oppressed wage the struggle to resolve the contradiction in which they are caught; and the contradiction will be resolved by the appearance of the new man; neither oppressor nor oppressed, but man in the process of liberation.[29]

The point to notice here is the intensely ethical character of the educational process; only the fullness of humanization brings liberation—anything less threatens to continue the endless cycle of oppression. Notice also what "conscientization" (full awareness) presupposes about the nature of human beings—that they have a transcendent capacity, first,

27. As described by Merlin Donald, *A Mind So Rare*, 120–21.

28. Paulo Freire, *Pedagogy of the Oppressed*, 30th Anniversary Edition, trans. Myra Bergman Ramos (New York: Continuum, 1970, 2002), 84, 85.

29. Freire, *Pedagogy of the Oppressed*, 48, 56–59.

for awareness (an understanding of themselves in relation to others) and, second, a capacity to love even those who oppress and hate them.[30] What is the significance of these capacities? In light of them, what does humanity tell us about reality?

The response suggested by the evidence of our knowing and loving—tragically imperfect though they are—is that there is far more to reality, far more to the universe and evolution than scientific materialism allows. The latter says that human knowledge evolved simply for the survival of genes. Further, it casts doubt on the value of the vast majority of human history and culture (especially its traditional myths and values) and suggests that human intelligence, awareness, and freedom are strictly qualified by their biological roots. Wilson is not at all sure that humans have any genuine free will,[31] which is a strange notion for an intelligent mind to choose to affirm! For scientific materialists, what ultimately defines us is our animal and evolutionary past. Our aspirations for knowledge, meaning, beauty, and goodness are sidelined by their account, and certainly are not permitted into the discussion as clues to our fundamental nature and the nature of the universe.

And yet, if we look carefully at the writings of the scientific materialists—Dawkins, Wilson, Rue, Dennett, and others—we see exemplified there also a passionate ethical drive. They are far from being detached scientists or philosophers when they tell us, for instance, that religion's "power as an external source of morality" needs to disappear "forever"[32] or that ultimate reality is characterized by "no design, no purpose, no

30. Freire calls "the act of rebellion" of the oppressed "a gesture of love," since it has to do with restoring "to the oppressors the humanity they had lost in the exercise of oppression" (*Pedagogy of the Oppressed*, 56).

31. *On Human Nature*, 71–97 (chapter on "Emergence"), affirms that we are "free and responsible persons" in the sense that "the mind is too complicated" and too subject to the influence of "social relations" to be predicted (77). Nevertheless, in a very real sense, "our freedom is only a self-delusion" (71), and *populations* follow predictable patterns of development (88), so that although "pure knowledge is the ultimate emancipator," it cannot "change the ground rules of human behavior or alter the main course of history's predictable trajectory." See also *Consilience*, chapter on "Mind," esp. 130–32, referenced in note 19 above.

32. Wilson, *On Human Nature*, 201; Richard Dawkins, Daniel Dennett, Sam Harris, Christopher Hitchens, Loyal Rue, Steven Weinberg, and others would all gladly endorse this idea. Ironically, though Wilson wants to see the end of "traditional religion," he is convinced that "the mind will always create morality, religion, and mythology and empower them with emotional force" (200), but he sees this as a purely physical process.

evil and no good, nothing but blind, pitiless indifference."[33] In their view, the world needs to wake up, recognize the foolishness of its traditional thinking, and espouse the new ethics of materialist philosophy. The ethical motivation in their endeavors is even clearer when they assure us that if we abandon the old wisdom, all will not be lost. Dawkins allows that "genuine altruism" might exist and that "we have the power to turn against our creators" (the selfish "gene machines" and "meme machines").[34] Where this capacity for love and transcendence comes from he does not say—surely not from selfish genes and memes!

In Wilson's account, "universal human rights"[35] is identified as a "primary value," but the "true reason" for it, he says, is its "raw biological causation." Once the latter is recognized, it will be found far more compelling, he thinks, than "any rationalization contrived by culture." In other words, we won't value human rights because of lessons learned from past violence and warfare, or from the inspirational teachings of a Ghandi, Martin Luther King Jr., or Jesus. No, it will be because "we are mammals" who value "personal reproductive success" and grant one another "grudging cooperation" so that we can "enjoy the benefits of group membership"![36]

Though both Dawkins and Wilson want to see humans as capable of moral ideals, the more they focus on the physical level alone, the more their accounts of it come across as unreasonable, not to say just plain false. Their own "pure desire for the truth," which I certainly take to be genuine, bespeaks a far vaster horizon than their method of science alone allows them to see.[37] They are reaching out for ultimate explanations of reality, explanations that go far beyond anything that could be subject to scientific observation, and yet they insist on doing so while denying

33. Dawkins, *River Out of Eden*, 133; again, an idea that is universal among scientific materialists.

34. *Selfish Gene*, 201. I will provide further critique of Dawkins on this point at the end of the present chapter.

35. He must be referring to the Universal Declaration of Human Rights of the United Nations, which is easily available at www.un.org. It includes in its preamble: "Whereas the peoples of the United Nations have in the Charter reaffirmed their faith in fundamental human rights, in the dignity and worth of the human person and in the equal rights of men and women . . ." Surely this is completely cultural, deriving from lessons learned from wars and genocides; how could it be improved by reducing its motivation to biology?

36. *On Human Nature*, 198–99.

37. I am trying, in my own way, to articulate rather briefly an important insight, and critique of naturalism, that has been explained at length by John Haught, *Is Nature Enough?* I am especially indebted here to his chapters on "Intelligence" and "Morality."

that any reality exists beyond the physical! The desire to explain reality, which Dawkins and Wilson illustrate so clearly, suggests that humans are continually being invited into knowing and understanding by a reality that far exceeds the animal drive for survival and reproduction. The fullness of the human vocation is liberation of the human spirit, not only from oppression, but for justice, love, truth, and other eternal values. Haught argues persuasively that

> even though critical intelligence is fully part of nature, its own quest for a fullness of truth is a reasonable clue that the world of being is infinitely larger than what naturalism [scientific materialism] is able to acknowledge.[38]

Ultimate explanations of reality will never have about them the clarity and simplicity of physical levels of explanation. The writings of the scientific materialists witness to this as clearly as the work of the most metaphysical philosopher. Dawkins and Wilson offer an ultimate explanation (scientific materialism) that they imagine to flow naturally from science. However, its fundamental assertion that science alone leads to true knowledge is not scientific at all; it is pure philosophy. And since science cannot demonstrate that "science alone leads to true knowledge," then it is a philosophy that contradicts itself!

Further, they want ultimate explanations to consider only physical evidence; indeed they cannot envisage that there is any other sort. But if the argument made here amounts to anything, it is that the broad panoply of human systems of knowing, and the pure desire for truth that undergirds those systems, all constitute significant evidence about human nature and the Eternal Mystery that evolved us into being. People are endemically spiritual, as is clear from our endless quests for meaning and truth, not to mention our perpetual fascination with God. Part of the argument I am making is that science also is part of the evidence of this spiritual longing, but scientific materialism (a philosophy) constricts the human spirit. We need liberation from it as much as we need liberation from the suffocating dogmatism of some religious traditions. The least we should expect of an ultimate explanation of humanity is that it allows enough breathing room for the fullness of the human mind and spirit.

Dawkins properly speaks of how "tragic" it is when religious fundamentalists close their minds to science due to their uncritical reading

38. *Is Nature Enough?*, 39.

of "a holy book."[39] I agree with him completely. But it is equally tragic when he confines the evidence only to the type of which he approves. We are obligated, in the search for truth, to consider all of the evidence, including the human quest for truth. Dawkins describes the universe as aimless and meaningless, but the only "evidence" for such a view is his interpretation of physical facts. What I am suggesting is that he and other scientific materialists would be well served to dig beneath their own acts of interpretation and ask what they mean. What is the significance of this endless desire to know and understand? Is evolution alone a sufficient explanation? Is "the human mind" only "a device for survival and reproduction," and reason merely "one of its various techniques"?[40] Dawkins and Wilson confine our gaze to science, physical causality and to the elements from which human life has emerged. They never encourage us to look up and to gaze ahead into the realm of promise and hope.

On the reading of the evidence suggested here, humanity is not explicable only in the terms of its evolutionary past. At least as important is our orientation toward the future, our longing for ultimate truth, our desire for the goodness of the promised kingdom of God. And the reason we have such an orientation is the beckoning of the Spirit of God. Everything in human nature points with passionate purpose toward the "unfinished" aspects of our being, and this is linked to the fact that the entire universe is in the process of becoming. Traditional religion has been accustomed to say that God "created" the universe, as though the action all belonged in the past; this is no doubt a hangover from an overly literal interpretation of the creation stories. Other parts of Scripture, however, also speak of God's creative action in ongoing terms (e.g., Ps 104:27-30; Isa 43:18-19). It is truer to say that God is creating the universe; we need to emphasize also the present and the future. John Haught, drawing also on other theologians, speaks of God in terms of the "Absolute Future."[41] It is because God, like a parent with a small child, constantly draws and encourages us into greater fullness of being that we are the purposive, hope-filled beings that we are.

39. *The God Delusion* (Boston: Houghton Mifflin, 2006), 283–84.

40. Wilson, *On Human Nature*, 2. If Wilson were correct in these assertions about the mind and reason, then how could anyone trust mind and reason? What would enable mind to jump from pursuit of food and sex to the quest for eternal truth? The minds of *animals* function as Wilson describes, but do not human minds have further capacities?

41. For example, *God After Darwin: A Theology of Evolution* (Boulder, CO: Westview Press, 2000), 90, 143–44.

The Many Facets of Knowledge

The argument I am making is that there is more to reality than meets the eye. "*All* of the evidence" has to include human minds and hearts and their purposeful search for ultimate knowledge and understanding. Scientific materialists interpret humanity in terms of the impersonal laws they see operative in the universe. Hence, for them, as the universe is just a machine, so also are humans; as the universe has no detectable meaning or purpose, neither do humans—it's all just "the outcome of a blind, uncaring shuffle through Chaos."[42] Such thinking turns into pure *object* what is also, and most quintessentially, *subject*; it turns "Thou" into "It." To do this, it strips from the universe the evidence that is closest and most compelling of all, the evidence of human subjectivity, and in the process strips sacredness from nature. If we follow this lead, then we are to look *at* the universe and stop there; what I am suggesting is that we need to also look at the universe *through* human eyes, taking time to consider the ones who are doing the looking, and the amazing reality of our ability to understand. It is not a coincidence that scientific materialists tend to downplay human consciousness and free will.

One of my hopes, in making this argument, is that some room will open up for taking the Bible seriously on its own terms along with the different type of knowledge that we have from science. My most basic thesis, after all, is that the Bible and science *together* provide a richer understanding of reality than either one alone. This means that different types of knowledge all need to be recognized and respected. Haught, again, is a wonderful guide here. He describes "five fields of meaning through which the desire to know must travel" in its quest for truth. One of these "fields" is "theory" that has to do with mathematical and scientific description. The other four are "affectivity," "intersubjectivity," "narrativity," and "beauty."[43] "Theory" in the ancient world was best exemplified in the Greek philosophers; its closest equivalent in the Bible is in the pessimistic, clinical observations of Ecclesiastes,[44] the gathering of received wisdom in the book of Proverbs, and the court chronicles found in the books of Samuel and Kings. But, of its very nature, the Bible

42. Daniel Dennett, *Darwin's Dangerous Idea: Evolution and the Meanings of Life* (New York: Penguin Books, 1995), 185, quoted in chapter 1 above.

43. *Is Nature Enough?*, 42 and 43–51.

44. This is the book (also named Qoheleth) that begins, "Vanity of vanities, all is vanity," and that Origen described as having to do with "the nature of each single [physical] thing." I quoted Origen in this regard in chapter 3 above.

is not much interested in theoretical knowledge; it is rich, however, in other forms of knowledge.

These other forms, which Haught describes as "pre-theoretical and nonscientific,"[45] are the ordinary stuff of knowledge by which the vast majority of us negotiate daily living. We have emotions about things and people (affectivity), and those emotions are necessary guides for how to understand and act. Try to imagine dealing with a child, a sick parent, or an angry boss without the instinctive knowledge that emotions provide. Galileo and his successors pushed emotions aside when devising theories based on what they observed through telescopes and microscopes, but that does not mean there is no emotion in science. Quite to the contrary, we have seen already the passion involved in the pursuit of truth, in arguing for a particular theory, or in choosing an area of research. Though emotions can sometimes be an obstacle to truth, in general they are as essential to it as is food for a journey. Wilson properly describes emotion as "the modification of neural activity that animates and focuses mental activity." As such, emotion impacts both the search for knowledge and its content, which means it also plays a crucial role in determining the value of our discoveries and insights for human life. Wilson goes on to say that "without the stimulus and guidance of emotion, rational thought slows and disintegrates."[46]

Intersubjectivity—knowledge as a shared endeavor—also plays a crucial role. Knowledge requires a sufficient empathy with other persons and things as subjects in order to learn both from them and about them. All human knowledge derives from shared cultures. As Haught says, echoing Michael Polanyi, this requires "a capacity to indwell the world of the other," in the manner of, say, an apprentice learning a craft, or students learning to play the piano or to fix the transmission in a Buick.[47] There is no knowledge without due attention to "the other" and its/their relation to "me."

Knowledge also naturally involves stories (narrativity) and aesthetics (beauty). As with other forms of knowledge, discernment is also needed

45. *Is Nature Enough?*, 48.

46. *Consilience*, 123. He also says that "the rational mind . . . cannot free itself to engage in pure reason. There are pure theorems in mathematics but no pure thoughts that discover them." In my view, this is right, though I would stress more than Wilson does reason's capacity to transcend emotion. Still, it may well be that there is no such thing as reason without emotion, just as there is no such thing as reason without faith.

47. Haught, *Is Nature Enough?*, 45. See Polanyi, *The Tacit Dimension* (Chicago: University of Chicago Press, 1966), 16–18.

here, but there can be no denying the power of stories in the search for truth. The stories of the Bible (e.g., Jesus' parables!) might spring to mind, but science also requires its stories. The narrative (or "mythology," to use Wilson's word) that guides science is not just "the evolutionary epic" but the story of science's rise over the last four hundred years, a story that inspires even further endeavors. Though theoretical knowledge rarely employs narrative, its facts and theories inevitably have to find their place within the larger framework of other facts and theories, otherwise consistency among them breaks down. Narrative, broadly understood, enables the construction of systems of knowledge.[48]

The place of beauty in relation to knowledge and truth is complex, far more so than there is space to discuss here. On the one hand, just as emotions, intersubjectivity, stories, and "secondary qualities," such as color, taste, and smell, were set aside by the first scientists, with their focus on matter in motion, so also was beauty. On the other hand, in more recent times, beauty has made something of a comeback in science, although in a way that is difficult to appreciate for those of us who are not experts in physics. Paul Davies (mathematical physicist) says:

> It is widely believed among scientists that beauty is a reliable guide to truth and many advances in theoretical physics have been made by the theorist demanding mathematical elegance of a new theory. . . . Paul Dirac [a physicist, famous for his "elegant equation for the electron"] . . . judged that "it is more important to have beauty in one's equations than to have them fit experiment" [!].[49]

Truth has a beauty about it that captures us when we encounter it. In such *eureka* (aha!) moments, we realize that we have discovered—even if only in a small way—some aspect of truth as a reality that existed before and apart from us. Certainly that is true for scientists discovering the

48. Narrative helps to *construct* systems of knowledge, but this is a different thing from the common notion that language lies at the root of thought; the latter turns out to be false. This is important for thinking about Michael Polanyi's concept of "tacit knowing" (below) and for understanding (in chap. 5) the prelinguistic "thoughts" and strivings of the mind that the symbolic language of the Bible represents. On language and stories as crucial for knowledge, see Donald, *A Mind So Rare*, 294–98; on thought as preceding language, see 274–79, 290–95.

49. *The Mind of God: The Scientific Basis for a Rational World* (New York: Touchstone Books, 1992), 175.

laws of nature, but it is no less true of the more abstract type of truth that we search for in ethics, philosophy, and theology. Davies reports that Roger Penrose (famous mathematician) "is frank about his belief in the creative mind 'breaking through' into the Platonic realm to glimpse mathematical forms which are in some way beautiful."[50] The reality and beauty of "the Platonic realm" was also important to Bertrand Russell (1872–1970), the philosopher and mathematician.

Russell was an atheist, but he insisted that "the [Platonic] world of *being*"—as opposed to the world of things *existing* in time—is real, and he described it as "unchangeable, rigid, exact, delightful to the mathematician, the logician, the builder of metaphysical systems, and all who love perfection more than life." Russell was so enamored of truth in this universal sense that, when he discussed "the value of philosophy," it was for the contemplation of this abstract eternal realm that philosophy, he believed, remained valuable in a science-dominated world:

> The free intellect will see as God might see, without a *here* and *now*, without hopes and fears, without the trammels of customary beliefs and traditional prejudices, calmly, dispassionately, in the sole and exclusive desire of knowledge—knowledge as impersonal, as purely contemplative, as it is possible for man to attain.[51]

But it was not just a matter of contemplation for its own sake. He believed that the mind, once accustomed to philosophical contemplation of the world of being, will carry "the same freedom and impartiality in the world of action and emotion"; the beauty of knowing transfers to the beauty of action. "The desire for truth" becomes the action of "justice," and the emotion of "universal love."[52]

Beauty is a "guide to truth," but, as Davies concedes, it is also "highly subjective."[53] Finding an idea attractive hardly guarantees its truth; it must

50. *Mind of God*, 176.

51. Bertrand Russell, *The Problems of Philosophy* (New York: Oxford University Press, 1912), 57 and 93 respectively, emphasis in the original.

52. *Problems of Philosophy*, 93 and 43–45. Russell does not mean that we know *a priori* the rightness or wrongness of particular ethical judgments; he is rather referring to "judgments as to the intrinsic desirability of things. . . . We judge, for example, that happiness is more desirable than misery, knowledge than ignorance, goodwill than hatred, and so on. Such judgments must, in part at least, be immediate and *a priori*." The judgments are *a priori* because they are "elicited by experience . . . but they cannot be *proved* by experience" (42).

53. *Mind of God*, 176.

be tested. And good ideas become better by being shared, discussed, and refined; this is apparent in all disciplines of learning. Even when knowledge is advanced by a lonely genius, such as Plato or Einstein, it only gains force by being shared, contemplated, and even corrected by other minds. At that point it starts to become part of the cultural narrative, and gains emotional power. Dawkins might say, it becomes a "meme," which is fair enough, except that memes are *not* our "creators."[54] Dawkins has it backwards; *we* are the creators or at least the discoverers, and on a regular basis we refine, dump, correct, and create ideas (memes) as we advance in knowledge and awareness. This is a process we engage in together, as cultural creatures. It is when we search for truth together in what Merlin Donald calls "cognitive communities" that we are best able to discern the beauty of truth.[55] Theory, beauty, stories, shared meaning (intersubjectivity), and emotions are all facets of knowledge, because knowledge partakes of the fullness of human nature; it is not just a head thing.

To the contrary, knowledge is a multifaceted diamond that involves every aspect of our humanity. Wilson appropriately says, "The rational mind . . . cannot free itself to engage in pure reason. There are pure theorems in mathematics but no pure thoughts that discover them."[56] Of course, knowledge has to do with theoretical (scientific) knowledge of the material world, the kinds of things that we can subject to measures and tests. But most of human existence is lived at far more complex levels, where we cannot easily distinguish hard fact from emotion, and where story might convey the truth far better than theoretical exposition. Knowing a beloved, for instance (whether child, friend, or lover), has nothing to do with measures and tests; indeed, in some circumstances,

54. Recall Dawkins, *The Selfish Gene*, 201. Merlin Donald, *A Mind So Rare*, 8, is far preferable: "Memes are simply the painstakingly generated products" of very active, conscious "processes." "If we want to know what makes human nature special," we must begin "neither with the end result (memes)" nor with "the genetically installed" inheritance of our animal forebears, but "with *the creative engine* itself . . . our capacity for consciousness" (emphasis added).

55. As Merlin Donald shows, *full* human consciousness only develops in the presence of culture (*A Mind So Rare*, 202–300), though the "capacity for consciousness" (note 51) is, paradoxically, the seedbed for culture. Early hominids first became "cognitive communities" (254), and thus began to develop the rudiments of culture (shared understanding and behavior) and symbolic communication. Complex language came comparatively late (293). We give each other the gifts of awareness and speech (279–326). Donald's insights from neuroscience confirm Polanyi's philosophy regarding "a society of explorers" (*Tacit Dimension*, 63–87; also *Science, Faith and Society* [Chicago: University of Chicago Press, 1946, 1964]).

56. *Consilience*, 123, part of a longer quote in note 46 above.

the latter might even be destructive of such knowing.[57] There is a type of knowing that we express in poetry and it is quite different from the knowing we seek in a history book. Fairy tales have their truth and it is not to be despised simply because it is not provable in the manner of a geometrical equation. The parables of Jesus are true in the most profound way, even though their stories may be pure fiction.

The point here is to make space for the types of truth represented in the Scriptures: creation stories, legends, prayers of anguish, prophetic denunciations, lamentations, proverbs, and so on. I will turn to some specific biblical texts in the next chapter and consider the types of truth they represent. But this chapter is making an argument about humanity: that we are far more than so much chemistry and biology, far more than evolved apes. Those facts (evolved apes, etc.) are the gifts that have come to us from our evolutionary past; they tell us, so to speak, about *how* God created us, and no doubt they add to the discussion about *why*. Before turning to specific Scripture texts, there is a little more to say about humanity, and about our relation to the universe from which we have emerged.

Michael Polanyi: Scientist and Philosopher

My argument is not that everyone should become religious in some traditional sense. Though I am religious myself—or maybe *because* I am—I have no wish to convert anyone to Christianity or any other religion. I know religion from the inside, and I am well acquainted with its pains and frustrations, as well as its inspiration. I do not need Dawkins, Wilson, Harris, Hitchens, or any of the other "new atheists"[58] to tell me that religion can sometimes be the devil's playground; theologians and just regular, observant believers know that well enough. But neither do I accept their mythology that the only type of evidence I should accept is that of which they approve, and the only sort of knowledge I should

57. There are times when seeking evidence is appropriate, but if a relationship calls for trust, seeking evidence only illustrates that there is something wrong with the relationship. This is what Dawkins misses in his misconstrual of the Doubting Thomas story in John 20:24-29 (Dawkins, *Selfish Gene*, 198 and 330–31). That, in other circumstances, faith requires testing is clear from Paul's injunction (1 Thess 5:19-21, "test everything"). It is a theme of John's gospel that though physical evidence might lead to *some* measure of faith, it is inadequate for the *fullness* of faith (John 2:23-24; 6:2, 26; 9:16; 11:48; 12:37, cf. Mark 8:11-21).

58. This is John Haught's phrase for these aggressively antireligious writers in his book *God and the New Atheism: A Critical Response to Dawkins, Harris, and Hitchens* (Louisville: Westminster John Knox, 2008).

consider worthwhile is the type that satisfies their purely materialist view of reality. Though I have no arguments with the science of writers like Dawkins and Wilson, I find their interpretations of it both intellectually and spiritually sterile. Their accounts of the universe lead nowhere, except to insist that we are "gene machines," and our minds are devices for "survival and reproduction" (food and sex). Those who wish to swallow that Kool-Aid are free to do so, but I hope they will first consider all of the evidence.

Another way to find and view evidence is provided by Michael Polanyi (1891–1976), whose ideas have featured briefly already. Polanyi was a scientist (chemistry) turned philosopher. His account of why he turned to philosophy, and specifically to research into the "art of knowing"[59] (epistemology), is relevant to our discussion. He was a practicing scientist in the 1930s when he encountered "the Soviet ideology under Stalin which denied justification to the pursuit of [pure] science," that is, the pure pursuit of truth for its own sake. Under Stalin, science was made to serve the interests of the State; it had to be practical, and therefore was wedded to technology. The pursuit of science for its own sake was seen "as a morbid system of a class society."[60] Soviet communism did not believe it needed to pursue truth as an unknown; it believed it had already discovered the ultimate framework of truth in its analysis of history as defined by class struggle. Science had to serve this social ideology, which was dominated by "scientific skepticism"; religion and all things spiritual were to be utterly repudiated—"scientific certainty" alone was the source of knowledge. Polanyi was alarmed that such an outlook produced "a mechanical conception of man and history in which there was no place for [pure] science itself,"[61] and which in its outworking led to the annihilation of millions.

59. "The Art of Knowing" is the title of the first part of Polanyi's book *Personal Knowledge* (below). It is also the subtitle of a book by Mark T. Mitchell, *Michael Polanyi: The Art of Knowing* (Wilmington, DE: ISI Books, 2006), to which I am indebted in this account of Polanyi's life and ideas. I am also using Polanyi's own work, specifically, *Science, Faith and Society* (1946); *Personal Knowledge: Toward a Post-Critical Philosophy* (Chicago: University of Chicago Press, 1958, 1962); and *Tacit Dimension* (1966).

60. *Tacit Dimension*, 3; see also *Science, Faith and Society*, 7–9; and Mitchell, *Michael Polanyi*, 13–14.

61. *Tacit Dimension*, 3. Polanyi continues: "This conception denied altogether any conception of power to thought and thus denied also any grounds for claiming freedom of thought. I also saw that this self-immolation of the mind was actuated by powerful moral motives. The mechanical course of history was to bring universal justice. Scientific skepticism would trust only material necessity for achieving universal brotherhood. Skepticism

Polanyi had moved from Hungary (his birthplace) to Germany in 1919 because of anti-Semitism; by the 1930s he had to abandon Germany for the same reason, and so moved to England, continuing his study and teaching of chemistry at Manchester University (1933–48). Even during those years he became increasingly concerned with the prevailing impersonal and objectifying understanding of science, and of knowledge in general, which was also making its presence felt well beyond the Soviet Union. To its credit, the university recognized the importance of Polanyi's turn to philosophy and created a chair to enable him to pursue his thinking. Polanyi spent the rest of his life developing his understanding of "personal knowledge," not as a philosophical theory for its own sake but because he was convinced that human existence must never be reduced to its physical components (survival and reproduction):

> To regard a meaningless substratum as the ultimate reality of all things must lead to the conclusion that all things are meaningless. And we can avoid this conclusion only if we acknowledge instead that deepest reality is possessed by higher things that are least tangible.[62]

He himself observed that it might seem "extravagant to hope" that the deep wounds of the modern mind-set might be healed by a reconsideration of "the way we know things,"[63] but of course thought dictates behavior; we deal with things and persons the way we think of them. Writing in 1966, Polanyi was motivated in his endeavor because he saw grounds for hope that people "are getting weary of ideas sprung from a combination of skepticism [the denial of transcendent reality] and perfectionism ["refashioning the world unhindered by transcendent moral restraints"]."[64] Perhaps Polanyi's hope will prove correct. The Soviet

---

[about knowledge and traditional ways of knowing] and utopianism [the desire for a classless, just society] had thus fused into a new skeptical fanaticism." What this Soviet ideology produced, of course, was far from "moral," and just as far from "brotherhood" of any sort. It led, in fact, to the annihilation of millions of people.

62. Polanyi, "On the Modern Mind," *Encounter* 24 (May 1965): 15, quoted in Mitchell, *Michael Polanyi*, 113.

63. *Tacit Dimension*, 60.

64. *Tacit Dimension*, 60. See Mitchell, *Michael Polanyi*, 147–50, for an explanation of Polanyi's idea of "perfectionism"; the quote in square brackets is from page 150. The examples of "perfectionism" that Polanyi seems to have had in mind were the Marxist-Stalinist Soviet Union and Nazi Aryanism, both of which were guilty of the most horrendous human atrocities.

Union collapsed in 1989, and the full revelation of its genocidal horrors (under Lenin and Stalin) has now come to light, and so perhaps also Alister McGrath may be vindicated in his view that atheism has reached its twilight.[65] Perhaps. But, as we have seen, there are strong, influential voices that define humanity purely in terms of chemistry and biology, and tell us vociferously that "all things are meaningless." The issue of what knowledge is and "the way we know things" is still very much before us. At stake is the question, what is a human being, and what is the value, the meaning, of humanity's existence?

Keith Ward, a Christian philosopher, well versed in modern science, says:

> There is a basic problem in modern science about the status of value, purpose, and consciousness. They have to enter into any complete account of the nature of things, but the natural sciences largely ignore them.[66]

Either ignore them or, in the case of the scientific materialists I have been debating, essentially deny them any reality. Polanyi, however, was convinced that human knowing, in its very structure, was the essential first clue to the reality of moral values and meaning. Only a brief account of his theory can be given here, but we can begin with a point already made, that we know something by "indwelling," in the manner that an apprentice learns a skill or a music student learns how to play an instrument. All human knowing, including within the sciences, has this character. Whether a child learning how to walk and talk or a young scientist learning the craft of experimentation, the learner is "impelled to imitate—and to understand better as it imitates further—[the] expressive actions" of the parent or teacher.[67]

All learning, therefore, has a fiduciary character, meaning that it involves community and trust. Not even the greatest scholars can begin to make their own contributions without first learning the language and skills of the craft they aspire to practice. As John Caputo says of Descartes

65. McGrath, *The Twilight of Atheism: The Rise and Fall of Disbelief in the Modern World* (New York: Doubleday, 2004), 230–35. I should clarify that though I disagree with atheism, I fully understand its motivations, and to the extent that anger at religion is one such motivation, I empathize with the anger. Atheism has a positive role, if only to keep theists honest and make them think rigorously about what they affirm and why they do so.

66. Keith Ward, *God and the Philosophers* (Minneapolis: Fortress Press, 2009), 39.

67. *Science, Faith and Society*, 44; see also Mitchell, *Michael Polanyi*, 77.

when, in the *Meditations*, he "put everything in doubt" and started out "from scratch," what Descartes failed to notice was that everything he said, "every last word of it, was deeply embedded in the words he used that he had inherited" from his parents, his schooling, "scholastic philosophers," and so on.[68] "No scientist," says David Lindberg, historian of science, "really begins at the beginning, without expectations, theoretical knowledge, or methodological commitments."[69]

What this means is that authority and tradition are basic to human learning of every sort. It also means that "the active participation of the knower is indispensable"[70] in the acquisition of knowledge; human subjectivity—with all its wisdom and warts—is "active [in the] shaping of experience."[71] Human knowing is never purely objective, having to do only with facts—not even within science is this the case. As surely as knowing involves emotion, story, beauty, and so on, so also it involves interpretation, evaluation, and meaning. Knowledge, therefore, is "personal" in the sense that it encompasses both the "objective" (the facts out there) and the "subjective" (the educated, inquiring mind of the knower).[72]

The reason for this is apparent in Polanyi's most basic insight about "the way we know things." All knowing derives from "tacit knowing," to which there corresponds "the tacit dimension." Tacit knowing refers to the fact—gleaned from Gestalt psychology—that "we can know more than we can tell." His parade illustration of this is the way we recognize a face. If asked to describe how we recognize a face, we cannot say. But we can see how it happens in the case of the police sketch artist who places before the observer various possible noses, chins, eyebrows, and so on, and thereby enables us to reconstruct a face we have seen but cannot describe. This process shows how we recognize even the most familiar faces, and further, what is happening when we see things in general.

What we do when we look at something is attend *from* its particulars (e.g., the details of a face) *to* the thing itself. Depending on what we

68. *Philosophy and Theology* (Nashville: Abingdon Press, 2006), 45–46.

69. Lindberg, *The Beginnings of Western Science*, 2nd ed. (Chicago: University of Chicago Press, 2007), 367.

70. Mitchell, *Michael Polanyi*, 79.

71. Polanyi, *Tacit Dimension*, 6. Polanyi used insights of Gestalt psychology in his theory of "tacit knowing," but over against its usual interpretation, Polanyi looked on Gestalt "as the outcome of an active shaping of experience performed in the pursuit of knowledge. This shaping or integrating," he continued, "I hold to be the great and indispensable tacit power by which all knowledge is discovered, and once discovered, is held to be true."

72. Polanyi, *Personal Knowledge*, 294–324; Mitchell, *Michael Polanyi*, 85–103.

are looking at, we may not be consciously aware of the particulars, but we are nevertheless guided by them to know the thing in its integrity. Recognizing a face or distinguishing, say, a hotel from a government building or a teenager from an old man, is something we do in an instant, but the same process is taking place when we are faced with far greater mysteries and challenges of knowing, like a doctor diagnosing illness or a mathematician puzzling over an equation.[73] As we attend from the particulars of what we seek to know, "it is their *meaning* to which our attention is directed."[74] Knowing is about integration, bringing the parts together to make the whole.

Polanyi liked to refer to the *Meno*, in which Plato puzzled over a paradox:

> To search for the solution of a problem is an absurdity; for either you know what you are looking for, and then there is no problem; or you do not know what you are looking for, and then you cannot expect to find anything.[75]

Polanyi's solution to the paradox was the process of tacit knowing. We might say that "the particulars" of the world invite our inquiry. People have an instinct, an "intimation of something hidden, which [they] may yet discover."[76] And, even against enormous odds or contrary to their own best interests, they research, experiment, reason, and question, somehow confident that out there is the truth, the discovery of a hidden aspect of reality. Over and over again, at every stage in their evolution, humans have faced "something hidden," and have broken through to further levels of reality, and further understanding of themselves and their universe.

To this, someone might respond, "Further understanding, sure, but 'further *levels of reality*'? What does that mean?" We have already met the notion with the discussion above about "the Platonic realm," which both Roger Penrose and Bertrand Russell took with complete seriousness. It simply refers to the fact that there are some things that are very real, the reality of which is quite different from other things. Russell distinguishes physical and mental things, and things that are neither physical nor men-

73. *Tacit Dimension*, 4–12; and Mitchell, *Michael Polanyi*, 70–79.

74. *Tacit Dimension*, 12.

75. Polanyi, *Tacit Dimension*, 22.

76. *Tacit Dimension*, 22–23.

tal, but are nonetheless real, like "relations," and abstract ideas—he calls them "universals"—like justice.[77] Polanyi would completely agree with this; he illustrated its value in his analysis of the concept of emergence.

Emergence

Emergence is a well-established scientific idea, though definition and understanding remain vague.[78] It refers to the fact that as the universe unfolds, things gain characteristics that cannot be accounted for only by the basic elements they are made of. From inanimate matter, for instance, animate being somehow emerged.[79] The animate depends on the inanimate for its physical composition, but the animate is also governed by other principles of which the inanimate knows nothing—striving, for example.[80] Consider a watch. Its parts function purely by physicochemical laws, but the watch as a watch functions by principles imposed on the parts by the watchmaker. The functional principles of a watch, which enable it to tell time, work through physics and chemistry but are not explicable by them. Physics and chemistry might account for the watch's *failure*, but they could never account for its *success*. From the physics and chemistry of a watch you would never know what the watch is for; to explain that, you would have to be acquainted with its higher principles that are determined by its purpose.[81]

77. *Problems of Philosophy*, 50–53. "Relations" refers simply to how one thing relates to another. In the example, "I am in my room," both I and the room exist, but so also does the relation "in." The relation is not merely mental, since a thing can be "in" something quite independently of any mind's perception (see also 55–56).

78. Morowitz (*The Emergence of Everything: How the World Became Complex* [New York: Oxford University Press, 2002]) describes "emergent properties" as "novelties that follow from the system rules but cannot be predicted from properties of the components that make up the system" (13); further, "nature yields at every level novel structures and behaviors selected from the huge domain of the possible" (14). His book describes twenty-eight "emergences" from the big bang, through stars, apes, and philosophy to "the Spirit." I doubt that I understand Morowitz fully, but he seems to suggest that "Spirit" (God) emerges (183–200); I would rather say that God is the *author* of emergence. Emergence does not account for God; it's the other way around.

79. In Morowitz's twenty-eight steps of emergence, "the world becomes Darwinian" only at the end of step eight, *after* the beginning of "cellular life" (29). In other words, the realm of biology, and of Darwinian evolution, follows long after the realms of physics and chemistry.

80. Polanyi, *Tacit Dimension*, 44.

81. Polanyi, *Personal Knowledge*, 328–32; and Mitchell, *Michael Polanyi*, 107–10.

Purpose is built into machines by levels of reality (human intelligence) that far exceed the laws of physics and chemistry while, of course, not contravening those laws but rather using them. Emergence refers to this endless potentiality in the universe for properties and principles that cannot be accounted for by earlier levels of development. This principle of potentiality (emergence) is an amazing fact about the universe. It tells us that though there has always been inanimate *matter*, there was never such a thing as an inanimate *universe*, at least in the sense that what created the universe was full of the potential for life, mind, and meaning.

Though emergence is well recognized within science, what it means is open to dispute. Edward Wilson titles his chapter on free will "Emergence," even though the chapter is not at all about emergence as such.[82] It deals rather with the sociobiological predictability of human behavior. Wilson seems to suggest that an emergent like free will was predictable, and in any event is reducible to nerves and neurons; "the brain," he says, "is a machine of ten billion nerve cells and the mind can somehow be explained as the summed activity of a finite number of chemical and electrical reactions."[83] Wilson's philosophy only enables him to see things in terms of their constituent parts. Paul Davies quotes Donald MacKay (1922–87), a Christian neurobiologist, who criticizes this reductionism as a "nothing-buttery" attitude. Davies agrees:

> In the case of living systems, nobody would deny that an organism is a collection of atoms. The mistake is to suppose that it is nothing but a collection of atoms. Such a claim is as ridiculous as asserting that a Beethoven symphony is nothing but a collection of notes or that a Dickens novel is nothing but a collection of words.[84]

Polanyi is even stronger in his rejection of such reductionism:

> It is taken for granted today among biologists that all manifestations of life can ultimately be explained by the laws governing inanimate matter. . . . Yet this assumption is patent nonsense. The most striking feature of our own existence is our sentience.

82. *On Human Nature*, 71–97.

83. *On Human Nature*, 1. Wilson is determined to keep God out of the picture. "Genetic chance and environmental necessity, not God, made the species," he says.

84. Davies, *God and the New Physics*, 61–62.

> The laws of physics and chemistry include no conception of sentience, and any system wholly determined by these laws must be insentient. It may be in the interest of science to turn a blind eye on this central fact of the universe, but it is certainly not in the interest of truth.[85]

I am not pointing to emergence, and nor was Polanyi, as some sort of miracle in the midst of physical laws; it is nothing of the kind. Physics does not understand the laws of emergence and may never do so, but emergence is in the domain of science, not theology. Theology can and must, however, include in its deliberations all types of knowledge, and what Polanyi, speaking as a philosopher, saw in regard to tacit knowing and emergence cries out for our attention. He not only saw a connection between emergence and tacit knowing but he even identified the one with the other.[86] He did so specifically in the idea that as emergents of the universe, humans know the universe by the emergent process of tacit knowing. In a sense, emergence is to the universe as tacit knowing is to human existence.

Let me explain this a little further. The physical laws of the universe are just that, physical laws—they are not, as Harold Morowitz seems to think, identical with "the immanent God." When we study the laws, we are not studying God any more than reading the menu is the same as having dinner with the chef.[87] Polanyi's beautiful idea—worthy of both scientific and theological thought—is that just as levels of reality have emerged over the eons of the universe, so the emergent mind, in its learning, mirrors the emergent process by which it arose. The mind reaches for and slowly grasps deeper levels of reality through tacit knowing, just as the universe itself reaches for and slowly attains deeper and deeper levels of reality. As a theologian, I would say that the universe, with its innate creativity, is reaching out for its Creator, and the mind, by its tacit knowing and in all realms of its learning, is doing the same.

85. *Tacit Dimension*, 37–38.

86. *Tacit Dimension*, 48–49, 88. On page 4 he writes, "My search has led me to a novel idea of human knowledge from which a harmonious view of thought and existence, *rooted in the universe*, seems to emerge" (emphasis added).

87. *Emergence of Everything*, 23 and 197 respectively. Though it makes for lovely poetry, I also cannot accept Morowitz's idea that emergence "is the process by which the word (immanence) becomes flesh (transcendence)." This follows on his assertion that "emergence has a divine aspect" (190). As I see it, *all* of the universe "has a divine aspect" in that it is God's creation, but only indirectly does it tell us of God.

The whole process originates, and continues, in God lovingly drawing creation forward.[88]

That is a theological interpretation. But even at a more common sense level, it is surely apparent that we can no more account for humanity in terms of physics and chemistry than we can account for "the Lord is my shepherd" (Ps 23) in terms of the ink and parchment on which it was written. Though no doubt chemical analysis of the ink and paper would be rich in information, it would not even begin to recognize the poetry, much less its meaning. Emergence happens when unanticipated, further principles come into operation. It is the way in which the universe has produced beings that can think about emergence, and not just understand but also employ the laws of physics. Morowitz says that "a physicist is the atom's way of thinking about atoms,"[89] which is no doubt correct. But in that case, what is the universe thinking of in Shakespeare, Bertrand Russell, Edward Wilson, or the eager mind of a university student? As Paul Davies says:

> Through conscious beings the universe has generated self-awareness. This can be no trivial detail, no minor byproduct of mindless, purposeless forces. We are truly meant to be here.[90]

Conclusion: All of the Evidence

If we are going to take into account all of the evidence, we must reckon with every level of reality that the universe and ordinary experience lay before us. Science is an endless store of riches in that regard; taken in its full context—not only objective facts but also the passionate commitments and desire for truth of the knower—science witnesses clearly to the depths of the human mystery, and the mystery of the reality from which we have emerged. In our explorations of the mystery, we sell ourselves short if we do not take into account every aspect of knowing, every field of meaning, and all of our capacities for discerning truth. Science, poetry, philosophy, art, theology, all of these and more reveal

88. See John Haught, *Christianity and Science: Toward a Theology of Nature* (New York: Orbis, 2007), 75, where he describes the vision of Teilhard de Chardin; also *Is Nature Enough?*, 77–97; and Arthur Peacocke, *Theology for a Scientific Age: Being and Becoming—Natural, Divine, and Human*, enlarged ed. (Minneapolis: Fortress Press, 1993), 300–303.

89. *Emergence of Everything*, 184.

90. *Mind of God*, 232; the final words of the book.

us to ourselves. Dawkins, however, rejects this. Quoting "the eminent zoologist G. G. Simpson," he begins *The Selfish Gene* by telling us that all responses to the question, "what is man?" that predate 1859 must be ignored.[91] If we were to specify that the answer must confine itself to physical morphology, then I would agree. If, on the other hand, we wanted to know why humans do science, write poetry, believe in God, seek to be loving, and so on, then I'm afraid Dawkins falls under the judgment he pronounces on all of those other answers; "there is such a thing as being just plain wrong."[92]

A concrete instance of his being just plain wrong involves the silly self-contradiction he creates with regard to altruism. Dawkins thinks that "we, and all other animals, are machines created by our genes." We are, therefore, liable to "ruthless selfishness," and are capable only of "a limited form of altruism." "Universal love," he says, simply does "not make evolutionary sense"; in fact, "pure, disinterested altruism . . . has no place in nature," and "has never existed before in the whole history of the world"! And yet, somehow, he believes we should "try to teach generosity and altruism," and even says that we are capable of cultivating it.[93] But this is utter nonsense! How are we to teach something that is not only contrary to nature but also has never before even existed? Dawkins here, like other scientific materialists, simply does not follow his own creed.[94] Indeed, the creed itself makes no sense.

An amazing aspect of the argument of the scientific materialists is that they define humans, and human intelligence, in the most minimal of ways—purely in terms of genes and memes, atoms and nerve cells. The natural conclusion would seem to be that we should be very circumspect about trusting any intelligence so constructed.[95] Scientific materialists, however, show no such caution about their own intelligence. Somehow or other, their brains have risen above the limitations of evolution, which—they assure the rest of us—demonstrates that we are really not much more than apes. Their brains, nevertheless, somehow have the

91. *The Selfish Gene*, 1; 1859, of course, was the year of publication of Darwin's *Origin of Species*.

92. *The Selfish Gene*, 267.

93. *The Selfish Gene*, 2–3, 200–201.

94. Haught, *Is Nature Enough?*, 97. A similar complaint can be made against Wilson with regard to free will; see the critique of Wendell Berry, *Life Is a Miracle*, e.g., 25–26.

95. See Haught, *Deeper than Darwin: The Prospect for Religion in the Age of Evolution* (Boulder, CO: Westview Press, 2003), 97–100. Haught has developed this critique of naturalism further in *Is Nature Enough?*, e.g., 110–13. I referenced this argument already in chapter 1.

ability to announce to the rest of us the ultimate truth about everything, that it is all just a massive accidental collocation of atoms that means nothing, and so on. One is tempted to ask, how did their brains manage this amazing feat? How come all the rest of us do not see things that way? The traditional religions were properly rebuked by the gains of the Enlightenment; let us hope that further reflection will also put this new mythology in its place.

Michael Polanyi contemplated "for the sake of argument that physics and chemistry could be expanded to account for [human] sentience," and so deliberated about the possible construction of a machine that could think like Shakespeare. He even considered whether "a perfect scientific knowledge would eliminate" any doubts about the possibility. In the end, however, he said:

> I am committed to a different belief . . . the works of Shakespeare offer a massive demonstration of a creativity which cannot be explained in terms of an automatic mechanism.[96]

In the end, perhaps personal belief is all we have, but if our beliefs are based on all of the evidence, then Polanyi—in my belief!—has the better of the debate. At least, in Polanyi's view, we can believe in the reality and value of our moral assertions and, by the explorations of tacit knowing, explore other levels of reality beyond the physical to account for what and who we are. As I have said already, we need liberation from ideologies that would confine us to the level of the physical every bit as much as we need liberation from the worst of religious fanaticism. Neither dogma is worthy of the depth and beauty of the human spirit.

In 1994, over the course of about a hundred days, 800,000 people—mainly Tutsis—were slaughtered in Rwanda. The following year, Archbishop Desmond Tutu, who was awarded the Nobel peace prize in 1984 for his nonviolent struggle against the humiliations of apartheid in South Africa, went to Rwanda in his capacity as president of the All Africa Conference of Churches. The message he preached was, "no future without forgiveness."[97] He knew what he was talking about, since in the previous years—at the behest of Nelson Mandela—he had headed

96. *Personal Knowledge*, 336.

97. Desmond Tutu, "No Future without Forgiveness," *The Impossible Will Take a Little While: A Citizen's Guide to Hope in a Time of Fear*, ed. Paul Rogat Loeb (New York: Basic Books, 2004), 390–96.

South Africa's "Truth and Reconciliation Commission," whose charge was both to uncover the atrocities of the apartheid period and, far from seeking revenge, to bring about peace, reconciliation, and even forgiveness. Even so, it was a stunning message: forgive those who slaughtered your family and friends!

Those of us spared such horrific experiences as apartheid and genocide can barely grasp the concept, and yet we know—though we cannot prove—the truth of what Tutu, Mandela, and others have embodied by their lives of courage and sacrifice. We *know* that violence, hatred, and revenge hold no future for the human animal. We know, as surely as we know ourselves, that our humanity has a genuine capacity for love, as it has capacities for freedom, forgiveness, and hope. Our capacities, however, are not automatically realized; we must begin by believing in them. To pursue them, and bring them to fruitful action, requires even more effort. So, though I am not trying to convert anyone, I am trying to make the case that the world's ancient spiritual traditions, which foster disciplines of prayer, compassion, universal love, forgiveness, and so on, are essential traditions that we abandon at our peril. And certainly I hope I have given reason to doubt the wisdom of the new mythology of scientific materialism. The self-contradiction of Dawkins, Wilson, and others is shown in the fact that in real life they espouse admirable values, like environmentalism, for instance, which certainly owes nothing to genes and—unlike universal love—has indeed, until very recent times, probably never existed before in the history of the world! But that's enough. It's time to return to the Scriptures, to experience their symbolism and to see the types of knowledge they embody that, in addition to science, we still very much need.

CHAPTER
5

TYPES OF KNOWING IN THE BIBLE

I prayed, and prudence was given me;
I pleaded and the spirit of Wisdom came to me.
I preferred her to scepter and throne,
And deemed riches nothing in comparison with her,
nor did I liken any priceless gem to her;
Because all gold, in view of her, is a little sand,
and before her, silver is to be accounted mire.

—Wisdom 7:7-9, NAB

Tacit Knowing and the Language of Scripture

I have argued that our fascination with scientific ways of knowing has caused us to constrict our ways of thinking about God, the world, and human beings. We have made God smaller than ourselves and subject to our scrutiny, and we have come to doubt our own powers of transcendence, even our powers of consciousness and free will. Such a science-only view of human beings is too narrow; we also need to draw on ancient spiritual wisdom. In this chapter I want to show that the types of knowledge embodied in the Bible also have value in the attempt to understand the full depth of existence. This is not because the Bible describes facts about humans and their world; theoretical knowledge is not the Bible's domain. The Bible reveals reality by presupposing infinite depths in the being of God, and by enabling us to understand humans in that context.

The Bible is properly seen as a product of consciousness and culture. Like other sacred texts,[1] it takes us into the heart of human awareness,

1. My focus will remain on the Bible, but I gladly acknowledge the relevance of what I am saying to the sacred texts of other religions. As I suggested in chapter 2 (note 69),

specifically as lived within the histories of ancient Israel and early Christianity. More specifically, the texts can be properly seen as illustrations of "tacit knowing" reaching out for the "tacit dimension" of reality. They represent restless longing for meaning in the face of the mystery of fleeting and fractured human existence. As such, biblical texts are assertions of God's presence not only in times of joy, when that presence was experienced as close and loving, but also in times of doubt and intense suffering, when God seemed remote or even absent and hostile.

A major obstacle, however, that constricts our reading of the texts, is an overly intense focus on the surface (the literal sense) of the words, almost as though words were exact representations of the things to which they point, which of course they are not. Sometimes we give the Bible too much credit—at other times, of course, not enough. We imagine that the texts represent answers or even doctrines,[2] when in reality they are closer to being—in the manner of tacit knowing—inquiries or first drafts that seek to discover or express new ways of seeing or knowing. Someone might quickly object that when, for instance, Leviticus 11 strictly forbids the eating of "unclean" meat, or when Paul, in apostolic fury, condemns his opponents (Gal 1:8-9), then the texts can hardly be said to represent "inquiries." There are times when they speak with unequivocal confidence, even with dogmatic certainty. All of that is true, but such texts have to be considered in their contexts; they are far from the last word on the issue. Further, even when people of the same time and culture share language, there is less than a one-to-one correspondence between speaker and hearer, all the more so if the topic is profound. We need, therefore, to consider how language functions in relation to thought, and to the acquisition and communication of knowledge.

Language did not evolve for the sophisticated purposes of modern society—business, technology, legal jargon, complex diplomacy, and so on. Neither did it evolve for the benefit of ancient Greek philosophers,

---

acknowledging that the literature of other religions is also sacred surely *strengthens*, rather than weakens, the case for the inspiration of the Bible. I should also emphasize the need within religion for critical discernment; I am *not* suggesting that just anything in religion is acceptable.

2. I do not mean to totally reject "the doctrinal approach" as a possible way to use the Bible, but the "reservations" about it as expressed by Avery Dulles (*The Craft of Theology: From Symbol to System, New Expanded Edition* [New York: Crossroads, 1992], 72) are serious, particularly the problem of "prooftexting" out of context, and the neglect of the "form" of the language (more on this below). We must also never forget that "many statements in the Bible . . . fall short of definitive truth"—*far* short (e.g., Deut 7:1-5).

or for the authors and scribes of the texts of the Bible. These are all very "modern" applications of a far more ancient set of skills that emerged among our African ancestors more than a hundred thousand years ago—maybe a lot more.[3] In its origins, language has more to do with "gossip," simple commands, and information-sharing than with technology or philosophy. Further, language is only one of the symbol-systems we use on a regular basis. "Song, art, dance, ritual and myth" are some of the more ancient; "writing, graphs, tables, data banks, printouts, and equations" are some of the more recent.[4] These, in turn, often involve speech and writing, but they also illustrate the symbolic, and inexact, character of language itself. Language brought people together and vastly accelerated the development of culture (tool-making, group-cooperation, etc.), but its power should not be overestimated. Contrary to the old orthodoxy that many of us learned, it is not the case that language is essential to thought—to the contrary, it is thought, in the sense of an ever-searching consciousness, which is in the driver's seat.[5] Full understanding always requires going deeper than the words.

That thinking far precedes speaking is evident both in animals and human infants. Animals can solve quite complex problems, and in some cases help one another to do so, all without the benefit of language. When a monkey solves the problem of how to get to the honey sealed in a container—check it out on YouTube—it is clearly thinking.[6] The pro-

3. I am indebted here especially to Merlin Donald, *A Mind So Rare: The Evolution of Human Consciousness* (New York: W. W. Norton, 2001), 252–300; see also Robin Dunbar, *Grooming, Gossip, and the Evolution of Language* (London: Faber & Faber, 1996); idem, *The Human Story: A New History of Mankind's Evolution* (London: Faber & Faber, 2004), 121–26; and Paul Ehrlich, *Human Natures: Genes, Cultures and the Human Prospect* (Washington, DC: Island Press, 2000), 139–63. According to Ehrlich (149), there is some evidence "that all extant languages [about 5,000 of them] share a fairly recent common origin, no more than 50,000 years in the past," but he favors an origin far older than that (150–56). Dunbar's research suggests (*Human Story*, 124–25) that language "in some form" "must have been in place" as early as 500,000 years ago. The gap between the numbers makes more sense with Donald's theory of the emergence of language from consciousness, culture, and mimesis.

4. Donald, *A Mind So Rare*, 276. Words, of course, are symbols in that they are arbitrary ways of designating something beyond themselves, from tables and chairs to isosceles triangles, and abstracts like "speech" or "justice."

5. I am following Donald's thesis here (277); Ehrlich, *Human Natures*, references the orthodoxy that "language is essential to thought," but properly says, "the data suggest otherwise" (146) and goes on to discuss the relation of the two. There are lots of theories, but thought's precedence is unquestioned. The real mystery is, what is thought?

6. "Monkey tool usage: Flint knife and probe," narrated by David Attenborough, http://www.youtube.com/watch?v=LThJWvJ2YNI.

cess by which a child learns language or anything else requires a great deal of conscious thought, and "aphasic patients who lose language altogether [e.g., due to stroke] . . . continue to be able to think in an artistic, mechanical or spatial sense."[7] A great deal of adult learning, in fact, comes by way of observation and imitation ("indwelling") that requires minimal language, but considerable thinking. The mind of Helen Keller is stunning evidence of the fact that an ever-searching awareness precedes and enables language, and that language requires culture and thought long before it makes its own contributions.[8]

The stunning success of language, its dominant place in human cultures, seduces us into overestimating its power to communicate thought. Since the Bible comes to us as language on a printed page, and since it has such enormous religious prestige, believers imagine that it is in some very literal sense the Word of God. And, of course—to be deeply paradoxical for a moment—*it is!* But it is such *only* inasmuch as it "indwells" the presence and love of God that reach out in creation and history. Perhaps a better description of the Bible might be "*thoughts* of God," leaving the *of* ambiguous. All of the language of the Bible is purely and only human; it is a product of culture(s), and of the "tacit" exploring of believers to reach beyond the surface into the mystery of existence. Given its limitations, the Bible's success is more than we should expect, but we inevitably get hopelessly confused if we fail to consider the limitations, as well as the possibilities, of its language. No language portrays thought perfectly; we all know this from our own failures to communicate.

"Language," says Merlin Donald, "regularly betrays us, misleads us, or proves completely inadequate to the task of capturing what it is supposed to capture."[9] He quotes the great French novelist Gustave Flaubert (1821–80), who was fastidious in his searching out of "the one precise word" and the "harmony of sounding syllables," so as to penetrate beyond "the mere sense of the words at their face value."[10] And yet Flaubert lamented that "language is like a cracked kettle on which we beat out tunes for bears to dance to, while all the while we long to move the stars to pity."[11] Words are attempts to convey thoughts; they evolved pursuant to mimesis—mime, imitation, skill-teaching, sign-gestures—as

7. Donald, *A Mind So Rare*, 277.

8. On Helen Keller, see Donald, *A Mind So Rare*, 232–51.

9. *A Mind So Rare*, 275.

10. "Flaubert, Gustave," *Encyclopædia Britannica Online*, accessed September 4, 2010, http://search.eb.com/eb/article-2350.

11. From *Madame Bovary*, quoted in Donald, *A Mind So Rare*, 252.

our early ancestors sought more and more to understand and communicate with one another.[12] "The great divide [from other primates] in human evolution," says Donald, "was not language but the formation of cognitive communities in the first place." In other words, "the first priority was not to speak" but "to bond as a group." "Symbolic thought" and language both derive from, and serve, that priority,[13] which helps to explain why emotions, stories, intersubjectivity, and desire for beauty are so intrinsic to the character of knowledge.

This means that beyond its "bread-and-butter functions" (gossip, simple commands),[14] language is heuristic; it is a searcher, driven by the mind's ever vigilant awareness as it attempts to frame its world meaningfully. Language partakes of the character of "tacit knowing," attending from the particulars toward integration and meaning, but what is in control is not language itself, but the subjectivity of mind that "knows" the problem, the idea—dare I say, the revelation?—long before it is able to express it in words:

> We evaluate all symbolic expressions from outside the symbol system, and from a region of mind that, in its principles of operation, is different from, and much more powerful than, the reach of any consensual expressive system [a language]. . . . We can recognize the value of ideas whose mere possibility we suspect, and whose reality still eludes us completely, to the point of pursuing them passionately for a lifetime.[15]

The Bible's symbolic language is itself a reaching out—a longing—for God, and in turn it enables such a pursuit in its readers. Theology has rarely attempted, and never agreed on, an explanation of how divine inspiration takes place, but any explanation would have to consider how thought, in reaching out to know its world more deeply, builds symbols and symbol-systems (language, art, ritual, and so on), and constantly refines these tools in search of better ones. It must be in "making us restless" (Augustine) for truth and meaning, and making us depend on one another for the search, that God finds ways to be Revealer:

12. See Donald, *A Mind So Rare*, 262–69.
13. *A Mind So Rare*, 254, 253.
14. Donald, *A Mind So Rare*, 276.
15. Donald, *A Mind So Rare*, 278.

> Awareness watches over and initiates all major symbolic performances . . . Consciousness is always on watch, and what is expressed is almost always less witty, less elegant, and less precise than what was intended. To our relief, our awareness knows this and compensates for it. Language has no autonomy from this conscious evaluative process, none. Our games with symbols may tease and twist our deep semantic spaces into novel shapes, creating new spaces between existing meaning states. Truly novel meanings have no other way to come into existence. But our symbolic universe serves only *one ultimate master, our drive for clearer states of awareness*, in both sender and receiver.[16]

Reading a text, therefore, is one mind inexpertly interpreting the symbolic communication of another mind that almost inevitably falls short of its communicative aims. Reading "seldom achieves what either author or reader originally intended, with any precision." But instinctively we know this; we know that reading the book does not lay bare the full mind of the author. What we are searching for is not "exact content" but "the possibility of a new domain of understanding"; it is in this "possibility"—in the "deliberate pursuit of enhanced awareness"—that "there is no longer any boundary between author and audience."[17] But if those sorts of limits obtain—as they do—between "authors" and "readers" who share the same culture, language, and moment in time, how much more hazardous are the communications between the ancient biblical authors and modern readers, where all of those distances are far more vast. And yet we can, and do, bridge the distance. Our desire for truth makes it possible.

Bridging the Distance

As already indicated, the "deliberate pursuit of enhanced awareness" on the part of both writer and reader delivers the possibility of new understanding. Putting thoughts into language has to do with both shaping and sharing them, in the hope of further awareness. Applied to the reading of the Bible, this means being open to the symbolic language—the symbolic universe, in fact—of the biblical authors. What did they experience? What do their texts, their language, reveal about their

16. Donald, *A Mind So Rare*, 279, emphasis added. I should clarify that Donald has no theological intentions in his description of consciousness and its evolution.

17. Donald, *A Mind So Rare*, 275.

understanding of God? What were they striving to express? There is no substitute for taking them seriously on their own terms, which is *not* the same as accepting at face value every claim or sentiment.

We return here to the necessity of the historical-critical method, which was a primary topic in chapter 2, but also, with due caution, to the guidance of the ancient interpreters, and the multileveled understanding of Origen. The Bible is perhaps best seen as symbolic communication, meaning that its images, persons, and events always point beyond themselves to realities they cannot define, but without which they could not be what they are. In a sense, all of Scripture has the character of the parables of Jesus.[18] But the communication has to be a two-way street. We cannot, in other words, be passive readers; we have to engage the texts sympathetically, but be prepared no less to argue with them—adopt the same freedom, in fact, that the authors of the Bible felt in relation to God. It is not the surface of the words that is our ultimate goal, but the being in communion, the real goal of language.

Also essential to bridging the distance are various methods of historical criticism. These will mostly be presupposed, but I will describe here one method that relates to the theme of types of knowledge, which has been important in our discussion. *Form criticism* is a well-tested method of analysis of biblical texts.[19] It builds on the fact that language, both oral and written, is shaped by the purposes and life settings in which it is employed. Letters, for instance, have quite definite purposes, and in fact they can be classified accordingly. Love letters have aims quite distinct from business letters, and so the life setting in which each type is found is also very distinct—romance in the one case, business in the other. Such well-established forms can also be classified by recognizable literary characteristics—"Dear Sir" being a dead giveaway of a business letter, "My darling" being characteristic of a love letter.

In every culture, people use various "forms" of language on a daily basis, slipping from one to another, recognizing automatically the conventions each requires. In modern society we regularly use and en-

18. On the Bible as symbolic communication, see Avery Dulles, *Models of Revelation* (New York: Orbis Books, 1983, 1992), 193–210; and Jeannine K. Brown, *Scripture as Communication: Introducing Biblical Hermeneutics* (Grand Rapids, MI: Baker Academic, 2007).

19. The method originated with Hermann Gunkel (1862–1932), especially with his analysis of Genesis, Psalms, and Prophets. It was applied to the New Testament, particularly the gospels and Acts, by Martin Dibelius (1883–1947), Rudolf Bultmann (1884–1976), and others. Its aims include trying to trace the forms back to their preliterary *oral* stage in the life of Israel and early Christianity.

counter letters (of various types), political and legal speeches, news announcements, recipes, greetings, sermons, sports reports, obituaries, jokes, gossip, editorials, dramas, novels, advertisements, fairy tales, histories, poems, endless varieties of each of these, and so on. We know instinctively how to distinguish a joke from a drama, since they are part of our everyday language. With a little thought, we could describe such forms in terms of their recognizable characteristics, their life settings, and, very important, what purposes they have. The purpose of a form has to do with what it aims to accomplish or, we might say, what type of truth it conveys. Obituaries, in that regard, are quite different from jokes, news reports from novels, and we would never mistake one for the other.

That instant recognition of forms disappears, however, the moment we are faced with the forms of a foreign culture, like the Bible. The major reason for this is simply that they are "foreign"; we do not know how to "read" them correctly, rather like someone unfamiliar with Western culture confusing a business letter for a love letter. If David could be fooled by Nathan's parable of the rich man who stole the poor man's lamb (2 Sam 12:1-6), even though David and Nathan shared the same culture, we can be fooled all the more easily. To this day, intelligent people read the Bible as though its purposes neatly conform to modern forms. Edward Wilson says he gave up on the Bible when he discovered that it "made no provision for *evolution*."[20] Apparently he thinks Genesis ought to be written in the form of a book on biology! His error is tantamount to dismissing *Macbeth* because it is not history, or the Prodigal Son (Luke 15:11-32) because we do not know the name of the "far country" in which the prodigal spent his father's money. We make similar errors when we read prophetic oracles as though they were infallible directives from God, miracle stories as though they were paragraphs from a biography, or the book of Jonah as though its purpose was to describe the prophet's experience in the belly of a fish.[21] Taking the texts of the Bible on their own terms requires a more nuanced understanding of their language, and of the types of truth they embody.

20. *Consilience: The Unity of Knowledge* (New York: Vintage Books, 1998), 6.

21. Even though Matthew's Jesus (Matt 12:40) refers to Jonah's "three days and three nights in the belly of a huge fish" (NIV), that does not make *Jonah* into history, much less does it change the actual point of the book, which is revealed only in the last paragraph—God's love and compassion for the enemies of Israel. Believers need to be careful about making Matt 12:40 into an argument for the literal interpretation of anything, since Matt 12:40 itself cannot be taken literally—Jesus was not *literally* "in the heart of the earth for *three* days and *three* nights."

But it is not only that biblical forms of speech and writing are unfamiliar to us. What is also unfamiliar is the symbolic and theological worldview in which they were generated and interpreted. In spite of their great diversity, what binds all of the texts of Scripture together is their presumption that all things have their being from God. Though not explicit, this is no doubt true even of the "godless"[22] Song of Songs, which justifies the rabbis and Origen taking it as an allegory. In doing so, they were at least close to the spirit of other biblical texts, which take it for granted that the presence of God suffuses the whole universe. It is essential to remember that long before the texts became sacred and "Bible," they were just texts—the Song originally was someone's love poems, large parts of Genesis were campfire stories about the ancestors. The Bible's divine character does not reside in the texts themselves, but in the persons, events, and experiences that—however imperfectly—they embody. The texts are sacred because Abraham and Sarah heard a divine call; because Israel "knew" that God is One, the Creator of all things; because the prophets felt divine pathos[23] in the face of injustice and religious hypocrisy; because Mary Magdalene, Peter, and others "knew" Jesus as "the Word" spoken from the heart of God; and so on.

The texts, in other words, are about the people and events that lie behind the texts, and about the dynamics of authoring and editing that are evident within the texts. Hence, the historical-critical method remains indispensable. It shows that the texts are products of long-lived "cognitive communities," which, over centuries, experienced and longed for God. The genius of their knowing was in their presumption, well exemplified in Origen, that all types of knowledge and every branch of learning cohere in the recognition of the sacredness of the universe. In that context, the modern splitting off of human subjectivity as though it has nothing to tell us of the nature of existence, as though everything is pure object, and only physical theory represents true knowledge, is singularly narrow, not to say destructive. We certainly cannot, and must not, agree with the Bible or Origen about everything, but we exhibit crass arrogance when we imagine that our discoveries and theories about the physical universe exclude all other knowledge and truth. Such a stance

22. "Godless" in the sense (recall chapter 3) that it makes no mention of God, God's commands, or God's rescue of Israel; it also contains no prayers or prophecy. On the surface, it looks throughout like erotic poetry.

23. I am reflecting here the interpretation of the prophets found in Abraham J. Heschel, *The Prophets*, vol. 1 (New York: Harper & Row, 1962), esp. 23–26.

is analogous to explaining the Good Samaritan (Luke 10:25-37) as mere paper and ink, a wedding ring as just a bit of metal, or a human being as just so many pounds of flesh and bone. Biblical thinkers interpreted the universe in terms of God and humanity; theology and anthropology are always intertwined.

This is why, as we read the texts, we must look beyond and behind the texts to the people, and to the events and experiences that brought them to their convictions. This is a different kind of knowing. It is not academic analysis or measured calculation. It is a knowing more akin to what lovers know than clinicians. "To comprehend what phenomena are, it is important to suspend judgment and think in detachment," says Abraham Heschel, in his book *The Prophets*. But such knowing, he explains, will not bring us where we need to be to get at the heart of the prophets or (we may add) other biblical writers. There are times when detachment aids knowledge; there are times when it impedes. "To comprehend what phenomena mean," he continues, "it is necessary to suspend indifference and be involved."[24] It is insufficient to look at the texts; we must learn more to look with them—through their eyes—and even occasionally to debate with them, without being too quick to assume that they are wrong. In any event, we must be involved with them and with their longing for God.

In addition to looking at the people and history behind the texts, we must also examine the experiences and convictions of the biblical writers, their interpretations of their ancestors and founding events. This also involves being sensitive to the conversations within the texts, as when Deuteronomy differs from Exodus, Chronicles interprets Samuel, Ezekiel rejects an Exodus maxim, Matthew elaborates on Mark, and Paul sharply rebukes Peter.[25] Such sensitivity rescues us from being overly bound to the surface level of the texts, and enables encounter with the deeper theological issues that lie both behind and within them. But—and this is a crucial point—we must attend not only to the dynamics behind and within the texts but also and no less to the dynamics in front of the

24. *Prophets*, xii–xiii.

25. Deut 5:15 gives a different motivation for the observance of the Sabbath over against Exod 20:11; 1 Chr 20 pointedly omits David's adultery with Bathsheba and his murder of her husband, as told in 2 Sam 11; Ezek 18 (cf. Deut 24:16; Jer 31:29-30) rejects the maxim of Exod 20:5 that children suffer for the sins of their ancestors; Matt 27:51-54 is dramatically different in several respects over against its probable source in Mark 15:38-39; Paul's sharp telling-off of Peter (Gal 2:11-14) is one of the most neglected and significant incidents in the entire New Testament.

texts.[26] *Our* sympathies matter, not only those of the ancients. The Bible's communicative intention is only accomplished when readers and hearers attend to its voices, listen to them carefully, and derive meanings that make sense in their own contexts. In other words, not only the text's context, but also the context of modern readers is essential to consider in the task of interpretation.

Readers as well as writers produce meaning. Readers must first strive to understand the purpose of the text, but they must also take their own situation into account as they "hear" it. We all have prejudices and needs—predispositions based on family background, education, social status, religion, and so on. Failure to recognize the lenses, through which we read the texts, leaves us prey to the way those lenses might as much hinder understanding as they might help. This is why interpretation is a slightly hazardous enterprise; it closely resembles tacit knowing, and therefore resembles also the mind's ever searching "drive for clearer states of awareness." When we read the Bible, we enter into a dialogue with it. The dialogue has to be characterized by an honest effort to hear the texts on their own terms, but also to bring our own selves, and context, to bear on the reading. Inspiration, remember, began long before the texts were written, and continues within and among its readers.

In the readings below, I will attempt to bring together a faithful hearing of biblical texts with some of the questions and insights of modern science. Our purpose is to discern the "thoughts of God" in and behind the various layers of the texts, and thereby to get at the types of truth they have to offer in the context of our science-dominated world. "Types of truth" does not mean particular truths, in the manner of doctrines; it has to do with looking through different lenses—the symbols and images of faith. This is more a search for *formation* than *in*formation. The reading will require some measure of humility and openness, not unlike how one might listen to representatives of a distant and different culture. The knowledge we attain from a sympathetic reading of biblical themes and texts challenges and enhances the view of reality that we gain from a science-only view. Certainly the discussion should make clear that there is no necessary conflict between scientific theories, and the images, stories, and God-centered views of the universe found in the Bible. The kind of coherence we seek from science has to do with the

26. See Joel B. Green, "The Challenge of Hearing the New Testament," in idem, ed., *Hearing the New Testament: Strategies for Interpretation* (Grand Rapids, MI: Wm. B. Eerdmans, 1995), 1–36; and Brown, *Scripture as Communication*, 120–29.

physical recipes and formulas by which the universe came into existence and now operates. The coherence we seek from theology and the texts of Scripture has to do with the Mind of the Universe that endows humans with capacities for awareness, contemplation, science, art, and theology.

The themes to be dealt with (suffering, miracles, life after death) are chosen because they are among the issues that most naturally spark discussion on the relationship between the Bible and science.

Suffering

Suffering is one of the most intractable problems that theology ever has to face, since at a moral and spiritual level it presents a clear challenge to belief in the presence and love of God. For its part, science can help in understanding suffering at the physical level; taken together, they can provide some measure of coherence on what will always remain a difficult issue. In the absence of the knowledge that modern science brings to an understanding of creation, ancient biblical thinkers sometimes attributed all suffering, natural disasters, and human violence alike to the will of God and left it at that. The initial response of Job[27] to the loss of his children exemplifies such an attitude:

> Naked I came from my mother's womb, and naked shall I return;
> The LORD gave and the LORD has taken away;
> Blessed be the name of the LORD. (Job 1:21, RSV)

David gives the same sort of stoic response when his baby son, born to Bathsheba as a result of David's adultery with her, dies: "Can I bring him back again? I shall go to him, but he will not return to me" (2 Sam 12:23, RSV). Guilty David and innocent Job both stare into the mysterious face of suffering, and indeed into the mystery of death, and trust God *in spite of* suffering. When Job's wife counsels him, in the face of even further suffering, to "curse God and die," Job rebukes her: "We accept good things from God; and should we not accept evil?" (Job 2:10, NAB).

The thought here is that all things ultimately derive from God, including suffering. For the believer, this can, though not easily, extend to being

27. "Job" here is not to be understood as a historical character; the book comprises a folktale that was known in and beyond Israel probably from at least the time of David and Solomon (10th c. BCE). Its writing involved several editions, ending in its present form perhaps around the 5th century BCE, but its date is very uncertain. Note that Job's suffering derives from both natural disasters and human violence (Job 1); Job blames God for both.

less afraid of suffering, since somehow God is present there also. This explains David's response on another occasion that if he and the people must suffer, "let us fall by the hand of the LORD, for his mercy is great; but let me not fall by a human hand" (2 Sam 24:14).[28] Much of modern theology shies away from the notion of God as the source of all things; we want to think of God only in terms of love and compassion. The notion of God as causing suffering, and especially the wrath of God, have become politically incorrect, even among theologians. Throughout most of Scripture, however, God is presumed to be the source of all things, life *and* death, good *and* evil (Lam 3:38). Though difficult, the biblical view bears a deep wisdom, as becomes apparent when we see the alternative.

The alternative, also entertained in the Bible, is to blame "Satan," including for the suffering caused by human evil.[29] In Job, "the *satan*," a kind of prosecuting attorney among "the sons of God" (Job 1:6), is the one who incites God to make Job suffer, but Job himself never mentions the *satan*, and blames only God for his suffering—and surely Job is correct. This is echoed in Jesus' prayer in the garden. Though it is presumed that Satan can harass him,[30] when Jesus prayed for deliverance from suffering, he prayed (and clearly believed) that everything depends upon God (Mark 14:36)—at most, Satan is a servant, a device; the One we truly have to deal with is God. In any event, the Bible does not permit letting God (or ourselves) off the hook too soon, so to speak. If we take

28. 2 Sam 24 is one of the most difficult, not to say strange, texts in the Bible. God's anger is inflamed against Israel for some unknown reason, so God incites David "against them," causing him to take a census of the people. No reason is given why a census should be regarded as offensive to God (taking control from God's hands?—24:3?), but David recognizes when it is completed that he has sinned. God then turns his wrath on Israel, giving David three choices of punishment, which is when David chooses to "fall by" God's hand rather than his enemies. The chapter is a vivid reminder of why not everything in the Bible can be taken as of equal value with everything else.

29. The version of the 2 Sam 24 story found in 1 Chr 21 breaks the tension of the original story, in which God both incites the evil deed and then punishes it, by saying that it was "Satan" who incited David! Satan here and in Job 1–2 is not "the Devil" (Satan, Prince of demons) of the gospels, but a servant of God whose job is to test virtue and prosecute sin. The notion that a demonic force (called by various names, including Satan) incites moral evil among people became a popular notion in the late Old Testament period, as seen in texts like Jubilees and Enoch. In the New Testament, the idea is especially prominent in the temptation-of-Jesus stories (Matt 4 and Luke 4) and in the book of Revelation. That demons caused sickness (e.g., Luke 13:16) was also a common idea. Jesus' ministry was seen as a breaking of the power of Satan (e.g., Matt 12:22-29; John 12:31).

30. Compare Luke 4:13 with 22:3, 31. By New Testament times, the *satan* (see the last note) had become a personal force named "Satan."

the Bible on its own terms, it forces us to wrestle with the question of why God at least permits so much suffering. In my view, it is ultimately a matter of creation, the sort of world God is creating, and it is in that regard that science can provide some help to understand the issue, as we shall see presently.

But first, both Job and other texts of Scripture provide far more complex responses to the mystery of suffering than its simple acceptance as the will of God. Job's three friends, for instance, represent a theology of retribution—suffering, they believe, derives from sin. Over and over again they imply that Job must have committed some sin that he is refusing to admit (e.g., 4:7-9, 17-21; 8:1-7). Such a theology, that sinfulness is the source of suffering, is well known elsewhere, and still makes its presence felt to this day. Psalm 37 is its most consistent articulation, but it appears also in Proverbs and in numerous other contexts (e.g., Prov 10:3; see 2 Kgs 21:10-15). In Job, however, such theology is rejected! The friends "did *not* speak rightly" and God instructs them to repent (42:7-9).[31] The problem with retribution theology is shown on its flip side, with the notion that prosperity derives from virtue, as though we are to believe that the rich are always virtuous![32]

Retribution theology receives a significant correction in John's gospel, at the beginning of the story of the man born blind. The disciples take it for granted that sin must have caused his blindness and so ask Jesus only whether the sin was his own or that of his parents. Reminiscent of Job, Jesus rejects both alternatives, "and what he says would apply equally to Job; he suffers not because of any sins but 'that the works of God may be shown forth in him'" (John 9:1-3).[33] Far from looking down on suffering, whether in ourselves or in others, perhaps we might regard it as a form of God's presence. But, of course, such a thought can easily become a platitude, and suffering—especially the suffering of the innocent—defies all platitudes and easy explanations.

The strongest biblical response to suffering is the prayer of complaint: "My God, my God, why have you forsaken me?" Those are the opening

31. Daniel C. Timmer, "God's Speeches, Job's Responses, and the Problem of Coherence in the Book of Job: Sapiential Pedagogy Revisited," *Catholic Biblical Quarterly* 71:2 (2009): 286–305, note 302–3.

32. To the contrary, notice how often in the Bible it is assumed that the poor, weak, and helpless are the ones who truly know and obey God (e.g., Ps 10:14-18; Matt 5:3-10) while the rich and powerful are those who oppress them (e.g., Jer 2:34; 5:27-28; Amos 4:1).

33. R. A. F. MacKenzie and Roland E. Murphy, "Job," in *The New Jerome Biblical Commentary* (Englewood Cliffs, NJ: Prentice Hall, 1968, 1990), 467.

words of Psalm 22 (NRSV), which according to Matthew (27:46) and Mark (15:34), Jesus "cried out with a loud voice" as he hung crucified, about to die. Psalm 22 is one of many psalms in which an individual—occasionally a whole community—laments harsh suffering.[34] In such psalms, prayers of complaint are a regular feature: "Why, O LORD, do you stand far off? Why do you hide yourself in times of trouble?" (Ps 10:1, NRSV); "You have cast us off and humiliated us . . . you have made us like sheep for slaughter" (Ps 44:9-11); "Has God forgotten to be gracious? Has he in anger shut up his compassion?" (Ps 77:9, NRSV). The prophet Jeremiah was more strident, even angry, in his complaints.

It is not for nothing that the word "jeremiad" derives from this prophet. He was a "young man" (1:6-7) when he began his ministry, but he grew old over its forty painful years (c. 620–580 BCE). He saw the land ravaged, the city besieged, the population reduced to cannibalism, and the final destruction (586 BCE). God instructed him not to marry (16:1-2). He was beaten and put "in the stocks" (20:2), threatened with death by his enemies (26:8), and placed in a muddy cistern to die (38:6). He had profound faith, but this seems only to have made him all the more bold in his complaints to God: "Why is my pain unceasing, my wound incurable, refusing to be healed? Truly, you are to me like a deceitful brook, like waters that fail" (15:18, NRSV). Jeremiah felt free enough in God's presence to complain bitterly:

> Cursed be the day on which I was born! The day when my mother bore me, let it not be blessed! . . . Why did I come forth from the womb to see toil and sorrow, and spend my days in shame? (20:14, 18, NRSV)

Religious piety sometimes thinks that prayer to God always has to be about praise and thanksgiving, but Jeremiah and Jesus also knew the value of the prayer of complaint. Mark and Matthew show Jesus quoting only the very opening words of Psalm 22; the next words are, "Why are you so far from helping me, from the words of my groaning? O my God, I cry by day, but you do not answer; and by night, but find no rest" (NRSV). One wonders how far into the psalm Jesus prayed. Even with

34. E.g., Pss 6, 10, 13, 38, 42, 43, 44, and 60 (the last two being communal laments). Lamentations mostly speaks of God in the third person, and so does not feature the direct prayers of complaint of the psalms. The prophet Jeremiah is famous for his laments (often referred to as his "confessions") and his complaints to God are very direct and sometimes quite harsh, not to say daring! See Jer 11:18–12:6; 15:10-21; 17:14-18; 18:18-24; 20:7-13, 14-18.

insights from science, there are no final explanations for deep human suffering; silence alone is appropriate. The apparent silence of God in the face of suffering is the experience behind the psalms of lament, and words like, "My God, my God, why have you forsaken me?"

The Silence of God

In *Night*, Elie Wiesel speaks of the silence of God in the context of his experiences in Birkenau, Auschwitz, Buna, and Buchenwald; of the murder of his mother and little sister; and the slow agonizing death of his father. Forced to witness the hanging of a child at Buna, he hears someone asking over and over, "'Where is God? Where is God?' And I heard a voice within me answer him: 'Where is he? Here he is—he is hanging here on this gallows.'"[35] A few weeks later was Yom Kippur, a day of fasting and repentance. The Jewish prisoners debated whether they should observe the traditional fast, though they were already starving to death:

> I did not fast, mainly to please my father, who had forbidden me to do so. But further, there was no longer any reason why I should fast. I no longer accepted God's silence. As I swallowed my bowl of soup, I saw in the gesture an act of rebellion and protest against Him. And I nibbled my crust of bread. In the depths of my heart I felt a great void.[36]

The apparent silence of God in the face of evil and suffering is the most painful problem faith ever has to face; it is a silence that sometimes erases faith. It is something of a mystery why it does not do so more often. Surely just hearing of Auschwitz and Buna, indeed of the deaths of millions of unremembered innocents throughout countless centuries, ought to be enough to erase all thought about the God of the Bible, a God who is supposedly "merciful and gracious, slow to anger, and abounding in steadfast love and faithfulness" (Exod 34:6, NRSV). Why have so many remained dedicated to that creed? Why do not more reach the

35. Elie Wiesel, *Night* (New York: Bantam Books, 1960), 60–62.

36. *Night*, 66. It should be stressed that, though his relationship with God was radically changed, Elie Wiesel did not lose his faith in God. Indeed, he regards it as "an interpretation bordering on blasphemy" when "theorists" take his words from *Night* "as justification of their rejection of faith"; see Elie Wiesel, *All Rivers Run to the Sea: Memoirs* (New York: Alfred A. Knopf, 1996), 84.

conclusion of Elie Wiesel's friend at Auschwitz, Primo Levi, that "if God is God, then He is present everywhere. But if He refuses to show himself, he becomes immoral and inhuman, the enemy's ally or accomplice"?[37] What is the experience that makes God inerasable from human minds and hearts, even in the presence of horrendous evil and suffering?

A common answer is that faith is some sort of perversion or at least a symptom of weak minds that cannot face up to reality.[38] But there was nothing weak-minded about Isaiah, Jeremiah, Mary Magdalene, or Origen. The same has to be said of Frederick Douglass (1818–95), Mohandas (Mahatma) Ghandi (1869–1948), Martin Luther King Jr. (1929–68), Mother Teresa (1910–97), Elie Wiesel, Desmond Tutu, and numerous others who have stared into the face of evil and suffering. None of them could solve the problem of why God allows the innocent to suffer, but whereas for nonbelievers that question does not even exist, for believers it is a matter of courage, prayer, and, on occasion, complaint. Wiesel properly says:

> The texts cite many occasions when prophets and sages rebelled against the lack of divine interference in human affairs during times of persecution . . . it is permissible for man to accuse God, provided it be done in the name of faith in God. If that hurts, so be it. Sometimes we must accept the pain of faith so as not to lose it.[39]

The complaints of Psalm 22—as in all the lament psalms—flow into an attitude of trust, without which there can be no sustained faith in God or any fullness of humanity. The psalmist remembers the ancestors who "were not disappointed" when they "cried out" in trust (22:3-5), but then he quickly complains again of his wretched condition: "I am a worm, not a man; scorned by humans, despised by people." The next remembrance is more intimate and personal: "Yet it was you who drew me from the womb, you entrusted me to my mother's breasts" (v. 9).[40]

37. Wiesel, *All Rivers Run to the Sea*, 83.

38. See especially the attacks of Sam Harris, *Letter to a Christian Nation*; and Christopher Hitchens, *God Is Not Great*. The same thought is implied in Dawkins's *God Delusion*.

39. *All Rivers Run to the Sea*, 84.

40. The translation can be disputed. RSV has, "thou didst *keep me safe* upon my mother's breasts"; NAB has, "[You] *made me safe* at my mother's breast." A very literal rendering is, "You *made me trust* when I was upon my mother's breasts." My translation is guided by the step parallelism of "took me from . . . *entrusted me to*." The verb *batach* denotes "trust" more than "safety"; it is causative, but in the context "*entrust*" makes more sense

This is the image of God as a midwife, but the metaphor switches in the next verse to God as *mother*: "On you I was cast from my birth, and since my mother bore me you have been my God" (v. 10, NRSV). Moses also, tired of the people's moaning in the desert, complained to God as Mother: "Did *I* conceive all this people? Did *I* give birth to them, that you should say to me, 'Carry them in your bosom, as a nurse carries a suckling child' . . . ?" (Num 11:12, NRSV). Consider what type of "knowing" is involved here: a mother's love for her child, a child's deep attachment to its mother. It is a knowing for which we have no words, and certainly no measures or tests.

God, Creation, and Suffering

But then how are the Holocaust and other genocides possible? To venture a thought (not an answer!), they are possible because God sets creation free. If God was a smothering presence,[41] who permitted no evil, then there would be no holocausts, but neither would there be any freedom or love, any risks or adventure. Perhaps something like this is what Wiesel means when he says, "Auschwitz is conceivable neither with God nor without Him." The "tragedy" of "faith within the barbed wire of Auschwitz," for both "believer and Creator alike,"[42] is that God and humanity are condemned, as it were, to freedom. God has to allow creation and humanity to be "other"; if not, there is no relationship, no trust or love. But the price of that freedom can be very high.

"God's suffering," to use Wiesel's imagery, is to "see the massacre of his children by his other children." In creation, as in Jesus, God "emptied himself" (Phil 2:7), and to his creatures became not so much designer or king as "servant" or loving parent. "No space is devoid of God," says Wiesel, "God is everywhere, even in suffering."[43] To make this point, Jesus suffered with, and for, creation—"he is hanging here on this gallows." He also taught that whatever we do, or fail to do, for those in need (the hungry, thirsty, sick, or imprisoned), we do, or fail to

---

than *"make to trust,"* especially in light of the synonymous parallelism of the next verse: "Upon you I was cast from birth."

41. In *God After Darwin: A Theology of Evolution* (Boulder, CO: Westview Press, 2000), 111–14, John Haught speaks of creation as God's "Letting Be," since an "annihilating 'presence'" would "overwhelm the world," denying it the freedom it needs to attain its own being.

42. *All Rivers Run to the Sea*, 84.

43. *All Rivers Run to the Sea*, 103–5, here 105.

do, for him (Matt 25:31-46). As noted several times, the Bible at its core is about "God with us"—*Immanuel* (Isa 7:14; Matt 1:23). And God enables in us trust and hope. As Paul says, with "all of creation" we "groan like a woman in labor" as we await "redemption," "the glorious freedom of the children of God" (Rom 8:21-24). Suffering will not disappear, but in the midst of it we can experience divine presence.

Science can add a little more to our reflections; it can be something of an ally, since it has delved into the recipe of creation, and enables understanding of the necessity for physical suffering. The more we know of nature, the more we know how necessary death is for life. From the first moments of creation, energy and fundamental particles have been in a dance of never-ending change. Astrophysicists properly speak of the "birth" and "death" of stars without which the elements for life would never have been made. And when life emerged and evolution began, the growth in beauty and diversity of living things depended at every step on the laws and rhythms of natural selection: life and death, death and life.[44] It was the pressures of natural selection, as well as the need for cooperation (symbiosis) and, in due time, the possibilities of communication and community, that have shaped living things from the amoeba to the human being. Jesus' spiritual principle that in order for life to be "saved," it must be "lost" echoes the natural order (Mark 8:35).

We only call earthquakes, tsunamis, and storms "disasters" when they impact human beings. Otherwise, we know that they are a part of the natural processes of creation—they are God making creation make itself, so to speak. Disease is also an inevitable part of an evolving world, and it always feels like a disaster; in one way or the other, it is the disaster none of us can escape. Human evolution also sheds light on moral evil, what Christians have traditionally called "original sin." We know now that "sin," in the sense of violence and selfish disregard of the needs and suffering of others, has always been with us. We cannot hold on to the picture of a literal garden of paradise in which there was no violence or selfishness—nor to a literal Adam and Eve who by their sin spoiled the fun for the rest of us.[45] We are, as Jared Diamond says, "The

44. Though stressing the rhythm of natural laws, I would also like to repeat and emphasize the presence of God in all circumstances. All of the laws, like all of creation, have their being in God and derive from God. God's presence is not therefore excluded by the laws, any more than a parent's love is excluded as a child grows to independence.

45. For a theological rethinking of original sin in light of evolution, see John Haught, *God After Darwin*, esp. 137–43; and Jerry D. Korsmeyer, *Evolution and Eden: Balancing Original Sin and Contemporary Science* (New York: Paulist Press, 1998).

Third Chimpanzee," and like our primate cousins we naturally desire to survive and prosper; a measure of selfish self-preservation is not only natural; it is also necessary.

Suffering—whether deriving from natural or moral evil—is the inevitable result of the universe God is creating and of which we are a part. Perhaps we might see suffering as the price we have to pay for the adventure of existence, and the capacities we have for learning, truth, relationships, and love. Without the emergence, unpredictability, and freedom of the universe there would be no suffering, but neither would there be everything that makes our existence human, our lives worth living. For such a universe, God has to be present not as an all-powerful designer, but as a loving guide, enabling freedom. Again, however, I want to be cautious about such an "answer" for suffering. It really is just a wrestling with the mystery.

As we saw in the last chapter, the distinction of humanity—what separates us from our animal heritage—is our capacity for transcendence and truth, and indeed for compassion and self-sacrifice. We go far beyond the requirements of natural selection when we embrace the gifts of transcendence—gifts we know best in art, science, longing for God, and love of neighbor, even love of enemies. Sin is the thwarting of those capacities. Though capable of truth, we are narrow-minded and stubborn; though capable of love and forgiveness, we hold onto our prejudices and hatreds; though capable of freedom, we surrender it to ideologies and tyrants for the sake of security and personal gain. The fullness of humanity is not easy to attain when we surrender so often to compromises, half-truths, "little faith,"[46] and little love. The best of what religion has to offer is summed up by Paul when he says, "Do not be defeated by evil, but rather defeat evil with good" (Rom 12:21).

The grace of suffering, if such a phrase can be permitted, is that it confronts us starkly with our limitations, and forces us to consider more carefully what we value. Its danger is that it might plunge us into despair; we might surrender to narrow, purely material views of humans, so that moral evil has a double victory—it not only slaughters the innocents but it also gets to define who they are. That is a victory we must never permit evil to have! Suffering and evil derive, in part, simply from the physical composition of the universe, but their worst manifestation is the moral evil that emerges when knowledge, community, love, and compassion

46. For Jesus' complaint about "little faith," see Matt 6:25-34, esp. v. 30; see also 8:26; 14:31; 16:8; 17:20. See also 28:17 and Luke 18:8.

are blotted out by ignorance, hatred, and apathy. The good news is, we have amazing capacities—we are children of God.

Miracles

For an understanding of suffering, science and theology can be seen as allies, but the same cannot be said regarding miracles. From the beginning of the rise of natural science, miracles were that aspect of the biblical tradition that was most called into question. Spinoza devoted a chapter of his *Theological-Political Treatise* to demonstrating that miracles are impossible, and the more that science revealed the mysteries of physical causality, the more difficult it became for traditional faith to insist on a historical understanding of the miracle stories. Some nineteenth-century theologians tried to defend the miracles by all sorts of rationalist explanations, and indeed some of these supposedly ingenious explanations persist to this day.

Very recently, for instance, "researchers at the National Center for Atmospheric Research and the University of Colorado" demonstrated with computer simulations that an event similar to the parting of the Red Sea, allowing the Israelites to escape from Egypt (Exod 14), could occur naturally, if "a 63 mph east wind" would blow "for 12 hours" across a chosen section of the Nile Delta.[47] In light of the "strong east wind" that, according to Exodus (14:21), "blew all night" prior to the crossing, some scholars both in the past, and today, take such natural explanations as proof of the accuracy of the biblical narrative. But they are nothing of the kind; all they demonstrate is physical possibility. The biblical texts are focused on God's action, which is never subject to such examination.

Similar rationalist explanations have been devised for some of the miracles of Jesus: he really did feed five thousand people with five loaves and two fish (Mark 5:38), because—so say the rationalists—others in the crowd were shamed into sharing their picnic lunches once Jesus and the disciples (or the little boy, John 6:9) shared theirs. Or the account of Jesus walking on the water makes sense, they assure us, once we consider that it was nighttime and the disciples were confused; they were closer to the shore than they realized, and Jesus was actually walking on the

47. Brad Lendon, "Where Did Waters Part for Moses? Not Where You Think," CNN.com, September 21, 2010, http://news.blogs.cnn.com/2010/09/21/where-did-waters-part-for-moses-not-where-you-think/?iref=allsearch.

shore or perhaps on stepping stones.[48] Such explanations seek to defend the accuracy of the *stories* by accounts of the *events* that deny the reality of the *miracle*. They are a perfect demonstration of how *not* to interpret the miracles, since they fail utterly to take the texts seriously on their own terms.

Three preliminaries are necessary to appreciate the miracle stories in their own terms and thereby to grasp what claims they are in fact making. These claims have nothing to do with rationalist explanations that only make the stories look ridiculous, trying in vain to make them compatible with science. First, we need to distinguish the events from the texts. Our concern has to be primarily with the texts, since the events as history—whether they happened or not—are out of reach. When it comes to individual miracle stories, their details are always beyond the grasp of certainty and definition. To claim too much is bad history. On the other hand, it is also bad history to see too little.

The great biblical scholar John Meier has written a massive study on the question of the historicity of the miracles, and properly concludes that the view of Jesus as "an exorcist and healer" is as certain "as almost any other statement we can make about the Jesus of history." This means, further, that any account of Jesus that tries to eliminate "his fame as a miracle-worker"—in the manner, say, of Thomas Jefferson's edition of the gospels—is condemned by its prejudice.[49] At the very least, we have to reckon with the fact that both Jesus himself and his eyewitnesses regarded healings of various kinds as characteristic of his public life. We can believe or not that Jesus performed miracles; we cannot deny that both he and his contemporaries took his healing actions with complete seriousness. Behind the texts, there were real people and real events.

Second, though we are cut off from the events, there is a great deal we can say about the theology both in and behind the texts, and about the symbolic universe of Jesus and those who interacted with him. Miracles always have a context; they are always attached to particular people, places, and times, and thus also are attached to particular cultures. Ancient cultures

48. See James D. G. Dunn, *Jesus Remembered: Christianity in the Making*, vol. 1 (Grand Rapids, MI: Wm. B. Eerdmans, 2003), 31–32, with other examples.

49. John P. Meier, *A Marginal Jew: Rethinking the Historical Jesus*, vol. 2: *Mentor, Message and Miracles* (New York: Doubleday, 1994), 970. Thomas Jefferson produced an edition of the gospels that focused exclusively on Jesus' teaching and completely cut out the miracle stories. Such a portrait of Jesus is inaccurate, because the miracles are intimately connected to Jesus' central teaching, and Jesus himself appealed to the miracles as illustrations of what his ministry was all about (e.g., Luke 7:22; 11:20).

allowed for miracles in a way that generally is not true of the modern West, but neither their naïveté nor our skepticism should be granted too much preference. Reading the Bible requires dialogue, which involves an honest attempt to see reality through its symbolic gaze. We cannot, and must not, relinquish our more analytical and scientific view, and therefore my appeal here is not for a wholesale acceptance of the stories just as written—far from it. On the other hand, they had a spiritual perspective that we, to a large degree, have lost in our science-dominated world. There is much to be said for giving a chance to an Origen-like, multileveled view of reality, so as to appreciate the purposes and insights of biblical thinkers.

A third preliminary is that the Bible contains paradoxical attitudes to miracles, occasionally within the very same author. No less important, Jesus himself seems to have been ambivalent about their value. Miracles are sometimes given too much importance in a way that goes beyond anything they deserve. The great classical prophets of Israel believed that they stood "in God's council" and had the authority to speak on God's behalf (e.g., 1 Kgs 22:19-23; Jer 23:21-22), but they went through their entire ministries without performing miracles, and only rarely mentioning miracles of the past. Elijah and Elisha were known as great wonder-workers, but their miracles were incidental to their message of fidelity to God. In his letters, Paul the apostle only rarely mentions "works of power" (e.g., Rom 15:19; Gal 3:5) and certainly does not make them the centerpiece of his gospel, nor does he ever appeal to the miracles of Jesus. Jesus himself was pointedly unimpressed with those who believed in him because of miracles. John comments that "many believed" in Jesus "when they saw the signs he was performing. Jesus himself, however, did not trust himself to them," nor did he feel any need of their "testimony" (2:23-25).[50] When asked to perform a "sign," Jesus sternly refused (Mark 8:11-13). Miracles often are just not the issue or, as in the case of Jonah, they are simply devices in service of the book's real message.

On the other hand, John also says that he has narrated "these signs [miracles] . . . so that you may believe that Jesus is the Christ, the Son of God" (20:30-31); indeed, throughout John's gospel, Jesus' "works" are revelations of who he is (e.g., 9:4; 10:25, 32, 37-38). And though Paul never appeals to Jesus' miracles, he certainly takes for granted his resurrection! This ambivalence about miracles is why theology has often observed

50. According to John, when Jesus perceived that the crowds were looking for him because of miracles, he rebuked them for missing their real point (6:25-27, note 6:2; see also 4:48 and Mark 8:11-13.)

that for those who believe no miracles are necessary, and for those who do not believe no miracles are sufficient. That is true, but only in part. I can certainly have faith without particular miraculous acts; indeed, as we have seen, faith can survive—sometimes even gather strength—in the midst of evil and suffering. But faith, of its very nature, must be able to see reality as sacred, and must on occasion have encounters with the sacred. This is surely what prayer and ritual are all about. Faith, in fact, arises from experiencing reality as more than just what it is on the surface, and thus also seeks to interpret reality in terms of its depths, not just its facts.

We see this interpretive tendency at work in narratives that are not classified as miracle stories, but where nonetheless the presence of God is presupposed. This is true even of the Bible's most "secular" texts. Second Samuel 11, as we have seen, features the story of David's seduction of Bathsheba and his arrangement for the death of her husband, Uriah, one of David's loyal soldiers. Second Samuel 11 is mostly pure history; there is no way the scribes would have invented such a story of Israel's greatest hero, were it not factual. No mention of God is made throughout the unraveling of the sinister story line—not until the very end, when the writer interjects: "But what David did displeased the LORD. And the LORD sent Nathan [the prophet] to David" (2 Sam 11:27–12:1). It was on this occasion that Nathan told David the parable of the rich man who stole the poor man's ewe lamb. Notice the biblical historian's presumption of God's presence; there are no circumstances from which God is absent. In that sense, from the perspective of faith, everything is sacred, everything is miracle.

Jesus' baptism by John the Baptist is another biblical incident that historians easily accept as factual. Since it might suggest Jesus' need to have sins forgiven, not to mention his subordination to a possible rival, there is no way the earliest Christians would have created the story unless John really did baptize Jesus.[51] Mark, in a somewhat matter-of-fact tone, says that "Jesus came from Nazareth of Galilee and was baptized in the Jordan by John" (Mark 1:9, NAB), but beneath the simple fact

51. For a full discussion of the baptism as a historical event, see Meier, *Marginal Jew*, 100–105. Notice that Matthew provides cover for the embarrassment of the event by inserting John's protest to Jesus, "*You* should be baptizing *me*," and by having Jesus say that in this way they fulfilled "all righteousness" (3:14-15). Luke's discomfort with the event is shown in the way that his narrative trips by it very quickly (3:21). The fourth gospel never even mentions that John baptized Jesus.

was its sacred meaning as the inauguration of Jesus' mission. Mark, therefore, tells us:

> Immediately he emerged from the water, he saw the heavens opening and the Spirit descending like a dove on him, and a voice from the heavens [said]: "You are my beloved son; in you I take delight." And immediately the Spirit drove him into the desert, and he was in the desert for forty days, being tempted by Satan, dwelling with wild beasts, and the angels ministered to him. (1:10-13)

How much fact there is in this further narrative is difficult to tell. Facts are not the issue; what dominates is the symbolism, which is multifaceted and complex. The hovering Spirit evokes both creation (Gen 1:2) and the Spirit that in Isaiah (42:1) is conferred on the "servant" in whom God's "soul delights." "Beloved son" identifies Jesus with Isaac (about to be sacrificed! Gen 22:2), with Israel's king at coronation (Ps 2:7), and with Israel itself (Hos 11:1; Jer 12:7). The time in the desert links him with Moses, the Exodus, and Elijah (1 Kgs 19:8). The story, in other words, shimmers with the sacred stories of Israel; it is full of "miracle."

A further example is Matthew's narrative of Jesus' death (27:45-54), which should be compared with its parallel (and source) in Mark (15:33-39). I will not dwell over the details, which are too numerous for comment, but notice at least the earthquake and splintering rocks, the tombs opening, and the bodies of the saints rising to walk around "the holy city." The fact that Jesus died as a common criminal does not tell the story properly; Matthew, therefore, with these dramatic details, takes his readers beneath the surface to the full significance of the event as God's action that transforms creation, and brings a new chapter to the ancient story of life and death. This is why Matthew, contrary to all other accounts, also introduces an earthquake (another one!) into the story of the resurrection, along with an "angel from heaven" who "rolled back the stone and sat on it" (28:2)—a powerful symbol of victory. None of these narratives is usually regarded as a miracle story, but they are nevertheless full of the sacred and miraculous.

When we turn, then, to miracle stories themselves, we can all the more easily recognize their theological character. None of them is primarily interested in historical detail, which is why even John Meier's careful historical investigations cannot pin down individual miracles; the main focus of the narratives is *always* theology. Nevertheless, as Meier shows, this does not mean that we can completely dispense with the reality of the miracles in the eyes of Jesus and those who knew him,[52] and our attitude to their reality depends on our assumptions. The theological creativity of non-miracle narratives shows that we cannot accept all of the miracles as historical, but it goes beyond the evidence to dismiss them *en masse*. In what follows, therefore, I will focus first on Jesus' actions and sayings about exorcisms, which almost certainly reflect his teaching and conduct during his ministry. Then I will focus on narratives that almost certainly reflect the theological creativity of his first believers. In all cases, the challenge of the texts lies in the questions, What spiritual experiences evoked them? What type of knowledge do they represent?

Jesus and the Demons

In our culture, demons are the stuff of Hollywood movies, weird clips on YouTube, and, to be sure, the serious religious beliefs of many people. Especially since the rise of modern psychiatry, science has understandably looked down on the notion of demons and demon possession, and there are many believers who are inclined to do so. With this discussion, I have no desire to foster belief in the notion that the devil literally "prowls around like a roaring lion, seeking whom he may devour" (1 Pet 5:8). Images of people, even children, in paroxysms of screaming rage, supposedly possessed by demons, are not only disturbing in themselves but they also raise some difficult theological issues. Though the Catholic Church has an official rite of exorcism, its stance when confronted with claims of possession is to remain skeptical and do the tests necessary to see if the phenomena can be explained in some more ordinary way. Demon possession has to be the diagnosis of last resort.

Biblical stories of demons are especially difficult for the science-theology dialogue, since the very concept of demons seems to fly in the face of everything modern science stands for. Of its very nature, the idea of demon possession stands for a realm of evil and chaos far beyond anything science can conceive, and since our modern worldview is so dominated by science, we naturally tend to dismiss the notion of demons out of hand. In this brief examination of the issue, my aim is simply to

52. Flavius Josephus, a first-century Jewish historian (c. 37–100 CE), only knew of Jesus by reputation, but in his *Jewish Antiquities*, 18, 3, he describes Jesus as "a doer of wonderful works," a clear reference to Jesus' reputation for miraculous deeds. See *The Works of Josephus, Complete and Unabridged*, trans. W. Whiston (Peabody, MA: Hendrickson Publishers, 1987), 480.

place the stories in their original context so that we can understand them for what they are. I would be foolish, not to say deceptive, if I claimed to understand the phenomenon; it is far outside of my experience. On the other hand, I believe that the stories have something deeply valuable to say about how humans experience the power of evil. They also tell us about Jesus' cultural context as a first-century Jew, his response to evil, and how he saw his own ministry. I will not suggest any easy way to reconcile the demon stories with modern scientific perspectives, but I do suggest that taken on their own terms their value should not be underestimated, and they could only constitute conflict between the Bible and science, if science imagines it can fully explain the phenomenon of whatever it is that demons represent.

Modern hesitations and skepticism about demons did not characterize the culture of Jesus. By his time, ancient Judaism had imbibed the notion that demons were responsible for evil in the world, including storms and disease. This is why, in Luke's gospel (4:39), in the description of Jesus' healing of Simon's mother-in-law, Jesus is said to have "rebuked the fever." This also explains, as we shall see later, the picture of Jesus "rebuking" the "wind and sea" (Mark 4:39). Belief in the agency of demons was fostered in Judaism by its contacts with other cultures, perhaps especially during the exile in Babylon.[53]

In the Old Testament, there are no demons such as those found in the New Testament. The exception that proves the rule is the "evil spirit from the LORD" (!) that "terrorized Saul," sometimes causing him to be violent (1 Sam 16:14-23; 18:10-11).[54] This spirit was exorcised by the young David playing a harp. By New Testament times, however, the idea had become established that "the Prince of this world" (John 12:31)—often named "Satan"—was an evil spirit that, in various ways, oppressed humanity (Acts 10:38) and caused them to do evil (John 13:27; Acts 5:3). There can

53. Zoroastrianism (from Zarathustra) may have been especially influential. For further background on demons, see T. H. Gaster, "Demon," in *The Interpreter's Dictionary of the Bible: An Illustrated Encyclopedia*, vol. 1, ed. G. A. Buttrick et al. (Nashville: Abingdon Press, 1962), 817–24.

54. Note also Dan 10:13, where "the prince of Persia" is a reference to a demon that opposed Gabriel, the guardian of Israel and Daniel's angelic helper (9:21). Only with the help of Michael, another of Israel's angels, did Gabriel escape to come to Daniel's aid. The book of Tobit features an evil spirit (see 3:8; 6:7-18; 8:3), and various Dead Sea Scrolls refer to Jewish exorcists (e.g., Abraham) being sought by foreign kings for their powers of exorcism. For more details, see Meier, *Marginal Jew*, 405, and note 61 below.

be no doubt that Jesus took very seriously the power of Satan and the demons, as did most Jews and many other peoples in the ancient world.

The gospel story that best illustrates the drama of Jesus' exorcisms is found in Luke (11:14-23) and Matthew (12:22-30); a somewhat different version is also found in Mark (3:22-27). Matthew and Luke both knew Mark's version and have combined it with the version they knew from Q, a collection of Jesus' sayings.[55] The heart of the story is not so much in what Jesus does as in what he says. In Q, it evidently began with a brief account of Jesus expelling a demon that caused its victim to be mute (Luke 11:14).[56] In Mark's version, the story begins with the accusation (also in Q) of "scribes from Jerusalem," that Jesus "is possessed by Beelzebul; it is by the prince of demons," they say, "that he casts out demons." Notice immediately that Jesus' opponents do not dispute that he successfully disposes of the demons; the issue is by whose power he does so—God's or Satan's. Jesus' response consists of a whole series of arguments that are striking in their imagery and their implications about Jesus. There are four distinct sayings to consider, which in their origins may well have belonged to differing contexts:[57]

1. "How can Satan cast out Satan? If a kingdom is divided against itself, that kingdom cannot stand. And if a house is divided against itself, that house will not be able to stand" (Mark 3:23-25, RSV; cf. Q, Luke 11:17-18).
2. "And if I cast out demons by Beelzebul, by whom do your sons cast them out? Therefore they shall be your judges" (Q, Luke 11:19, RSV; not in Mark).

55. "Q" (for "Quelle," source) was a brief written collection of sayings of John the Baptist and Jesus that was incorporated by Matthew and Luke into their gospels; it was apparently unknown to Mark. It only exists now in its Matthew and Luke forms; see John S. Kloppenborg et al., *Q-Thomas Reader* (Salem, OR: Polebridge Press, 1990). Rarely, both Mark and Q contain versions of the same saying, and that occurs here: Mark 3:24-26 = Luke (Q) 11:17-18; and Mark 3:27 = Luke (Q) 11:21-22.

56. For reasons of his own, Matthew adds that the victim was also blind.

57. In other words, Mark 3:23-27 and Luke (Q) 11:17-23 probably contain originally *separate* sayings of Jesus, all defending his activity as an exorcist. 1 and 4 are together in Mark and may always have been so, but comparison of Mark with Q, and literary analysis of 2 and 3, shows that Q brought these four sayings together for the first time. Specifically, note that the "you" of "your sons" in 3 must be quite a different "you" from the audience envisaged in ". . . then the kingdom of God has come upon *you*." The former "you" denotes opponents, the latter Jesus' disciples and those he has healed. For full discussion, see Meier, *Marginal Jew*, 407–11.

3. "But if it is by the finger of God that I cast out demons, then the kingdom of God has come upon you" (Q, Luke 11:20, RSV; not in Mark).

4. "No one can enter the house of a strong man to plunder his goods, unless he first binds the strong man, and then he will plunder his house" (Mark 3:27; cf. Q, Luke 11:21-22).

Saying 3 ("finger of God") is the gem of the collection. In the landscape of the New Testament, it stands out like a diamond on dark velvet. What is particularly unique is the phrase, "by the finger of God"; also very striking is the assertion, "then the kingdom of God has come upon you." The image of "the finger of God" is never used elsewhere in the New Testament. It was not picked up by the exorcists of the early church, and it has only one true—very telling—parallel in the Old Testament and ancient Jewish literature.[58] The image of God's finger writing on "the two stone tablets of the covenant" appears in Exodus (31:18) and Deuteronomy (9:10), but that action is rather different from that of Jesus casting out demons. Exodus 8:15[59] is the only true precedent for Jesus' phrase. In Exodus 7–8 the "magicians" of Pharaoh, "by their magic arts" (e.g., 8:3), have, prior to this point, been able to duplicate the amazing acts (the plagues) that Moses and Aaron have performed in their efforts to convince Pharaoh to set the Israelites free from slavery. But the third plague (gnats) and all the plagues thereafter confound them; they say to Pharaoh, pointing to the staff of Moses and Aaron, "This is the finger of God."

We have before us, then, an amazing little historical fact: Jesus quoted the magicians of Pharaoh as they surrendered before a power that defeated them. Jesus tries to bring his opponents to the same recognition as the magicians: the power by which he casts out demons has nothing to do with "magical arts" or Satan; it has to do, rather, with the coming, even with the presence, of "the kingdom of God." In any event, Jesus' opponents are at a loss in the face of his exorcisms. They can try to demean his power over the demons, but they cannot deny or duplicate it. In the terms of saying 4, Jesus is the one who has entered "the house" of Satan ("the strong man") and has bound him, so that now in setting

58. See Meier, *Marginal Jew*, 416.

59. The Hebrew text and most modern Bibles have this verse at 8:15, but the RSV and the NIV, following the old American Standard Bible (also KJV), begin Exod 8 at what is 7:26 of the Hebrew text, and so have this verse at 8:19. There is no difference in the story; it's just a difference in the numbering of verses.

people free of demons he is plundering Satan's possessions. The Luke (Q) version of this saying, reflecting believers' further interpretation, describes Jesus as "the stronger one" who like a military hero defeats "the well armed man," divests him of his weaponry, and shares the spoils of victory with his allies. Mark's simpler version is almost certainly more original to Jesus,[60] but the vivid imagery is true to the point; Jesus is in a contest with Satan, and Satan is being despoiled. This is consistent with the argument of saying 1 that by the exorcisms Satan is losing power, not gaining it and therefore Jesus cannot be an agent of Satan, since in that case he would represent "a house divided against itself," bound for destruction. Jesus is Satan's worst nightmare, not his ally.[61]

This brings us to the most remarkable claim of saying 3: "if it is by the finger of God that I cast out demons, then the kingdom of God *has come upon you.*" "Kingdom of God" has long been recognized by biblical scholars as the phrase that was most characteristic of Jesus' preaching. The phrase is very rare in the Old Testament, though the concept of God as ruler of history was ancient.[62] Most fundamentally the phrase denotes God as creator and ruler of the universe, but its particular nuance varies from context to context.[63] What is remarkable about Jesus' usage is that, though it always connected to the idea of God as king as articulated in the Old Testament and other texts, Jesus did not follow any particular text or tradition. Jesus is the one who truly put "kingdom of God" on the map, and did so with a stamp all his own.

Our problem with the phrase is that we too easily identify it with "heaven," as though it either had to do with a totally otherworldly reality or merely denoted life after death, which seriously misses the point. Even

60. Meier, *Marginal Jew*, 418.

61. Saying 2, in which Jesus implicitly accepts that there are other Jewish exorcists, places him solidly within his culture and its easy acceptance of the reality of exorcism. According to Josephus, Solomon had been a great exorcist and had left behind "wisdom" for expelling demons; Josephus claims to have witnessed an exorcism that was performed by a Solomonic technique. See Josephus, *Antiquities*, 8, 2, 5, in *Works of Josephus*, 214; also Meier, *Marginal Jew*, 405.

62. The phrase itself is found only in Wis 10:10 and in the apocryphal Psalms of Solomon 17:3. For the general notion, see, e.g., Exod 15:18; Ps 103:19; 145:11-13; Isa 52:7; Dan 4:25-27; 7:13-14. As Meier shows in a lengthy survey (*Marginal Jew*, 243–70), the *concept* is common in the OT and ancient Judaism, but not totally pervasive. For the importance of "kingdom of God" in Jesus' preaching, see Meier, *Marginal Jew*, 289–351; and Norman Perrin, *Rediscovering the Teaching of Jesus* (New York: Harper & Row, 1967), 54–108.

63. For example, contrast Ps 145:11-13 with Psalms of Solomon 17:3, and Dan 4:25-27 with Rom 14:17.

when Jesus spoke of the kingdom as a future reality,[64] he did so not for the sake of describing the future reality (which he simply took for granted), but for the sake of illuminating the situation of his listeners in the present (e.g., Luke 6:20-26). Jesus' distinctive focus was on God's nearness. John the Baptist, who undoubtedly influenced Jesus (Luke 7:24-28),[65] had proclaimed God's nearness in apocalyptic terms: "the axe is laid to the root of the trees; every tree therefore that does not bear good fruit is cut down and thrown into the fire" (Matt 3:10, RSV). That threat of imminent judgment was also a part of Jesus' teaching (e.g., Luke 13:1-9), but when Jesus began his own ministry, separate from John, his focus changed.

Unlike John, he went *to* the people, traveling round the towns of Galilee and Judea; he sought out "the lost," and, more than the threat of punishment, focused on God's desire to forgive and reconcile—hence the parables of finding the lost sheep, the lost coin, the prodigal son (Luke 15:11-32), the repentant sinner (18:9-14), the unforgiving servant (Matt 18:23-35), the laborers in the vineyard (Matt 20:1-16), and so on. The kingdom is about God's present, as well as future, action; it is religious by way of being social, even political. When Jesus says, therefore, that in the exorcisms, "God's kingdom has come upon you," his unique focus is evident—the kingdom is not only an object of longing (1 Cor 15:50) but also an experience of here and now; it has "come near" (Mark 1:15) and is "in the midst of you" (Luke 17:20-21). Jesus' implicit claim is that in casting out the demons, he exerts God's power; in a very real sense, the kingdom is present in Jesus himself.

In his historical evaluation of the seven demoniac stories of the gospels, John Meier judges that the exorcism of "seven demons" from Mary Magdalene (Luke 8:2) is one that most probably reflects a "historical event in Jesus' ministry." Early Christians would be unlikely to invent the story, since Mary was such an important witness of Jesus' crucifixion and resurrection.[66] In fact, she is the *only* person—man or woman—who is named in all four gospels as a witness of both events; picturing her as a former demoniac would not enhance her status in the ancient world. We cannot know anything meaningful about her experience of being set free of demons; indeed, our skepticism about ancient diagnoses is surely well placed.

64. For example, "Thy kingdom come" (Matt 6:10), a petition of the Lord's Prayer; see also Matt 8:11-12 and Mark 14:25.

65. On the relationship between John and Jesus, see Meier, *Marginal Jew*, esp. 116–30.

66. Meier, *Marginal Jew*, 658, 661.

Nevertheless, what we can see is that behind the texts were real human beings whose lives were transformed by the actions and words of the Galilean prophet. The flowering of Christianity from such inauspicious beginnings attests to the truth of this, whether we like it or not. Between Jesus and his audience, on the one hand, and "the demons," on the other, there was some exercise of power, which led to healing that is beyond our calculation. However we evaluate the exorcisms from our modern perspective, they were real for Mary and others; we cannot deny that any more than we can deny the reality of evil in our own world.

I have to admit that the notion of demons that have the power to possess and torment people does not sit at all well with my own theological preferences. But none of us gets to impose our particular philosophies on the texts; they are what they are. Another philosophical view might be that such phenomena remind us of the limits of our knowledge, which is not to say those limits prove anything supernatural—they do not. The limits pertain equally to science and theology, and should leave us all humbled. Jesus' healings are not a denial of modern science, since there is nothing science can say in their regard, and even faith has to approach such a topic with a great deal of humility, not to mention caution.

These stories and sayings about exorcism are deeply symbolic and theological, but they also have a historical core that cannot be dismissed. It is that core that makes them strange and challenging to our modern perspectives; if they were more like fairy tales, then we would understand them more easily. The next stories we will consider will return us to the pure theological creativity of the early Christians as they thought about Jesus' identity, who he was, who he *is*. It is not the facticity of these stories that is challenging—everything points to them being fiction—but it is the fact that at such an early point, strict Jewish monotheists were telling stories about a human being that implicitly claimed he was far more than human. Once again, they pose the question, what experience, what sort of knowing, lies behind the stories?

Spiritual Experience and Theological Creativity among Jesus' Earliest Followers

The most amazing aspect of human existence, to which science also bears witness, is our extraordinary desire and ability to understand. We are at every moment tacit knowers, somehow aware that there are further questions and problems drawing us forward into new endeavors, and new knowledge. Our consciousness, like a searchlight, sweeps into the surrounding darkness and mystery. It questions everything and longs for coherence. And when, as in the case of the followers of Jesus, it discovers a revelation that is pure grace and that sheds so much light, it hurries on its way to find the most lucid and compelling ways in which to express the discovery. As with the equations of physics, so also in the realm of religious knowledge, beauty is a hallmark of truth, meaning the discovery must not only answer to the deep questions but it must also shed light that enables new explorations and discoveries.

For Mary Magdalene, Peter, Paul, and the first generations of believers, Jesus met the criterion of beauty. Given his all too brief ministry (barely two years) and then his agonizing death as a criminal, mostly abandoned even by friends, we would normally expect that, far from the volcanic growth that actually followed, there would have been a gradual but fairly brief period of his followers disappearing into disillusionment. That did not happen. What stands between that expected outcome and the actual events of history seems to be the experience of the resurrection. Jesus became the seed sown into the ground that dies, and then miraculously grows and bears fruit (John 12:24). No more than the other "miracles" can we account for this experience. Unlike them, this one as such is not even susceptible of historical investigation; Jesus is not said, like Lazarus, to have reentered society and history. All we can contemplate of the resurrection is its effect. As John Meier says, "Once the early Christians believed that Jesus had been raised from the dead, a theological explosion was set off that assured both creativity and disorder for the rest of the 1st century A.D."[67] The creativity had to do with how in the world to express who and what Jesus was, and is—what sort of a ripping of the veil was he? The disorder had to do with the myriad ways they answered that question.

We have already seen some of the theological creativity of the gospels within the narratives of Jesus' baptism and death. Sometimes, as in those cases, the stories theologize from real events, introducing symbols and images that first-century hearers and readers could not miss. The exorcism story we considered above is somewhat arresting and challenging for modern readers because of its *lack* of theological elaboration; it is a very restrained report, simply recounting the hostile evaluation of Jesus'

67. *Marginal Jew*, 919. See also N. T. Wright, "The Self-Revelation of God in Human History: A Dialogue on Jesus with N. T. Wright," in Antony Flew, *There Is a God: How the World's Most Notorious Atheist Changed His Mind* (New York: HarperOne, 2007), 185–213, esp. 209–13, on the empty tomb stories.

opposition, and Jesus' brief, punchy retorts, probably from a few different occasions. Careful historical investigation, as exemplified by Meier, will not allow us just to dismiss all of the miracle stories, though Meier by no means regards all of them as historical,[68] and neither do I. The point is that if we wish to be "scientific" in our examination of Jesus as a miracle worker,[69] we will be hard-pressed to deny that Jesus had such power and effected genuine healings. Regardless of our assessments, Jesus' first witnesses (even to some degree, his opposition!) were convinced.

Very shortly after Jesus' death and the disciples' experience of the resurrection, the Jesus movement was vibrant and growing. We know this because it so quickly attracted the attention of opponents, most notably Paul of Tarsus, who, in his own later words, "persecuted the church and tried to destroy it" (Gal 1:13). His subsequent conversion, only about three years after Jesus' death, shows that the earliest followers did not spend long sitting on their hands. As they spread out into the cities of the eastern Mediterranean, they had to express, in ways that made sense to the people of that culture, who Jesus was. They told the stories of his ministry, quoted his words, and repeated his parables, but it was not enough to portray him simply as God's "anointed" (*Messiah* in Hebrew; *Christos* in Greek), and to think of him only as a human being. For some reason, whether modern minds like it or not, at a very early point, they began to apply to Jesus imagery and symbolism from Old Testament texts, which were all about the unique power of the God of Israel.

Until very recent times, theologians and historians worked with the assumption that the process of ascribing divine status to Jesus began slowly and only truly developed when Christianity became popular in the Gentile world beyond Judaism, perhaps under the influence of the Greek mystery religions. In the early period, according to this framework, all of the Christology (claims regarding Jesus' identity) was "low," and there is indeed plenty of Christology in the New Testament that is reticent about Jesus as divine.[70] The "high" Christology (that Jesus was divine) only truly began after Christianity broke into the Gentile world. Such was the older view. That view is now gradually being abandoned,

68. For example, note his overall evaluation of the exorcisms, *Marginal Jew*, 661.

69. Those interested in a precise definition of "miracle" should consult Meier, *Marginal Jew*, 512–17, which includes discussion of modern miracles, such as those claimed at the shrine of Lourdes, France.

70. For a survey of the types of Christology in the New Testament, see Raymond E. Brown, *An Introduction to New Testament Christology* (New York: Paulist Press, 1994).

however, thanks especially to the studies of the New Testament scholar Larry Hurtado.[71]

The earlier view had argued, for instance, that giving the title "Lord" (*kyrios*) to Jesus primarily happened under the influence of pagan cults. But more careful review of the evidence, beginning with Paul, shows that it originated among Jewish believers. This is significant, because *kyrios* ("Lord") is the word that the Greek translation of the Old Testament always used to translate God's most sacred name *Jahweh*. But not only did they give Jesus the title *kyrios,* they also invoked him by it in prayer and worship, and this in spite of their strict monotheism, which forbade placing any human being alongside God in the context of worship.[72] This is not to say that every time *kyrios* is used of Jesus in the New Testament it carries overtones of divinity, but on many occasions it clearly does.[73] A dramatic example is found in a hymn Paul quotes in Philippians (2:6-11). The hymn probably did not originate with Paul, but was part of the Christ-devotion of the earliest believers, including Jewish believers. It is remarkable because it applies to Jesus words from Isaiah (45:22-25) that are themselves remarkable for their emphatic proclamation of the unique power of the God of Israel. Paul got into trouble for things he said in his letters, particularly in regard to the Jewish law, but nowhere is there evidence that his ascribing Scripture texts about God to Jesus ever got him into trouble.[74]

To the contrary, the evidence is that he learned to do this from the believers whom he had once persecuted. And that can only point to some remarkable religious experiences on the part of Jesus' earliest Jewish followers. These experiences presumably began during his ministry, but must primarily have to do with the disciples' experiences of his resurrection. The latter, as already said, fall outside of any historical or scientific investigation; they point to realms of knowledge that one accepts, dismisses, or wonders about on philosophical grounds. But we can say without fear of contradiction that the experiences had profound effects,

71. Larry W. Hurtado, *Lord Jesus Christ: Devotion to Jesus in Earliest Christianity* (Grand Rapids, MI: Wm. B. Eerdmans, 2003); and *How on Earth Did Jesus Become a God? Historical Questions about Earliest Devotion to Jesus* (Grand Rapids, MI: Wm. B. Eerdmans, 2005).

72. Hurtado, *Lord Jesus Christ*: on the use of *kyrios*, 20–21 and 108–18; on the strict monotheism of Judaism contemporary with Jesus and early Christianity, see 29–53.

73. Sometimes *kyrios* seems to be no more than a polite form of address (e.g., Matt 8:6-8, 21; Mark 11:3; Luke 8:12), but on other occasions, it clearly means far more (e.g., Matt 14:28-30; John 20:28; Rom 10:13; 1 Cor 8:6).

74. Hurtado, *Lord Jesus Christ*, 165–66.

and they gave rise to religious creativity and social transformations of amazing proportions. The hypothesis that ascribes all such experiences to psychopathology of some sort looks as weak in this case as when it is applied to such figures as Jeremiah, Gandhi, Martin Luther King Jr., and so on.[75]

Jesus as L*ORD of the Sea*

The stories of Jesus on the sea are instances of the creativity that was unleashed in Christianity's early decades with the experiences of the resurrection. I will not spend any time defending them as historical accounts. I agree with John Meier in saying that both the calming of the storm (Mark 4:35-41) and the walk on the water (6:45-52) are products of early Christian theology.[76] Their value for us is not with regard to any historical occurrence in Jesus' ministry but as witness of the first believers' profound experience with regard to who Jesus was. When believers called upon Jesus in prayer as *kyrios*, they thereby placed him alongside the God of Israel as worthy of divine worship. These stories do something very similar, but they do it not in the form of prayer or confessional statement but in the form of narratives that have the character of saga or legend. To understand their peculiar force, we need to examine how they echo Old Testament images of God.

Prior to its incorporation into the Gospel of Mark, and its later inclusion in Matthew (8:23-27) and Luke (8:22-25), the calming of the storm would have been a part of the church's preaching and teaching about Jesus. We cannot know to what degree its first framers and hearers took it as a factual narrative, but for those who would understand its imagery, the message was clear regardless. At creation, God disciplined the watery chaos and created light to put the darkness in its place (day 1), the firmament (dome) to corral the waters (day 2), and the land to set boundaries for the sea (day 3). God takes chaos and molds it, and in the Bible nothing exhibits this divine majesty more dramatically than power over the threatening deep. To portray Jesus as calming the stormy sea

75. On the formative character of religious experience, and a response to the claims that it has to do with psychopathology and so on, see Hurtado, *Lord Jesus Christ*, 64–70. For a defense of the reasonableness of faith in Jesus, see Flew, *There Is a God*, 185–213, which mostly comprises a response by N. T. Wright (Anglican bishop and New Testament scholar) to Flew's questions on the issue.

76. Meier, *Marginal Jew*, 921 (re: walk on water), and 933 (re: calming the storm).

anticipates, though it has not yet arrived at, the formulations of later centuries that confess Jesus as "true God from true God."

Meier suggests that the storm story may have been intended to echo, "with a certain type of paradoxical reversal,"[77] the story of the storm in Jonah (1:7-16). In both stories, the prophet is asleep in the boat as a great storm threatens to destroy it. In both the prophet has to be wakened: in Jonah, the captain complains at Jonah and urges him to pray that they will not perish, and in Mark, the disciples waken Jesus with the complaining words, "Do you not care that we are perishing?" In Jonah, when the sailors reluctantly throw the prophet overboard, and the sea immediately calms, "they feared the Lord greatly," which is nearly word-for-word how Mark describes the disciples of Jesus (Jonah 1:16; Mark 4:41).

The "reversal" is in the contrast between Jonah, a disobedient prophet fleeing from God, and Jesus who is "obedient unto death" (Phil 2:8). Jonah has no power over the storm at all, whereas Jesus displayed the power of God; "he rebuked the wind and said to the sea, 'Quiet, be still.'"[78] Focusing on the story as history would miss the point; its point is the identity of Jesus as God. Theologically it is not unlike the great confession at the end of the Gospel of John (20:28), when Thomas finally sees the risen Jesus for himself and says to him, "My Lord (*kyrios*) and my God," where *kyrios* designates Jesus as divine in a very "high" sense. Matthew's version of the storm story brings this out further in that he has the disciples not complain at Jesus, as in Mark ("Teacher, do you not care . . . ?"), but address a prayer to Jesus as *kyrios*, "Lord, save us, we are perishing" (Matt 8:25). Matthew adds further theological punch when, in reverse of Mark's order, he has Jesus correct the disciples while the storm *is still raging*; "Why are you afraid, people of little faith?" says to all believers that faith has to show itself precisely in the middle of the storm. The chaos cannot confound Jesus' divine power.

The theological, as opposed to any historical, intent of the story becomes even clearer when we compare it to Psalm 107, which describes sailors caught in a fearful storm: "Then they cried to the Lord in their trouble, and he delivered them from their distress; he made the storm be still, and the waves of the sea were hushed" (Ps 107:27-29, RSV). Only God has such power over the deep; what is amazing about the storm story is the forthright way in which it depicts Jesus as wielding a power that, throughout the Old Testament, belongs only to God. This theme

77. *Marginal Jew*, 931–32.

78. The Greek word *pephimoso* actually suggests, "Muzzle yourself."

is also vividly clear in the walk on the water story (Mark 6:45-52). Jesus had made the disciples get into the boat and set off by themselves for the far shore, while he dismissed the crowds and went alone to pray. In the darkness, with the wind against them,

> he came to them, walking upon the sea and meant to *pass by* them, but when they saw him walking on the sea, they thought it was a ghost and all of them cried out, for they saw him and were terrified. But he immediately spoke with them, and said to them, "Take heart, it is I [*Ego eimi*], don't be afraid."

This story has many similarities to the storm story in that both depict Jesus doing what only God can do. But whereas the storm story applied the ancient images to Jesus so as simply to describe him, third-person style, as the Lord of the sea, the walk on water story is told from Jesus' personal perspective. By "the fourth watch of the night" (3–6 a.m.), the disciples should have been miles from where they left Jesus, but the text says that "he saw them making headway painfully, for the wind was against them." So "he came to them . . . and meant to *pass by* them." "*Pass by* them" is a strange phrase that has caused a lot of confusion, but as Meier shows, it is an aspect of the story as a divine epiphany.[79] It is a story of Jesus wanting to reveal to his disciples who he is as *kyrios* of creation.

In fact, it echoes one of the most solemn events in the entire Old Testament. Moses asked for assurance that God would accompany the people on their journey to the Promised Land. He asked God, "Let me see your glory" (Exod 33:19). In response God promised to "pass before" (*ʿabar*) Moses and to say the sacred name, Jahweh (*kyrios*), a promise God duly fulfills (34:6). The same Hebrew word (*ʿabar*) is used in 1 Kings (19:11-13) when God "passed by" the prophet Elijah to reassure him, also on Mount Sinai. The Greek text of the Old Testament translates *'abar* with the word *parerchomai*, which is the word used in Mark of Jesus wanting to "pass by" the disciples on the sea. In other words, the walk on water story intends to show Jesus as revealing himself to the disciples, and comforting them in the same way as God had reassured Moses and Elijah when they were in distress.

That Jesus "walked upon the sea" deliberately evokes Old Testament images of God controlling the sea at creation, and walking upon it (Job 38:8-11, 16). It also easily recalls the exodus story of Israel's rescue

79. *Marginal Jew*, 917.

through the sea "when the waters saw you, O God, and were afraid," and when God made "a way through the sea . . . a path through the great waters" (Ps 77:16, 19).[80] But perhaps the most striking aspect of the story is how Jesus identifies himself to the disciples when they cry out in fear: "it is I [*Ego eimi*], don't be afraid." *Ego eimi* recalls the revelation of the divine name from the burning bush (Exod 3:14) when God said to Moses, *ʿehyeh ʿasher ʿehyeh* ("I am who I am," or "I shall be who I shall be"), which the Greek text translates as *ego eimi ho on* ("I am the One Who Is"). Second Isaiah[81] (43:1-13) dwells at length on this revelation of God as "I am," and it may well have been in mind when believers framed the walk on water story, since all of its major elements are found there. God says to Israel, "Don't be afraid . . . when you pass through the waters, I will be with you . . . that you may know and believe me and understand that I am He [*Ego eimi*] . . . I, I am the LORD."[82]

In Matthew and Mark (Luke omits it), it is only in the walk on water story that "I am" surfaces as a way to identify Jesus with the God of Israel. John, however, takes the "I am" and makes it a drumbeat throughout his gospel, culminating at the arrest of Jesus in the garden. Jesus goes to meet Judas and the soldiers and asks them, "Who are you looking for?" When they answer, "Jesus of Nazareth," he says *Ego eimi*, which can be translated simply as "That's me," but the New American Bible is quite correct to render the phrase, "I AM" each time that it occurs (John 18:5-8). This is clear from the fact that when Jesus says *Ego eimi*, the Judas group "fell backwards to the ground," involuntarily bearing witness to the divinity they face, and to the deep irony of their imagining that by killing him they will defeat him. The drumbeat of Jesus revealing himself this way begins in John with the woman of Samaria (4:26), and resounds again and again at key points in the gospel (e.g., "Before Abraham was, I am," 8:58).[83]

80. See Meier, *Marginal Jew*, 915, for further Old Testament allusions.

81. Isaiah 40–55 comprises oracles from the aftermath of the exile in Babylon at the end of the 6th c. BCE. They have been attached to the book of Isaiah, but date from close to two hundred years after his time. Isaiah 56–66 is named Third Isaiah, deriving from a yet slightly later period.

82. See Meier, *Marginal Jew*, 918, for longer discussion.

83. Jesus reveals himself as "the bread of life" (6:35), "the light of the world" (8:12), "the gate of the sheepfold" (10:7), "the good shepherd" (10:11), "the resurrection and the life" (11:25), "the way, the truth and the life" (14:6), and on several occasions as simply "I AM" (8:24, 28, 58; 13:19).

This is consistent with the fact that the miracles in John are all more spectacular and more obviously theological than the miracles in the other three gospels. They tell of Jesus curing the blind (e.g., Mark 10:46-52), but in John Jesus cures a man who was blind from birth (9:1); they recount stories of Jesus raising the dead (e.g., Luke 7:11-17), but in John Jesus raises Lazarus after he has been four days in the grave (11:1-44). John attaches to the miracles long discourses, providing commentary on what they mean, and thereby making it explicit that it is not the miracle as an event that matters most, but rather its interpretation, its significance for human existence. At the end of the man born blind story, for instance, Jesus says, "I came into this world for judgment, so that those who do not see might see, and that those who do see might become blind" (9:39, NAB). The story, in other words, is about far more than an individual instance of blindness; it is about the blindness that afflicts everyone. We are all blind in some degree, none more so than those who insist, with a measure of arrogance, that they have no blindness (9:40-41).

In differing ways, all of the miracle stories have this symbolic character, whether they have a historical core or derive from pure theological creativity. They were told and repeated, and finally incorporated into the gospels, because they answered to the longing for healing that goes far beyond the pains of physical illness. We all know what evil is, how it far exceeds our control even in ourselves, and we all long for it to be dismissed from our world and from our own minds and hearts. We are all blind; we are all Lazarus, wrapped in death, longing for light and freedom. What John has made explicit and prominent, the Synoptic Gospels articulate more quietly, with more reserve, almost as though they are still trying to find the language to express who and what Jesus was, and is.

Truth be told, that same tacit searching is also present in John's language and in all religious confessions. Faith, contrary to some popular perceptions, is not about the certainty of knowledge when—at least on the surface—the answers are all known, and the puzzles have been solved. Religious faith has the character of hope; it always involves, as Paul says, "groan[ing] within ourselves as we wait for adoption, the redemption of our bodies" (Rom 8:23, NAB). Paul goes on to say that "we were saved in hope," which means we cannot "see" what we "hope for" (8:24). Faith never reaches the end of its longing and searching, and so it compels us to inquire further, and to seek deeper coherence. This is why faith is always an ally of the honest search for truth of whatever kind, including when science and historical investigation ask hard questions about the miracles. The hard questions are necessary for faith itself, lest we imagine that the absence of miracles means the absence of God, which would be a complete contradiction of what the texts are all about.

Conclusion

This section has been about trying to see the miracles on their own terms. They are primarily theological texts. Even when they comprise, as best we can tell, some remembrance of actual persons or events in the ministry of Jesus, it is nevertheless clear that they were preserved and incorporated into the gospels not primarily as history but as confessions about Jesus' identity and as stories of spiritual power. On the one hand, the miracles are a challenge to us and to our science-dominated view of existence. If we are to be honest in our investigations, we cannot be satisfied with cynically brushing them aside as though such things are impossible (a philosophical prejudice) or as though no one can believe them (which is simply not true).[84] In that sense, the miracles sit a little uncomfortably with the notion that nothing can happen beyond the rules of causality as we understand them. This can be disconcerting for the religious mind as well as the scientific. If miracles are an option, why does God not bring them about more often? Further, if miracles were easy for Jesus, how truly human could he be?

On the other hand, therefore, we must maintain a critical stance toward miracles, both those claimed in the Bible and—perhaps even more so—those claimed today. We must never forget that Jesus was impatient with those who looked for miracles (Mark 8:11-13), was dubious of the faith of those who believed because of miracles (John 2:23-25), and had to rebuke people who completely misinterpreted them (Luke 11:14-23; John 6:14-15). The critical stance toward religion in general, and the Bible in particular, that we learned from the Enlightenment was salutary. The gullible acceptance of everything claimed by religious texts and authorities has never been good for society or for religion itself.

What, then, is the value of the miracle stories? This is pretty much the equivalent of asking, What is the value of the gospel narratives as a whole?—since as we have seen, they are sprinkled liberally with the miraculous, even when they narrate facts. Their value resides, at least in part, in the spiritual experience that lies behind them. They are not primarily records of facts; they are witnesses of spiritual experience and faith. They are, so to speak, Mary Magdalene liberated from demons,

84. On this, see Meier, *Marginal Jew*, 520–21.

the blind who attain sight, the despairing who discover hope, the poor who hear good news. They are religion in its ability to foster attitudes of faith, hope, compassion, tolerance, humility, forgiveness, and so on.

The miracles represent types of knowing that make no sense in a world where we think we have everything under control, and we understand precisely how the universe works. The problem is, of course, that we have no such control, no such complete understanding. Miracles seem to conflict with science only when we hold on too tightly to those modern mythologies. If, on the other hand, we recognize our limits and that, in addition to all that science has to offer, we also need our spiritual traditions, then there is no conflict between biblical stories and scientific theories. To the contrary, they might function as complementary lenses through which to contemplate the mystery of reality.

That brings us to a final topic, the issue of life after death, where it might seem to many that the Bible and science are bound to clash. If suffering and miracles are beyond easy explanation, that is all the more true of the belief that we survive into eternity. I will first focus on some common misunderstandings of what the Bible says, and on what belief in life after death entails. I will conclude with some thoughts on near-death experiences and what value they might have for telling us about eternal life.

Life after Death

The Old Testament

Many assume that belief in life after death is found everywhere in the Bible, but in fact it is not. Just about all of the Old Testament is either silent about the afterlife or is close to denying its existence. Ecclesiastes (3:19) is the clearest example of the latter, insisting that "the fate of humans and the fate of beasts is the same; as one dies, so dies the other, . . . humans have no advantage." In interpreting Ecclesiastes, one has to remember its generally pessimistic nature; it is probably not representative of most Israelites. Psalm 88, a psalm of lament, is probably closer to the dominant attitude:

> I am reckoned among those who go down to the Pit; . . .
> like one forsaken among the dead, like the slain that lie in the grave,
> like those whom you remember no more, for they are cut off from your hand . . .

> Do you work wonders for the dead? Do the shades rise up to
> praise you?
> Is your steadfast love declared in the grave, or your faithfulness
> in Abaddon?[85] (vv. 4-5, 10-11)

Psalm 115:17 answers the questions exactly as Psalm 88 would expect: "The dead do not praise the LORD, nor do any that go down into silence" (RSV; cf. Isa 38:18). It is a remarkable fact about ancient Israel that, although its surrounding cultures, Egypt to the south and Mesopotamia to the north and east, had many myths about the land of the dead, and many beliefs about how to consult the dead, Israel's Scriptures are almost totally silent on the topic.[86] Until very late in the Old Testament period, most ancient Israelites seem to have entertained only vague ideas about the afterlife, and had no concept at all of the afterlife as involving reward and punishment.

A major reason for avoiding speculation about the afterlife may have been Israel's abhorrence of the religious practices of Canaanite and other cultures. This is clear in Deuteronomy (18:9-14), which forbids various practices of the other nations, especially consultations with "a charmer, or a medium, or a wizard, or a necromancer." The other nations "pay heed to soothsayers and diviners, but the LORD your God has forbidden you to do so" (18:14). Soothsayers and the rest were known for consulting with the dead in order to help in making decisions or predicting the future. Why this was so offensive is not clear, but a clue appears in the immediately following text, where God promises to provide for the people a prophet like Moses: "I will put my words in his mouth, and he shall speak to them all that I command" (18:18, RSV). Consulting the dead, maybe also involving worship of the dead, would represent for Israel an idolatrous practice, a substitute for trust in God (Isa 8:19). Perhaps Israel's abhorrence of consultation with the dead translated into a suspicion of the afterlife altogether, at least on the part of some. We know, however, that the practice did occur; in fact, the very forbidding of the practice is evidence for that.[87]

85. Abaddon means place of destruction; it is paralleled with Sheol (Job 26:6; Prov 15:11; 27:20), but neither term denotes "hell" in the sense of a place of punishment. The latter is a much later idea and is denoted by the term Gehenna (e.g., Matt 23:33).

86. For an extensive study of the issue, see Alan F. Segal, *Life After Death: A History of the Afterlife in the Religions of the West* (New York: Doubleday, 2004), 27–170, esp. 120–70.

87. Segal, *Life After Death*, 126–30.

There is also a very famous example describing an actual consultation (1 Sam 28:3-25). It is a significant text for what it shows about living a life of obedience to God and what that means or does not mean in relation to the afterlife. King Saul had angered God, and so when the Philistines gathered for battle against him, he could get no response about what he should do "either by dreams or Urim or prophets" (1 Sam 28:6).[88] He became desperate, so although he had "put the mediums and wizards out of the land" (28:3), he nevertheless decided to consult the witch of Endor. The witch was reluctant, but at Saul's insistence she conjured up the spirit of the dead prophet Samuel, who rose "like a god coming up out of the earth" (28:13). Samuel complained: "Why have you disturbed me by bringing me up?" Saul explained his plight and asked Samuel what to do, but Samuel told him only what he already feared: that he was to be defeated and would die.[89]

The most interesting figure, for our purposes, is the dead Samuel. He had lived a life of complete faithfulness to the covenant; "all Israel had mourned for him" at his death (28:3). But the text shows not the slightest hint that in the afterlife he was receiving any reward beyond quiet rest in his grave. The writer does not presume that Samuel now lives in paradise; if he is alive in the afterlife, "it is not an afterlife to be desired."[90] The silence about the afterlife suggests that the motivation for worshiping God and obeying God's commands had nothing to do with the hope of eternal reward. To the contrary, the only rewards expected—if there were rewards at all—were blessings and long life *before* death. After death, not only did humans have no advantage over the beasts, neither did the virtuous necessarily have any advantage over sinners. Religion was about obeying God, and being just to one's neighbors simply because that was what God demanded. This is important to note, since there is a common presumption that the Bible teaches people to have faith in God so as to gain eternal life, but such an idea does no justice to the fullness of faith as understood in the Scriptures.

Consider, for instance, the preaching of the great prophets, and their demands for true worship that went along with practicing justice for the poor, and defending the rights of the orphan and widow (e.g., Isa

88. Urim, usually paired with Thummim, were associated with the breastplate of the high priest and were used as lots to determine divine judgment (1 Sam 14:3 and 42).

89. It is possible that the story was told and written precisely to reinforce the prohibition against consulting the dead; Saul tried it, and even succeeded, but all he got for his efforts was defeat and death.

90. Segal, *Life After Death*, 143.

1:10-17; Jer 7:1-7; Amos 5:21-24). The prophets never demanded justice and righteousness with an attendant motivation or promise that those who obeyed would live with God forever. Such an understanding of religion, whether on the part of believers or nonbelievers, is a misunderstanding of faith's true motivation: it is a matter simply of being "God's familiar servants," to use James Kugel's phrase (see Luke 17:7-10). In Old Testament religion, God's care for Israel does not seem to have included the afterlife. God's promise in the covenant was to give Israel, as a nation, a land and posterity (e.g., Gen 12:1-9). Individuals also were expected to obey the laws, of course, and blessings and curses were enumerated for obedience and disobedience (Deut 27–28). None of them, however, had to do with the afterlife, and as Job and the psalms of lament show, there was no guarantee that virtue would translate into rewards even in this life.

Job 19:25-26 has often been interpreted as though it was proof of this book's belief in eternal reward for fidelity to God. Job, of course, exemplifies total obedience to God. The book even expands the problem of why the innocent suffer by locating Job in the land of Uz,[91] which means he was not an Israelite. The problem is global: why does God not consistently protect and reward the virtuous? Why do the obedient suffer, while the evil so often seem to prosper? Job is staunch in his own defense against his friends, who suggest that he must have sinned and so earned God's wrath. The reader of the book knows what Job does not know, that God is fully aware of Job's innocence. Indeed, Job is suffering *because of* his innocence, since God has consented to the *satan*'s proposal of testing Job to see if his virtue is genuine, or if he obeys only for the sake of reward (1:8-12; 2:3-6). A major idea in the book, therefore, is that there is such a thing as goodness for its own sake—that is precisely why Job is a true model of devotion to God.

In his anger and frustration, Job (really, the author of the book) puts God on trial, a total reversal of the usual divine-human situation. In 19:23-24, Job wants to have his case against God inscribed "with an iron pen," in letters of "lead" "graven in the rock for ever." But then he has a stronger thought, about a "redeemer," an advocate, who will plead his cause:

> I know that my Redeemer lives, and at last he will stand upon the earth; and after my skin has been thus destroyed, then from my flesh I shall see God, whom I shall see on my side, and my eyes shall behold, and not another. (19:25-27, RSV)

91. Perhaps modern-day Jordan or Syria.

The text is notoriously difficult, and so occasions numerous different interpretations. It is highly unlikely, however, that the text is articulating any hope of life after death. The entire situation of the book forbids such an interpretation, since life after death would mean that God could not be charged with failing to keep the bargain of reward for obedience.[92] Further, an afterlife is no part of the book's resolution. Job's words here are an expression of hope that God will appear personally and hear what Job has to say. He envisages that this might happen after his body has borne further destruction, and that in the end, before death, God will vindicate him. And, of course, that is what happens in the book's conclusion; God appears out of the whirlwind, vindicates Job against the accusations of his friends, and restores him to health and prosperity in *this* life. Heaven has nothing to do with it; for ancient Israel, "the heavens" (*shamayim*) were God's dwelling. With only two exceptions (below), humans did not get to go there.

Psalm 23 is another text that is sometimes taken as evidence of belief in an afterlife, but again it is near certain that no such idea is present. The psalm begins with the famous words, "The LORD is my shepherd," and continues with expressions of trust in the protecting hand of God. Its final verse reads: "Surely goodness and mercy shall follow me all the days of my life; and I shall dwell in the house of the LORD for ever" (RSV). "Forever," in the minds of many, denotes eternal life, but the Hebrew phrase (*le'orek iamim*) simply denotes "length of days"; the NAB translation, "for years to come," catches the sense. "The house of the LORD" denotes the temple. What Psalm 23 envisages, as also Psalm 27:4, is the joy of being able to "dwell in the house of the LORD." For the priests and Levites, this was literally the case, but for others it was an apt figurative expression for the desire to be close to God by being in God's temple—an idea expressed with great poignancy in Psalm 42 (see 42:4; 43:3).[93]

The "two great exceptions to the biblical notion that all must eventually die . . . [were] Enoch and Elijah"[94]; at the end of their lives God simply "took" them. In Genesis (5:23-24), after Enoch lived for "three hundred sixty-five years, he walked with God and was no more, for God took him." In ancient Judaism, at the end of the Old Testament period, when belief in life after death had become a clear and accepted concept,

92. Segal, *Life After Death*, 146–47.

93. Psalms 42 and 43 are actually a single psalm; it was improperly divided into two psalms when the Bible was divided into chapters and verses in the sixteenth century.

94. Segal, *Life After Death*, 154.

this cryptic text about Enoch's end gave rise to many writings about him as a source of wisdom about the end of days. Elijah's end was even more dramatic. In 2 Kings (2:11), as Elijah and Elisha walked together, "a flaming chariot and flaming horses came between them, and Elijah went up by a whirlwind into heaven [*shamayim*]." In ancient Judaism, even before the development of the Enoch tradition, this memory of Elijah's assumption into heaven gave rise to the notion that Elijah would return before "the great and terrible day of the LORD comes" (Mal 4:6). People wondered if perhaps John the Baptist were Elijah (Mark 6:14-15), and in fact, according to Matthew (11:14; 17:9-13), Jesus believed that he was (note Luke 1:17). Enoch and Elijah were exceptional because they did not die like ordinary people, which is why it was conceivable that they were in heaven with God. In ancient Israel, such a fate was not conceivable for ordinary people.

As we turn to the belief in life after death, which is so much a part of the New Testament texts, we need to think carefully about what such a belief represents. Life after death is not the primary reason for believing in God or the main motivation for religious practices of prayer, love of neighbor, and so on. Faith and devotion were expected of believers in Israel long before there was a clear belief in life after death. Belief in the afterlife certainly can enrich or even provide motivation for doing good, but the latter was required long before the former was clearly articulated.

The idea of life after death came to Israel and Judaism rather slowly. The first clear indication that it had reached a mature level of reflection is the book of Daniel (12:2-3), which is perhaps the last book of the Old Testament to have been written—probably around the middle of the second century BCE. The belief probably gained ground among Jews during the exile in Babylon in the sixth century BCE, under the influence of Persian religious ideas, and grew from there. In any event, by the time of Jesus, it was a standard part of the religious understanding of most Jews, though not all.[95] There is no doubt where Jesus stood on the matter.

The New Testament

The Sadducees of Jesus' time believed "there is no resurrection" (Acts 23:8), so they presented Jesus with the case of a woman who had seven husbands in the course of her life, and asked him, "To whom will she belong in the resurrection?" Jesus gave a double response: first, "when

95. Acts 23:8 says that "the Sadducees say that there is no resurrection, nor angel, nor spirit, but the Pharisees acknowledge them all." In this regard, the Sadducees were the traditionalists; the Pharisees and Jesus were the innovators!

they rise from the dead, they neither marry nor are given in marriage, but are like angels in heaven." Then he pointed them to God's self-appellation as "the God of Abraham, the God of Isaac, and the God of Jacob" (Exod 3:6) and concluded, "He is not God of the dead, but of the living; you are quite wrong" (Mark 12:18-27, RSV). Before the God of the living, in eternal life, the woman does not belong to anyone; she is free.

Unlike the Pharisees, the Sadducees did not believe in the resurrection, "nor in angels or spirits" (Acts 23:8). With regard to all three, Jesus was on the side of the Pharisees. As I have indicated, these were comparatively new ideas for the ancient religion of Israel; they were a testimony to its power to renew itself, to learn from other traditions for new situations. From about the time of the writing of Daniel (c. 150 BCE), apocalyptic ideas about the end of the world had started to become popular with many Jews. Like John the Baptist and many other of his contemporaries, Jesus seems to have believed that history was drawing to a close: "The time is fulfilled, and the kingdom of God is at hand; repent, and believe in the gospel" (Mark 1:15, RSV).

The key saying here is, "the kingdom of God is *at hand*," which is ambiguous, perhaps deliberately so. "Kingdom of God" denotes God's exertion of power as the sovereign creator of the universe. The saying is ambiguous in that it suggests both that the kingdom is already sufficiently present that believers can experience it here and now, and at the same time that the kingdom is still not completely present—there is yet more to come. When Jesus began his own ministry, separate from John, he neither forgot the imminent expectation of his teacher nor felt bound by it. His focus fell, as I have indicated, on God's longing to restore "the lost sheep." Jesus, therefore, devoted his energies to gathering and instructing a community of disciples that would include "tax collectors and sinners," and perhaps also a few Gentiles (Luke 15:1-2; Matt 8:10-12).

With his death and the experience of the resurrection, that process of gathering communities continued, and so also did the expectation that history was drawing to a close. But history has not done so, of course. Over the centuries, the expectation of the end was largely transferred to a longing for eternal life. This transference was all the easier in that the expectation and hope for the end of history, in both Judaism and Christianity, was not always necessarily focused simply on a future consummation. John J. Collins makes the point:

> The future hope of late post-exilic Judaism cannot be understood as the expectation of a purely future event, and . . . it is

> not primarily concerned with the end of anything. Rather it is concerned with the transcendence of death by the attainment of a higher, angelic form of life. This hope shows considerable affinities with the Greek doctrine of the immortality of the soul.[96]

Writing to the Philippians, Paul is in two minds as to which he should prefer, to stay for the sake of believers or "to depart and be with Christ" (Phil 1:21-24). He actually says that "it is far better" to die! (One should note that there is a vast difference between longing to *die* for a cause and longing to *kill* for one.) The experience common to Jesus and his followers was a deep longing for God; the kingdom is so close that even now it casts its shadow and transforms the present. We see this in Paul's words to the Corinthians when he tells them that in light of the nearness of the end, they should live now "as though" the present were already transformed: "Let those who mourn be as though not mourning, those who rejoice as though not rejoicing, and those who buy as though they had no goods" (1 Cor 7:29-30). This is not an instruction to be detached from society, but to live from a wider context—to see the present in terms of eternity, so that in a sense death is defeated in the midst of life.

In his public life Jesus had to reckon with the threat of a violent death (e.g., Luke 13:31), but unlike Paul, Jesus seems to have felt no eagerness for death. He did not want to die; the prayer for deliverance in Gethsemane that is so heartfelt and poignant in Mark's version of the story (14:34-36) is somewhat softened by Luke (22:42)[97] and is totally silenced by the high Christology of John.[98] It was a genuine prayer, so much so that some may have found it scandalous on the lips of Jesus. Like any person, Jesus wanted to live; he certainly did not want to die by Roman crucifixion, and so he prayed, "Take this cup from me." He could nevertheless face death with as much courage as he did, like others before and since, because of his faith in "the God of the living." We totally

96. John J. Collins, "Apocalyptic Eschatology as the Transcendence of Death," in Paul D. Hanson, ed., *Visionaries and Their Apocalypses* (Philadelphia: Fortress Press, 1983), 78; quoted in Carol Zaleski, *The Life of the World to Come: Near-Death Experience and Christian Hope* (New York: Oxford University Press, 1996), 15.

97. Luke 22:43-44, which describes Jesus as "strengthened by an angel, and being in agony . . . with his sweat becoming like great drops of blood," is not original to the gospel; it was added by an editor and subsequently copied by others. Hence the description is missing from many modern Bibles.

98. In John, the prayer is transferred to the end of the public ministry, long before the arrest narrative, and is turned into a question ("Shall I say, 'Father, save me from this hour'?"), which Jesus immediately rejects ("But it was for this that I came to this hour," 12:27).

misunderstand Jesus, if we imagine that death was in some sense easy for him. The agonizing cry, "My God, my God, why have you forsaken me?" speaks for itself.[99]

Jesus in particular and much of religious spirituality generally give the lie to the idea that belief in an afterlife has to do with trying to deny the reality of death. Several of Jesus' parables have to do with the nearness of death and with how awareness of it is a necessary part of life (e.g., Luke 12:4-5, 13-21; 16:19-31). As Carol Zaleski shows, "the world's religions have universally counseled humankind to keep death in mind, to keep death real."[100] To deny the reality of death or to run from one's own mortality leads to a diminution of life and to distorted understandings of oneself and others. Both Benedictine and Buddhist monks, in their spiritual exercises, encourage their novices to remember death every day as a means to recall the graciousness of God, one's own limitations, and to learn compassion for others.[101] Faith is the very opposite of an attempt to deny death or one's mortality; to the contrary, faith embraces death as a necessary feature of life. In Christianity, as in other religions, there is no true life without death (e.g., John 12:24-25).

There is no evidence that belief in the afterlife arises simply from the fear of death. The people of the Old Testament must have feared death as much as any other humans, but they and their descendants resisted the notion for hundreds of years. Are we to suppose that the belief was adopted because somehow the fear of death had increased? Jesus had as strong a belief in survival after death as anyone we can imagine, but it did not stop him from being horrified at the prospect of dying; he still prayed to be spared. Belief in the eternity of the soul—"the resurrection of the body and life everlasting,"[102] according to the Creed—functions in human existence similarly as belief in God; the latter, in fact, is the ground of the former. The belief in eternity is a foundational response

99. As I have indicated earlier, Matthew and Mark both report that those were Jesus' last words. Luke (23:46) puts the words of a different psalm on his lips: "Father, into your hands I commend my spirit" (Ps 31:6). In John, he simply says, "It is finished" (19:30). We cannot know for sure what Jesus' last words actually were, but the prayer of dereliction in Mark and Matthew could be disturbing to some and was less likely to be invented.

100. Zaleski, *Life of the World to Come*, 15.

101. Zaleski, *Life of the World to Come*, 16.

102. The Jewish and Christian belief in the resurrection of the body, borrowed from Persian religion, is quite a different concept from the immortality of the soul, which derives from Greek philosophy, especially Plato. On the influence of Persian religion and Platonic philosophy on Judaism and Christianity in this regard, see Segal, *Life After Death*, 173–396.

to the question, what is a human being? Carl G. Jung (1875–1961), one of the great founders of modern psychology, said:

> The decisive question for man is: Is he related to something infinite or not? That is the telling question of his life. Only if we know that the thing which truly matters is the infinite can we avoid fixing our attention upon futilities, and upon all kinds of goals which are of no importance.[103]

Belief in God and eternity makes sense because it is consistent with the way humans experience themselves and their encompassing reality. Our minds and the universe itself pull us forward, goading us into further inquiry about the tacit dimension and the mystery of God. As the Old Testament shows, belief in God does not require belief in eternal life, but the first tends to lead to the second—they are two sides of the same coin.

Near-Death Experiences

The question of life after death is, to some degree, one of those borderline issues that touches on both theology and science. When it comes to physical death, medical science obviously has the expertise; theology's concerns in that regard simply gravitate around human dignity. Science, especially neuroscience, is interested in the experience of the dying person, specifically what happens as the brain shuts down in the course of bodily death. In recent years, interest has grown in the phenomenon of near-death experiences, with the work of Raymond A. Moody, and more recently of Carol Zaleski and others.[104] The issue has to be considered with a great deal of respect. What do these experiences mean?

If the question is eternal life, meaning life with God after the complete destruction of the body and brain, then it is purely a philosophical and theological matter. But near-death experiences all have to do with persons who do not die in the full sense; they revive and are able to report amaz-

103. Carl G. Jung, "Visions/Life After Death," excerpted from idem, Memories, Dreams, Reflections (1961), in Lee W. Bailey and Jenny Yates, eds., *The Near-Death Experience: A Reader* (New York: Routledge, 1996), 110–11.

104. Raymond A. Moody, *Life After Life: The Investigations of a Phenomenon—Survival of Bodily Death* (San Francisco: HarperSanFrancisco, 1975, 2001); idem, *Reflections on Life After Life* (New York: Bantam Books, 1977); Bailey and Yates, *Near-Death Experience*; and Zaleski, *Life of the World to Come*. I should also mention the very personal account of Elisabeth Kübler-Ross (1926–2004), *On Life After Death* (Berkeley, CA: Celestial Arts, 1991), in which she claims complete certainty of "knowing" of life after death (3).

ing experiences that suggest the reality of the afterlife. The questions then arise: to what extent are such experiences tied to the still living brain and body or are they totally independent of the physical self? In the absence of the body, what is the self? Neither medical science nor philosophy can answer these questions in a decisive manner. In the absence of understanding the phenomenon of near-death experiences, it is foolish for theology to claim them as proof of life after death in the theological sense. There is no such definitive proof, any more than there is final proof of the existence of God. God is the ground of all existence, but is not available for our inspection or measurement, and neither is eternal life.

What, then, can we say about near-death experiences? First, we have to be honest about some difficult questions. Why do only some of the people who come back from a close call with death have the experience of departing from their bodies, feeling at peace, a being of light, and so on?[105] Why such apparent selectiveness? Second, what is the relationship between the experience reported and the report of the experience? Literary studies, including biblical studies, have long known that a report of an event is far from the same thing as the event itself. In the discussion of miracles, I had to distinguish the experiences people had in Jesus' company from the stories that were later composed. This is the simple recognition that we can never capture in words the reality of a person or a complex event. Robert Kastenbaum (psychologist) fully accepts the reality of near-death experiences and that they are significant, but he properly critiques undue trust in the reports of them.[106] It is not a question of rejecting such reports, but it is important to be aware of the limitations of language and memory, as also of cultural conditioning, personal biases, and so on. There is "striking evidence for the cultural shaping of near-death experience."[107] When Christians meet a being of light, they invariably take it to be Jesus or God, but Hindus will identify it as Krishna or some other deity.

On the other hand, near-death experiences and related phenomena have always been part of human experience; they are "nothing new."[108] No doubt they have played an important role in the evolution of religion.

105. For some statistics, see Bailey and Yates, *Near-Death Experience*, 7. In addition to the fact that they just did not have any such experience, other explanations include forgetting and repression. As with other things, some persons may be more sensitive to such experiences; Jung is an instance of the latter.

106. Robert Kastenbaum, "Near-Death Reports? Evidence for Survival of Death?," in Bailey and Yates, *Near-Death Experience*, 247–48, and 254–58.

107. Zaleski, *Life of the World to Come*, 20; see also Segal, *Life After Death*, 715.

108. Zaleski, *Life of the World to Come*, 23.

Though the reports are culturally conditioned, there is also an amazing commonality among them, across lines of age, culture, and personal beliefs. In other words, the visions and images of the experience "have a reality and spontaneity of their own,"[109] but the *interpretations* of them vary according to culture and background. The commonality of the basic images has impressed researchers. Michael Grosso (a philosopher) says:

> Apparently, a pattern of images and feelings occurs to people on the verge of death with striking regularity. It is hard to avoid the conclusion that the [near-death experience] pattern is, so to speak, "built in" to the deep psyche.[110]

As described by Carol Zaleski, the "pattern of images and feelings" includes the following:

1. Separation from the body, sometimes accompanied by a "spectator" perspective, watching the scene or crisis from a distant or elevated vantage point.
2. Journey motifs, such as drifting through darkness, outer space, a "void" or a tunnel.
3. Encounter with deceased relatives or friends, or with a godlike or angelic presence (Moody's "being of light").
4. Review of one's past deeds in the form of a panoramic visual replay of memories (the life review). In cases of sudden encounter with life-threatening danger, this life review often takes precedence over other features.
5. Immersion in light and love. Many confess that this experience is indescribable. Cognitive and affective characteristics are fused. The keynote is a profound sense of security and protection, accompanied by a sense of receiving special messages or hidden truths. For some, this takes the form of an instantaneous, timeless, and comprehensive vision of the totality of existence.
6. Return to life, either involuntarily or by choice, to complete unfinished business on earth.

109. Carl G. Jung, "Visions/Life After Death," 110.

110. "The Archetype of Death and Enlightenment," in Bailey and Yates, *Near-Death Experience*, 131.

7. Transforming aftereffects, such as loss of fear of death, newfound zest for everyday life, and renewed dedication to the values of empathetic love, lifelong learning, and service to others. For some, these positive effects are accompanied by difficulties in adjusting to normal life.[111]

By no means are all of these elements present in every near-death experience; on the other hand, in some experiences there are even further elements. In that regard, there seems to be a lot of variety. That in general the experiences are authentic is beyond question; even hardened skeptics have been unable to refute their reality.[112] Scientific analysis, however, has to be given its due. Neurobiology long ago established that the brain has its own chemistry, which responds to events and stimuli of the outside world. Naturally, therefore, an extreme event such as a close encounter with death triggers neurochemical responses, and some theorists have quite reasonably proposed that these responses may help to explain features of near-death experiences. Such explanations are helpful, as far as they go, but as I shall argue presently, we cannot leave explanation for human experience to neurobiology alone. Extreme skepticism, which dismisses near-death experiences as explainable *solely* in biological or psychological terms,[113] is typical of scientific materialism that reduces

111. Zaleski, *Life of the World to Come*, 19. For a longer list, dependent on the research of Raymond Moody, see Bailey and Yates, *Near-Death Experience*, 5–6. Carol Zaleski, in "Evaluating Near-Death Testimony," Bailey and Yates, *Near-Death Experience*, 331–54, steers a middle ground between emphasizing the culture-bound character of the reports and being overly impressed with the commonality of the features of the experiences. The former can lead to too much skepticism, the latter to too much gullibility. She properly interprets the visions of near death as instances of the religious imagination, not unlike conversion stories and visions of new life that already fill religious literature. As such they are "real" products of the "imagination" as humans strive to put life here and now into the wider context of ultimate reality.

112. The large numbers of studies that have been done make it impossible to simply dismiss the phenomenon as fraudulent or mass hallucination or anything of the kind. Apparently, A. J. Ayers (1910–89), philosopher and vigorous atheist, "had a NDE in old age . . . 'My recent experiences,' he mused, 'have slightly weakened my conviction that my genuine death . . . will be the end of me, though I continue to hope that it will be. They have not weakened my conviction that there is no god'" (Bailey and Yates, *Near-Death Experience*, 15).

113. For examples of this, see Bailey and Yates, *Near-Death Experience*, 12–15. For a lengthy discussion of the possible brain chemistry involved in near-death and analogous experiences, see Karl Jansen, "Neuroscience, Ketamine, and the Near-Death Experience: The Role of Glutamate and the NMDA Receptor," in Bailey and Yates, *Near-Death Experience*, 265–77. For the view that neurobiology can never explain away religious experience,

all human existence to the physical level. A presumption that they represent more than some sort of pathology seems warranted. We need an understanding of this phenomenon that gives due consideration to both the physical and spiritual aspects of our humanity.

We have such an understanding in ancient spiritual traditions, including within the Bible, and as we shall see presently, neuroscience helps in achieving an integrated understanding. The creation stories place humans within creation, as material beings alongside the birds of the air, the creeping things of the earth and the beasts of the field. God created the *ʿadam* from the *ʿadamah*, and so also God created the animals; as Ecclesiastes says it, "humans have no advantage over the beasts (Eccl 3:19)." The psalmist (Ps 8:4) therefore wonders, "what are human beings that you care for them?" And yet, that is precisely the great revelation of the Scriptures, that God creates humans in the divine image and loves them. We know ourselves to be, in so many ways, just like other animals, and yet we cannot deny our capacities for transcendence, all of those qualities that make possible art and literature, science and philosophy, longing for truth and longing for God.

Eternal Life

The extreme skeptics of near-death experiences settle for neurobiological explanations, and leave it at that. Since scientific materialism will not allow the reality of the transcendent in human existence, then any experience suggesting the reality of a spiritual world must have to do with the pathology of the brain under duress, and nothing more. Not only near-death experiences are dismissed by such skepticism but so are all the prayers and religious experiences of humanity in all cultures down throughout the ages. So also is any human knowing that is not compatible with purely chemical and biological explanations. If the gospels tell us that Jesus "spent the night in prayer to God" (Luke 6:12), scientific materialists will assure us that it was all just brain chemistry. If Prince Siddhartha (Buddha) sat under the Bodhi tree, and contemplated the way to enlightenment, he ought really to have studied neurobiology. The problem with such skepticism is not its appeal to science, but its inability to see anything else.

---

see Andrew Newberg, Eugene D'Aquili, and Vince Rause, *Why God Won't Go Away: Brain Science and the Biology of Belief* (New York: Ballantine Books, 2001).

I am not suggesting that neurobiological explanations have no role to play in the discussion. The brain is a receptor for the mind as a radio is for radio waves or a telescope for light rays. The brain chemistry, therefore, which goes along with our experiences, is very real, but the chemistry is not what the experience itself *is*. For example, the emotion (the chemistry!) you feel as you gaze at the sun setting into the sea is evidence of your ability to be in touch with a beauty that is really out there; it is not evidence that "it's all just in your head." To be sure, there are physical phenomena that go along with spiritual experience, and drugs, therefore, can mimic such experiences, but that is only what we should expect. The issue is not whether chemicals are present in the brains of persons who have near-death and other out-of-body and spiritual experiences; it is clear that they are. The issue is, why do we have brains that function as seekers and receptors of beauty and love? The presence of brain chemicals in response to an experience says nothing about the reality or value of the experience itself.

Andrew Newberg (neurologist and professor of religious studies) and Eugene D'Aquili (1940–98, neuropsychologist)[114] conducted experiments, in which they recorded SPECT[115] scans of the brains of Buddhist monks and Carmelite nuns during the most intense moments of their meditating. Speaking of years of research that he did with D'Aquili, Newberg says:

> Gene and I began, as all scientists do, with the fundamental assumption that all that is really real is material. We regarded the brain as a biological machine, composed of matter and created by evolution to perceive and interact with the physical world.
>
> After years of research, however, our understanding of various brain structures and the way information is channeled along

114. According to his obituary by Margaret and John Bowker in *The Independent* (British newspaper), August 29, 1998, Eugene D'Aquili "was a faithful Catholic, though he had no time for what he regarded as the current follies of the Vatican. He lived a life of loyal dissent, writing letters of protest (in Latin) to Cardinal Ratzinger, yet always keeping the Easter Triduum in a private but passionate way. Not surprisingly, his research was not reductionistic in the manner of the more ephemeral sociobiologists when they approach the subject of God. In his view, the naturalising of our religious behaviours in detailed brain research is not a comment, one way or the other, on what there is, outside our brains, waiting to be apprehended and known."

115. SPECT = single photon emission computer tomography.

> neural pathways led us to hypothesize that the brain possesses a neurological mechanism for self-transcendence. . . .
>
> This hypothesis was later supported by our SPECT scan studies, which began to shed light on the neurological correlates of spiritual experience. In the narrowest scientific view, it would be possible to believe that we had reduced all spiritual transcendence . . . to a neurochemical commotion in the brain. But our understanding of the brain would not allow us to rest with that conclusion.[116]

It was impossible to rest with that conclusion because knowing the mechanism of the brain in no way determines the reality or nature of the things that the brain perceives. Newberg gives the example of a person recalling an experience of a moving performance of "*Nessun Dorma*" from Puccini's opera *Turandot*. The opera lover's brain waves would "fire" very much as if she were actually in the theater; indeed, tears might stream from her eyes all over again, recalling the plaintive and passionate lyrics of the aria. Brain chemistry could certainly provide clues that her emotions were singularly active. But no theory of how her brain works can say anything about the majesty of the opera, the inspiring artistry of the tenor's voice, or the depth of the opera lover's experience. The theory, like the SPECT scan, would only be a picture of brain activity that could say nothing of the beauty that the brain/person had encountered. Perhaps the administering of drugs could even provide a person with an analogous experience, but such an experiment would have nothing to do with the beauty and drama of an opera; the experience would be something else entirely.

Near-death experiences deserve to be taken seriously, therefore, as possible pointers to reality beyond themselves, and theologians should not be intimidated into silence about them for fear of inevitable criticisms.[117] It is not a matter of substituting near-death experiences for the visions and messages of the Bible. There is no either-or here any more than there is an either-or between the Bible and knowledge gained from some other area of human experience. It is also not a matter of selling out the biblical notion of the resurrection of the body in favor of the Platonic concept of the immortality of the soul. Those two notions have long

116. Newberg, D'Aquili, and Rause, *Why God Won't Go Away*, 145–46.
117. See Zaleski, "Evaluating Near-Death Testimony," 332–34.

been uneasily wedded in theological thought.[118] No doubt theologians will revisit this problem again and again, but it is not an issue to which ordinary believers give much thought. As for such accounts becoming escapist, not to mention saccharine, and occasions for shallow theologies, the response has to be the same sort of rigorous, reasoned criticism that would be applied to any other challenges. These are real problems, but we cannot, therefore, simply shrug aside what are clearly real experiences. The more pressing problems today gravitate around our ability to have any faith at all in the transcendent, and thus to have any faith that humans are more than just so much accidentally put together star stuff. We need an understanding of ourselves that is true to all of our knowledge, and that can encompass both our material and our spiritual nature. Near-death experiences may have a role to play.

One of the problems is that near-death stories describe the soul as rising from the body like a ghost from a machine. This very dualist picture of humans has a long and complex history, but it is a notion that most modern thinkers want to abandon. Science has everyone convinced that dualism is bad, since everything has to be in causal continuity.[119] Theology's sympathy with this aversion to dualism, however, can go only so far. In fact, human experience and recent neuroscience make it clear that there is a lot of space, and considerable need, for a reasonable sort of dualism, as we have already seen. The continuity of the inner self even as the outer self disintegrates, as in aging or suffering a physical injury, tells us that the mind is not simply in continuity with the body. Indeed, the whole field of psychosomatic medicine[120] tells us that the mind has powerful effects on both the body and the brain. Jeffrey Schwartz (psychiatrist) has demonstrated just how powerful the mind is with his development of a revolutionary technique for helping patients with obsessive-compulsive disorder. His technique involves, among other things, meditation and an effortful focusing of attention so as to achieve "relabeling, reattributing, refocusing and revaluing." The object of each of those verbs has to do with the particular obsessions and

118. See Alan Segal's account of the contests in this regard between "the orthodox" and the Gnostics (*Life After Death*, 532–95).

119. On this problem in relation to the philosophy of Descartes, see Keith Ward, *God and the Philosophers* (Minneapolis: Fortress Press, 2009), 29–40.

120. The professional, scholarly journal *Psychosomatic Medicine* can easily be found online at http://www.psychosomaticmedicine.org/reports/mfr1.dtl. Its two most frequently read articles are "Social Isolation Kills: But How and Why?" and "Alterations in Immune Function Produced by Mindfulness Meditation."

compulsions that paralyze a patient's life, and then with the patient's mind and the truth of his or her situation. The technique has achieved a better than 80 percent success rate, without the use of drugs, even with patients suffering severe cases of the disorder.[121] With the help of brain scans, Schwartz has established that by the concentrated focusing of the *mind*, the *brain* is physically altered.

Human beings, we might say, are embodied souls. The soul is foundational to human existence, just as the outpouring of the Spirit of God is foundational to the creation of reality. We saw in the last chapter that the universe is characterized by emergence, the constant flowering of the wholly new from elements that of themselves seem unable to account for the new principles and properties that emerge. This is a good analogy for understanding the way in which God constantly draws creation forward into further complexity, diversity, and beauty. The soul, in this view, "is a distinctive sort of reality."[122] If God is Supreme Being and Consciousness who has endowed creation not just with existence, but with being, then a human being, a human soul, is the universe as it responds to God and even begins to stammer its thanks, though also its fears and questions. Soul/Spirit has always been an aspect of the universe by virtue of the Spirit of God. Soul is already present in animals to a degree; it reaches in humans enough maturity to make possible the knowledge of God, and eternal life with God.

Though it is very difficult to describe what near-death experiences represent, they seem to be encounters with deeper reality, closer to God, in moments when everything else is stripped away—when the self is forced into silence and submission. Carol Zaleski, who is adamant that the experiences cannot be proof of an afterlife, describes them as "at once imaginative and real. It is a real experience mediated by the religious imagination."[123] To understand this, it helps to recall how foundational to human existence are imagination, symbol-making, ritual, and narrative (myth, saga, legend). Imagination, symbol, and ritual existed in human evolution prior to language and were its roots. Along with the rhythms

121. Jeffrey M. Schwartz and Sharon Begley, *The Mind and the Brain: Neuroplasticity and the Power of Mental Force* (New York: HarperCollins, 2002); see 54–95 for the history and specifics of the four-step technique; see also Sharon Begley, *Train Your Mind, Change Your Brain: How a New Science Reveals Our Extraordinary Potential to Transform Ourselves* (New York: Ballantine Books, 2007).

122. Ward, *God and the Philosophers*, 38. See also Carol Zaleski's thoughts on the need for "some form of soul-body dualism" (*Life of the World to Come*, 58–64).

123. *Life of the World to Come*, 20–21.

of birth, life, and death, image and symbol were the generators of myths and, no doubt, of what Jung calls the archetypes of the collective unconscious.[124] Without symbol, image, myth, and narrative, we would not have the most potent means we have devised to communicate with one another—not merely words, but art, literature, ritual, music, and drama. Silencing or ignoring near-death accounts, when they are genuine, is to silence powerful symbols coming from our shared unconscious that can reveal us to ourselves. And if they reveal us to ourselves, then they may be glimpses also of the reality from which we have emerged and even of the Eternal Mystery that is the ground of all being.

Zaleski persuasively suggests that reports of near-death experiences are analogous to conversion stories that feature regularly in religious literature.[125] When Paul, for example, was on the Damascus road, intent on destroying the embryonic Jesus movement, he had a vision that, by his own account, completely transformed him (Gal 1:13-18). We have no reason to believe that it was a near-death experience, but its similarity to those narratives is quite striking, particularly in his encounter with a being of light,[126] receiving a special message, and returning to ordinary life totally transformed. Conversion stories in general, though far less dramatic than Paul's, follow this pattern of a surprising encounter with the divine in which a new way of seeing reality is given, so that life thereafter is never the same. Conversions, like near-death experiences, are often described in terms of "entering another world," "emerging from a sepulcher, from an abyss of darkness" or of coming to new life, even "new creation."[127] They function to remind us that our sense of the sacred in existence is not simply to be ignored. Near-death reports are compelling to the extent that our vision of ourselves has become too narrow and pessimistic; we need to break free, to regain a sense of ourselves as spiritual beings.

Near-death experiences cannot prove for everyone the reality of eternal life, though for those who experience them, they seem sometimes to constitute such proof. In general, however, we never escape the challenge

124. See Grosso, "Archetype of Death and Enlightenment," in Bailey and Yates, *Near-Death Experience*, 129–42.

125. Zaleski, "Evaluating Near-Death Testimony," 347–50.

126. It is actually Acts that describes "a light from heaven" (9:3; 22:6; 26:13), but Paul's words in 2 Cor 4:6 are sometimes understood, quite appropriately, as a reference to his own experience: "For it is the God who said, 'Let light shine out of darkness,' who has shone in our hearts to give the light of the knowledge of the glory of God in the face of Christ" (RSV).

127. See Zaleski, "Evaluating Near-Death Testimony," 348–49; and 2 Cor 5:17; Gal 6:15.

of faith. But close encounters with death are, paradoxically, privileged moments. Ordinarily, we do all we can to avoid death, but among those who have had near-death experiences, it is remarkable how common is the theme that they were reluctant to return. Jung says it took him about three weeks to make up his mind to live again.[128] It is also remarkable that the experience changes those who go through it, often in quite notable ways. For everyone else, the stories are a challenge; they invite our meditation and remind us that we have every reason to see ourselves as the Bible would have us believe, as children of God.

Conclusion

Near-death experiences and eternal life are appropriate topics on which to close since in some respects they straddle the borderline between the Bible and science. Overall, the Bible is somewhat ambivalent about the afterlife, since, as we have seen, the Old Testament writers had no clear vision of it. Ancient Judaism, Jesus, and the New Testament step into this uncertainty, however, and—we might now say—complete the picture. They take it for granted that God's love reaches from the creation to the final consummation—not just of humans, however, but of the entire universe. Genesis begins with creation, and Revelation concludes with "the new heaven and the new earth" (Rev 21:1).

The cosmic sweep of the biblical vision has a lovely correspondence with the discoveries of modern science. From both cosmology and Darwinism we now know how completely bound up with all of creation human beings are. Not only have we evolved from animals, so that our very DNA makes us not-too-distant cousins of the animal world, but every atom in our bodies was forged in the heart of the stars and was released by their deaths. It might sound like poetry to say it, but it is literally true: we are born from the stars and someday all of our atoms will return there. John Haught says it well:

> The thrust of much recent science, and especially evolution, is that we truly belong to the universe. Theologically this would mean that the revelatory promise that gives us our hope extends backward to cosmic beginnings, outward to the most remote galaxies, and forward to the future of the whole of creation.[129]

128. "Visions/Life After Death," 105.

129. Haught, *God After Darwin*, 164.

Paul Davies appropriately says, "I cannot believe that our existence in this universe is a mere quirk of fate, an accident of history, an incidental blip in the great cosmic drama. Our involvement is too intimate."[130] Our capacities of knowing and contemplation, faith and reason, were built into the universe from its first moments. Faith proclaims that they were there from their origin in the Mind and Love of God. Even from a scientific perspective, the case can easily be made that the most reasonable way to account for the human mind is not with an accidental and mindless universe, but with an eternal intelligence—with what Mariano Artigas (priest, physicist, philosopher) calls "the Mind of the Universe."[131]

This book has been something of a protest against overly narrow views of God and human beings. It is encouraging to consider that the Bible and science agree on a vision of humans as truly cosmic beings. We are simultaneously made from star stuff and from the Spirit of God, in whom we also have our final destiny. If the biblical writers could have known what we now know, they would only have had all the more reason to say that "the heavens proclaim the glory of God" (Ps 19:1) and that "creation itself waits with eager longing . . . for the glorious liberation of the children of God" (Rom 8:19, 21).

130. *The Mind of God: The Scientific Basis for a Rational World* (New York: Touchstone Books, 1992), 232.

131. Artigas (*The Mind of the Universe: Understanding Science and Religion* [Philadelphia: Templeton Foundation, 2000], xvi, xvii) says, "God can be referred to as 'the mind of the universe' not in a pantheistic sense, but to express the idea that our universe exhibits rationality, information, and creativity; that it makes possible the existence of human beings who are strictly rational and creative; and this requires a divine foundation: a participation in God's creativity"—"the contemporary scientific worldview suggests that the universe is permeated in its innermost being by a rationality whose explanation requires the authorship of a personal mind."

BIBLIOGRAPHY

Adelard of Bath. *Conversations with His Nephew: On the Same and the Different, Questions on Natural Science, and on Birds*. Edited and translated by Charles Burnett, with Italo Ronca et al. (New York: Cambridge University Press, 1998).

Armstrong, Karen. *The Case for God* (New York: Alfred A. Knopf, 2009).

Artigas, Mariano. *The Mind of the Universe: Understanding Science and Religion* (Philadelphia: Templeton Foundation, 2000).

Augustine, Saint. *The Literal Meaning of Genesis*. Translated and annotated by John Hammond Taylor (New York: Newman Press, 1982).

Bailey, Lee W., and Jenny Yates, eds. *The Near-Death Experience: A Reader* (New York: Routledge, 1996).

Ball, Philip. "Triumph of the Medieval Mind." *Nature* 452 (April 17, 2008): 816–18.

Barbour, Ian G. *Religion and Science: Historical and Contemporary Issues* (New York: HarperCollins, 1997).

Barr, Stephen M. *Modern Physics and Ancient Faith* (Notre Dame: University of Notre Dame Press, 2003).

Begley, Sharon. *Train Your Mind, Change Your Brain: How a New Science Reveals Our Extraordinary Potential to Transform Ourselves* (New York: Ballantine Books, 2007).

Behe, Michael J. *Darwin's Black Box* (New York: Free Press, 1996).

Berry, Wendell. *Life Is a Miracle: An Essay Against Modern Superstition* (Washington, DC: Counterpoint, 2000).

Brown, Jeannine K. *Scripture as Communication: Introducing Biblical Hermeneutics* (Grand Rapids, MI: Baker Academic, 2007).

Brown, Raymond E. *An Introduction to New Testament Christology* (New York: Paulist Press, 1994).

Caputo, John D. *Philosophy and Theology* (Nashville: Abingdon Press, 2006).

———. "Open Theology—Or What Comes After Secularism?" *Bulletin of the Council of Societies for the Study of Religion* 37:2 (April 2008): 45–46.

Cochrane, Louise. *Adelard of Bath: The First English Scientist* (London: British Museum Press, 1994).

Collins, John J. "Apocalyptic Eschatology as the Transcendence of Death." In *Visionaries and Their Apocalypses*, edited by Paul D. Hanson (Philadelphia: Fortress Press, 1983).

Coyne, George V. "Evolution and the Human Person: The Pope in Dialogue." *Science and Theology: The New Consonance*, edited by Ted Peters, 153–61 (Boulder, CO: Westview Press, 1998).

Davies, Paul. *God and the New Physics* (New York: Simon & Schuster, 1983).

———. *The Mind of God: The Scientific Basis for a Rational World* (New York: Simon & Schuster, 1992).

———. *The 5th Miracle: The Search for the Origin and Meaning of Life* (New York: Simon & Schuster, 1999).

Dawkins, Richard, and Lawrence Krauss. Stanford University Forum on "Science Education." Q&A Part 7. March 9, 2008. http://richarddawkins.net/article,2472,Richard-Dawkins-and-Lawrence-Krauss,RichardDawkinsnet.

Dawkins, Richard. *The Selfish Gene*. 30th Anniversary Edition (New York: Oxford University Press, 1976, 2006).

———. *The Blind Watchmaker: Why the Evidence of Evolution Reveals a Universe without Design* (New York: W. W. Norton, 1986, 1996).

———. *River Out of Eden: A Darwinian View of Life* (New York: Basic Books, 1995).

———. *The God Delusion* (Boston: Houghton Mifflin, 2006).

Dennett, Daniel C. *Darwin's Dangerous Idea: Evolution and the Meanings of Life* (London: Penguin Books, 1995).

Diamond, Jared. *The Third Chimpanzee: The Evolution and Future of the Human Animal* (New York: HarperCollins, 1992).

———. *Guns, Germs and Steel: The Fates of Human Societies* (New York: W. W. Norton, 1999).

Donald, Merlin. *A Mind So Rare: The Evolution of Human Consciousness* (New York: W. W. Norton, 2001).

Dulles, Avery. *Models of Revelation* (New York: Orbis Books, 1983, 1992).

———. *The Craft of Theology: From Symbol to System—New Expanded Edition* (New York: Crossroads, 1992).

Dunbar, Robin. *Grooming, Gossip and the Evolution of Language* (London: Faber & Faber, 1996).

———. *The Human Story: A New History of Mankind's Evolution* (London: Faber & Faber, 2004).

Dunn, James D. G. *Jesus Remembered: Christianity in the Making*, vol. 1 (Grand Rapids, MI: Wm. B. Eerdmans, 2003).

Ecklund, Elaine Howard. *Science vs. Religion: What Scientists Really Think* (New York: Oxford University Press, 2010).

Ehrlich, Paul R. *Human Natures: Genes, Cultures and the Human Prospect* (Washington, DC: Island Press, 2000).

"Flaubert, Gustave." *Encyclopædia Britannica Online*. Accessed September 4, 2010. http://search.eb.com/eb/article-2350.

Flew, Anthony. *There Is a God: How the World's Most Notorious Atheist Changed His Mind* (New York: HarperOne, 2007).

Freire, Paulo. *Pedagogy of the Oppressed*. 30th Anniversary Edition. Translated by Myra Bergman Ramos (New York: Continuum, 1970, 2002).

Garner, Dwight. "Many Kinds of Universes, and None Require God." *New York Times.* September 7, 2010. http://www.nytimes.com/2010/09/08/books/08book.html.

Gaster, T. H. "Demon." In *The Interpreter's Dictionary of the Bible: An Illustrated Encyclopedia*, vol. 1, edited by G. A. Buttrick et al. (Nashville: Abingdon Press, 1962).

Giberson, Karl W., and Mariano Artigas. *Oracles of Science: Celebrity Scientists versus God and Religion* (New York: Oxford University Press, 2007).

Giberson, Karl W. *Saving Darwin: How to be a Christian and Believe in Evolution* (New York: HarperOne, 2008).

Gilkey, Langdon. *Religion and the Scientific Future: Reflections on Myth, Science and Theology* (New York: Harper & Row, 1970).

Goodenough, Ursula. *The Sacred Depths of Nature* (New York: Oxford University Press, 1998).

Green, Joel B. "The Challenge of Hearing the New Testament." In *Hearing the New Testament: Strategies for Interpretation*, edited by idem (Grand Rapids, MI: Wm. B. Eerdmans, 1995).

Gribbin, John. *Science: A History: 1543–2001* (London: Penguin Books, 2003).

Grosso, Michael. "The Archetype of Death and Enlightenment." In *Near-Death Experience*, Bailey and Yates (cited above), 127–43.

Harris, Sam. *Letter to a Christian Nation* (New York: Vintage Books, 2008).

Harrison, Peter. *The Bible, Protestantism, and the Rise of Natural Science* (New York: Cambridge University Press, 1998).

———. *The Fall of Adam and the Rise of Natural Science* (New York: Cambridge University Press, 2007).

Harrisville, Roy A., and Walter Sundberg. *The Bible in Modern Culture: Baruch Spinoza to Brevard Childs* (Grand Rapids, MI: Wm. B. Eerdmans, 1995, 2002).

Haught, John F. *God After Darwin: A Theology of Evolution* (Boulder, CO: Westview Press, 2000).

———. *Deeper Than Darwin: The Prospect for Religion in the Age of Evolution* (Boulder, CO: Westview Press, 2003).

———. *Is Nature Enough? Meaning and Truth in the Age of Science* (New York: Cambridge University Press, 2006).

———. *Christianity and Science: Toward a Theology of Nature* (New York: Orbis Books, 2007).

———. *God and the New Atheism: A Critical Response to Dawkins, Harris, and Hitchens* (Louisville: Westminster John Knox, 2008).

Hawking, Stephen, and Leonard Mlodinow. *The Grand Design* (New York: Bantam Books, 2010).

Hawking, Stephen. *A Brief History of Time* (New York: Bantam Books, 1988, 1996).

Heschel, Abraham J. *The Prophets*, vol. 1 (New York: Harper & Row, 1962).

Hick, John. *The Fifth Dimension: An Exploration of the Spiritual Realm* (Oxford: Oneworld, 2004).

Hurtado, Larry W. *Lord Jesus Christ: Devotion to Jesus in Earliest Christianity* (Grand Rapids, MI: Wm B. Eerdmans, 2003).

———. *How on Earth Did Jesus Become a God? Historical Questions about Earliest Devotion to Jesus* (Grand Rapids, MI: Wm. B. Eerdmans, 2005).

Jansen, Karl. "Neuroscience, Ketamine, and the Near-Death Experience: The Role of Glutamate and the NMDA Receptor." In *Near-Death Experience*, Bailey and Yates (cited above), 265–77.

John Paul II, Pope. "Message of His Holiness Pope John Paul II." *Physics, Philosophy and Theology: A Common Quest for Understanding*, edited by R. J. Russell et al. (Vatican City: Vatican Observatory, 1988), M1-14.

———. "Faith Can Never Conflict with Reason." *L'Osservatore Romano* N. 44 (1264). November 4, 1992. http://www.its.caltech.edu/~nmcenter/sci-cp/sci-9211.html.

Johnson, Elizabeth A. *Quest for the Living God: Mapping Frontiers in the Theology of God* (New York: Continuum, 2007).

Josephus, Flavius. *The Works of Josephus, Complete and Unabridged*. Translated by W. Whiston (Peabody, MA: Hendrickson Publishers, 1987).

Jung, Carl G., and Aniela Jaffé. *Memories, Dreams, Reflections*. Translated by Richard and Clara Winston (New York: Vintage Books, 1961, 1989).

Kastenbaum, Robert. "Near-Death Reports? Evidence for Survival of Death?" In *Near-Death Experience*, Bailey and Yates (cited above), 245–64.

Kloppenborg, John S., Marvin W. Meyer, and Stephen J. Patterson. *Q-Thomas Reader* (Salem, OR: Polebridge Press, 1990).

Korsmeyer, Jerry D. *Evolution and Eden: Balancing Original Sin and Contemporary Science* (New York: Paulist Press, 1998).

Kübler-Ross, Elisabeth. *On Life After Death* (Berkeley, CA: Celestial Arts, 1991).

Kugel, James L. *The Bible As It Was* (Cambridge, MA: Belknap Press of Harvard University, 1997).

———. *How to Read the Bible: A Guide to Scripture Then and Now* (New York: Free Press, 2007).

Kung, Hans. *Does God Exist? An Answer for Today* (New York: Doubleday, 1980).

Lendon, Brad. "Where Did Waters Part for Moses? Not Where You Think." CNN.com. September 21, 2010.http://news.blogs.cnn.com/2010/09/21/where-did-waters-part-for-moses-not-where-you-think/?iref=allsearch.

Lindberg, David C. *The Beginnings of Western Science: The European Scientific Tradition in Philosophical, Religious, and Institutional Context, 600 B.C. to A.D. 1450* (Chicago: University of Chicago Press, 1992).

Mackenzie, R. A. F., and Roland E. Murphy. "Job." In *The New Jerome Biblical Commentary* (Englewood Cliffs, NJ: Prentice Hall, 1968, 1990).

Maier, Gerhard. *The End of the Historical-critical Method*. Translated by E. W. Leverenz and R. F. Norden (Eugene, OR: Wipf & Stock, 1977).

Mayr, Ernst. *What Evolution Is* (New York: Basic Books, 2001).

McGrath, Alister, and Joanna Collicutt McGrath. *The Dawkins Delusion? Atheist Fundamentalism and the Denial of the Divine* (Downers Grove, IL: InterVarsity Press, 2007).

McGrath, Alister E. *Dawkins' God: Genes, Memes, and the Meaning of Life* (Malden, MA: Blackwell, 2005).

———. *The Twilight of Atheism: The Rise and Fall of Disbelief in the Modern World* (New York: Doubleday, 2004).

Meier, John P. *A Marginal Jew: Rethinking the Historical Jesus, vol. 2: Mentor, Message, and Miracles* (New York: Doubleday, 1994).

Mitchell, Mark T. *Michael Polanyi: The Art of Knowing* (Wilmington, DE: ISI Books, 2006).

Moody, Raymond A. *Life After Life: The Investigations of a Phenomenon—Survival of Bodily Death* (San Francisco: HarperSanFrancisco, 1975, 2001).

———. *Reflections on Life After Life* (New York: Bantam Books, 1977).

Morowitz, Harold J. *The Emergence of Everything: How the World Became Complex* (New York: Oxford University Press, 2002).

Morris, Desmond. *The Naked Ape: A Zoologist's Study of the Human Animal* (New York: McGraw Hill, 1967).

———. *The Human Zoo* (New York: McGraw Hill, 1969).

Newberg, Andrew, Eugene D'Aquili, and Vince Rause. *Why God Won't Go Away: Brain Science and the Biology of Belief* (New York: Ballantine Books, 2001).

Nichols, Robert Hasting. "Fundamentalism in the Presbyterian Church." *The Journal of Religion* 5:1 (January 1925).

Origen. *The Song of Songs: Commentary and Homilies*. Translated and annotated by R. P. Lawson (Westminster, MD: Newman Press, 1957).

Paley, William, Matthew Eddy, and David M. Knight. *Natural Theology: or, Evidence of the Existence and Attributes of the Deity, Collected from the Appearances of Nature* (New York: Oxford University Press, 2006).

Peacocke, Arthur. *Theology for a Scientific Age: Being and Becoming—Natural, Divine, and Human*, Enlarged Edition (Minneapolis: Fortress Press, 1993).

Perrin, Norman. *Rediscovering the Teaching of Jesus* (New York: Harper & Row, 1967).

Peters, Ted, and Martinez Hewlett. *Theological and Scientific Commentary on Darwin's Origin of Species* (Nashville: Abingdon Press, 2008).

Peters, Ted, ed. *Science and Theology: The New Consonance* (Boulder, CO: Westview, 1998).

Philo. "The Special Laws." *The Works of Philo Complete and Unabridged*. Translated by C. D. Yonge (Peabody, MA: Hendrickson Publishers, 1993).

Polanyi, Michael. *Science, Faith and Society* (Chicago: University of Chicago Press, 1946).

———. *The Study of Man* (Chicago: University of Chicago Press, 1958).

———. *Personal Knowledge: Towards a Post-critical Philosophy* (Chicago: University of Chicago Press, 1958, 1962).

———. "On the Modern Mind." *Encounter* 24 (May 1965).

———. *The Tacit Dimension* (Chicago: University of Chicago Press, 1966).

Rachels, James. *Created From Animals: The Moral Implications of Darwinism* (New York: Oxford University Press, 1990).

Ratzinger, Joseph, Pope Benedict XVI. *Jesus of Nazareth: From the Baptism in the Jordan to the Transfiguration*. Translated by Adrian J. Walker (New York: Doubleday, 2007).

Rees, Martin. *Just Six Numbers: The Deep Forces that Shape the Universe* (Lymington, UK: Basic Books, 2000).

Rolston III, Holmes. "Does Nature Need to be Redeemed?" *Zygon* 29:2 (June 1994): 205–29.

Rue, Loyal. *By the Grace of Guile: The Role of Deception in Natural History and Human Affairs* (New York: Oxford University Press, 1994).

Russell, Bertrand. *Problems of Philosophy* (New York: Oxford University Press, 1912, 1998).

Sagan, Carl. *Cosmos* (New York: Ballantine Books, 1980).

Schneiders, Sandra. *The Revelatory Text: Interpreting the New Testament as Sacred Scripture* (Collegeville, MN: Liturgical Press, 1999).

Schroeder, Gerald L. *The Science of God: The Convergence of Scientific and Biblical Wisdom* (New York: Broadway Books, 1997).

Schwartz, Jeffrey M., and Sharon Begley. *The Mind and the Brain: Neuroplasticity and the Power of Mental Force* (New York: HarperCollins, 2002).

Segal, Alan F. *Life After Death: A History of the Afterlife in the Religions of the West* (New York: Doubleday, 2004).

Shea, William R., and Mariano Artigas. *Galileo in Rome: The Rise and Fall of a Troublesome Genius* (New York: Oxford University Press, 2003).

Spinoza, Benedict. *Theological-Political Treatise* (Gebhardt Edition). 2nd ed. Translated by S. Shirley (Indianapolis: Hackett Publishing, 2001).

Timmer, Daniel C. "God's Speeches, Job's Responses, and the Problem of Coherence in the Book of Job: Sapiential Pedagogy Revisited." *Catholic Biblical Quarterly* 71:2 (2009): 286–305.

Trible, Phyllis. *God and the Rhetoric of Sexuality* (Philadelphia: Fortress Press, 1978).

Tutu, Desmond. "No Future without Forgiveness." In *The Impossible Will Take a Little While: A Citizen's Guide to Hope in a Time of Fear*, edited by Paul Rogat Loeb (New York: Basic Books, 2004).

Van Biema, David. "The Case for Teaching the Bible." *TIME In Partnership with CNN*. March 22, 2007. http://www.time.com/time/magazine/article/0,9171,1601845-1,00.html.

Von Rad, Gerhard. *Old Testament Theology: volume I: The Theology of Israel's Historical Traditions.* Translated by D. M. G. Stalker (New York: Harper & Row, 1962).

Ward, Keith. *Pascal's Fire: Scientific Faith and Religious Understanding* (Oxford: Oneworld, 2006).

———. *God and the Philosophers* (Minneapolis: Fortress Press, 2009).

Weinberg, Steven. "Without God." *New York Review of Books* 55:14 (September 25, 2008): 73–76.

Weinstein, David. "Herbert Spencer." *The Stanford Encyclopedia of Philosophy*. Summer 2009 Edition. Edited by Edward N. Zalta. http://plato.stanford.edu/archives/sum2009/entries/spencer/.

Whitcomb, John C., and Henry M. Morris. *The Genesis Flood: The Biblical Record and Its Scientific Implications* (Philadelphia: Presbyterian and Reformed Pub. Co., 1961).

Whitehead, A. N. *Science and the Modern World: Lowell Lectures, 1925* (New York: The Free Press: 1925, 1967).

Wiesel, Elie. *Night* (New York: Bantam Books, 1960).

———. *All Rivers Run to the Sea: Memoirs* (New York: Alfred A. Knopf, 1996).

Wilson, Edward O. *On Human Nature* (Cambridge, MA: Harvard University Press, 1978).

———. *Consilience: The Unity of Knowledge* (New York: Vintage Books, 1998).

Wright, N. T. "The Self-Revelation of God in Human History: A Dialogue on Jesus with N. T. Wright." In Flew, *There Is a God* (cited above), 185–213.

Zaleski, Carol. *The Life of the World to Come: Near-Death Experience and Christian Hope* (New York: Oxford University Press, 1996).

———. "Evaluating Near-Death Testimony." In *Near-Death Experience*, Bailey and Yates (cited above), 331–54.

INDEX OF PEOPLE AND SUBJECTS

ʿadam (*ʿadamah*)/Adam, 22, 70, 94–96, 98, 100, 152, 188
Abraham, 2, 3, 46, 52, 57, 59, 60, 92, 93, 96, 160, 172, 181
Adelard of Bath, 11
Altruism, 104, 106, 113, 131
Aristotelian Philosophy, 12, 90
Armstrong, Karen, 64, 65, 75, 76, 77, 79
Arrogance, 19, 20–21, 96, 99, 142, 173
Artigas, Mariano, 9, 21, 22, 75, 195
Atheism/Atheists, 6, 8, 13, 32, 62, 66, 75, 77, 79, 97–98, 106, 124
Augustine, Saint, 20, 72, 74, 96, 97, 138
Auschwitz (death camp), 149–51

Bailey, Lee W., 184, 185, 186, 187, 193
Ball, Philip, 11
Barbour, Ian G., 5, 77, 79
Barr, Stephen M., 5, 22, 76, 79, 80
Begley, Sharon, 192
Behe, Michael J., 7
Berry, Wendell, 107, 131
Bible
    ancient interpreters of, 42–49, 52–57, 70, 72, 73, 140
    as partner with science, 17–19
    canon of, 26–30, 40, 44, 66, 67
    inerrancy of, 33, 35
Big Bang, 89, 90, 127
Brown, Jeannine K., 54, 140, 144
Brown, Raymond E., 167

Caputo, John D., 12, 13, 21, 40, 62, 64, 72, 75, 76, 81, 124
Christianity, 26, 28, 38, 44, 54, 58, 59, 60, 69, 73, 77, 85, 96, 97, 106, 121, 135, 165, 167, 168, 169, 181, 183
Church, 10, 27, 29, 35, 58, 71, 77, 92, 159, 169
Cochrane, Louise, 11
Collins, John J., 181, 182
Consciousness, 107, 108, 111, 116, 120, 124, 134, 136, 139, 165, 192
Copernicus/Copernican Revolution, 79, 102
Coyne, George V., 19
Creation stories, 20, 102, 115, 121, 188
Creationism, 7, 20
Curiosity, 16–17, 110

D'Aquili, Eugene, 188–90
Darwin/Darwinism, 7, 9, 10, 16, 17, 18, 33, 56, 79, 81, 106, 127, 194
David (biblical), 46, 48, 52, 70, 71, 96, 141, 143, 145, 146, 157, 160
Davies, Paul, 5, 87, 89, 90, 100, 118, 119, 128, 130, 195
Dawkins, Richard, 4, 6–9, 13–15, 16, 17, 18, 21, 30–33, 35, 36, 60, 62, 69, 82, 88, 101, 104, 105, 112–15, 120, 121, 122, 131, 133, 150
Deism, 78
Dennett, Daniel C., 9–10, 16–17, 18, 21, 112, 116
Descartes, René, 12, 75–78, 81, 108, 124, 125, 191
Diamond, Jared, 21, 152
Dirac, Paul, 118

Documentary Hypothesis (Pentateuch), 47
Donald, Merlin, 108, 111, 120, 136, 137
Douglass, Frederick, 150
Dualism, 12, 191–92
Dulles, Avery, 54, 78, 135, 140
Dunbar, Robin, 136
Dunn, James D. G., 155

Ecklund, Elaine Howard, xii, 4
Eddy, Matthew, 78
Ehrlich, Paul R., 107, 136
Einstein, Albert, 120
Elijah (biblical), 156, 158, 171, 179, 180
Elisha (biblical), 156, 180
Elohim, 31, 93, 94, 102
Emergence/Emergent Universe, 89, 99, 105, 112, 127–30, 136, 153, 192
Enlightenment, 11–13, 17, 18, 21, 38, 40, 42, 54, 58, 62, 69, 74, 76, 81, 98, 132, 174
Ethics, 67, 68, 69, 72, 83, 85, 105, 107, 113, 119
Evidence (and faith), 3, 4, 83, 87, 88, 99, 114, 116, 121, 122, 130–33, 189
Evil, 9, 10, 82, 86, 95, 96, 98, 99, 103, 113, 145, 146, 149, 150–53, 157, 159, 160, 165, 173
Evolution/Evolutionary, 6–9, 16–18, 33, 36, 56, 57, 79, 80, 89, 95, 103–7, 110, 112, 115, 118, 121, 126, 127, 131, 138, 139, 141, 152, 185, 189, 192, 194
Exorcism/Exorcist, 71, 155, 159–65, 166, 167

Faith (*see also* Evidence), 2–4, 5, 6, 10–13, 17, 18, 21, 22, 25, 28, 29, 35, 37, 46, 48–60, 62–63, 69–72, 74, 80, 82, 83, 87, 90, 97, 99, 101, 102, 113, 117, 121, 144, 148, 154, 157, 165, 169, 173, 174, 177, 178, 180, 183, 191, 194, 195
  and suffering, 149–51
  biblical, xi, 7, 11, 24, 42, 51, 55–57, 59, 60, 62
  distinct from belief, 84
  Historical Criticism and, 43, 49–53
  "little faith," 153, 170
  of Jesus, 182
  people of, 2, 55, 65, 98, 105
Flaubert, Gustave, 137
Flew, Anthony, 4, 88–91, 109, 166, 169
Form Criticism, 140
Free Will, 22, 72, 77, 80, 107, 112, 116, 128, 131, 134
Freire, Paulo, 111, 112
Fundamentalism (biblical), 6, 20, 33–36, 47, 69

Galileo, 11, 74–76, 78, 81, 102, 108, 117
Gandhi, Mohandas, 169
Garner, Dwight, 1
Gaster, T. H., 160
Genocide, 32, 62, 98, 106, 113, 133, 151
Giberson, Karl W., 7, 9
Gilkey, Langdon, 17, 68, 83
God (*see also* Elohim *and* Jahweh)
  as Absolute Future, 115
  as beyond all knowing, 64–66
  council of, 100, 156
  declared dead, 1, 62, 81
  images of, 65, 90, 92–94, 169, 171
Goodenough, Ursula, 80
Green, Joel B., 144
Gribbin, John, 12
Grosso, Michael, 186, 193

Harris, Sam, 6, 30, 32, 33, 112, 121, 150
Harrison, Peter, 73, 74
Harrisville, Roy A., 20, 33, 42
Haught, John F., xii, 2, 5, 6, 8, 15, 16, 30, 76, 87, 90, 105, 110, 113–17, 121, 130, 131, 151, 152, 194
Hawking, Stephen, 1, 108–9
Hermeneutics (*see also* Interpretation), 37

Heschel, Abraham J., 142–43
Hewlett, Martinez, 5, 79, 101, 107
Hick, John, 76
Historical Criticism, 8, 25, 33, 38, 41, 42, 43, 49–56, 78, 80, 140
Hobbes, Thomas, 39, 47
Hubble telescope, 100
Human/Humanity (*see also* *ʿadam*/ Adam)
  as distinct from animals, 109–11, 188
  as related to animals, 94–95, 103, 109
  capacity for truth, 13, 16, 17, 110, 115, 118, 120, 173
  capacity to know God, 2, 64, 86, 95
  evolution of, 57, 95, 104–7, 110, 138, 152, 192
  humanization, 111
Hurtado, Larry W., 168, 169

Immanuel, 97, 152
Inspiration (biblical), 2, 6, 39, 46, 52, 53, 55, 57–59, 91, 135, 138, 144
Intelligence, 5, 15–17, 56, 82, 88, 103, 109, 112, 114, 128, 131, 195
Intelligent Design, 7
Interpretation (biblical), 21, 24–60, 69, 73–74, 91, 115, 144
Intersubjectivity, 116–17, 120, 138
Irreducible Complexity, 7

Jahweh (*see also* God *and Elohim*), 50, 51, 168, 171
Jansen, Karl, 187
Jefferson, Thomas, 155
Jeremiah (biblical), 35, 52, 71, 148, 150, 169
Jerome, Saint, 27
Jesus, 26, 34, 38, 58, 60, 70, 71, 91, 92, 96, 97, 101, 113, 118, 121, 140, 142, 146, 147, 148, 151, 152, 154–74, 180–83, 185, 188, 193, 194
Johnson, Elizabeth A., 66, 69
Josephus, Flavius, 159, 163
Judaism, 10, 26, 38, 44, 53, 58–60, 97, 160, 163, 167, 168, 179–81, 183, 194
Jung, Carl G., 184–86, 193, 194

Kant, Immanuel, 84
Kastenbaum, Robert, 185
Keller, Helen, 137
Kepler, Johannes, 11, 78, 81
King, Martin Luther, Jr., 113, 150, 169
Kingdom of God, 71, 96, 97, 115, 161–63, 181
Kloppenborg, John S., 161
Knight, David M., 78
Knowledge
  facets of, 116–21
  modern expansion of, 73, 80
  tacit, 117, 125–27, 129, 132, 134, 135, 138, 144, 165
  types of, xii, 19, 79, 106, 116, 129, 133, 134, 140, 142
Korsmeyer, Jerry D., 152
Krauss, Lawrence, 14
Kübler-Ross, Elisabeth, 184
Kugel, James L., 42–61, 70, 178
Kung, Hans, 92

Language
  biblical, 40–41, 45, 134–35, 137, 138, 140–42
  evolution of, 135–36
  limitations of, 135–39, 185
Laplace, Pierre, 78–79
Lendon, Brad, 154
Lenin, Vladimir, 124
Lindberg, David C., 12, 72, 75, 90, 125
Luther, Martin, 27–29, 38, 73–74

MacKay, Donald, 128
MacKenzie, R. A. F., 147
Maier, Gerhard, 35, 42
Mandela, Nelson, 132, 133
Mayr, Ernst, 109–10

McGrath, Alister, 4, 5, 8, 76–79, 82, 92, 97, 98, 124
McGrath, Joanna Collicutt, 8
Meier, John P., 155, 157, 158, 160–64, 166, 167, 169, 171, 172, 174
Memes, 104, 113, 120, 131
Middle Ages/Medieval, 5, 10–12, 72, 102
Mind (*see also* Subjectivity)
 and desire for truth, 110, 119, 129
 and language, 134–39
 as adaptive instrument, 15, 107, 115
 capacities of, 75, 82
 modern, 67, 68, 92, 123
 of God/Universe, 88, 90, 108–9, 145, 195
Miracles, 41, 71, 78, 145, 154–75, 185
Mitchell, Mark T., 122–27
Mlodinow, Leonard, 1
Moody, Raymond A., 184, 186, 187
Morowitz, Harold J., 99, 127, 129, 130
Morris, Desmond, 109
Morris, Henry M., 7, 91
Moses (biblical), 31, 47, 52, 57, 151, 154, 158, 162, 171, 172, 176
Mother Teresa, 150
Multiverse, 1, 63, 89, 90
Murphy, Roland E., 147

Napoleon Bonaparte, 78
Natural Selection, 14, 15, 152, 153
Naturalism, 5, 7, 13, 20, 22, 34, 75, 80, 103, 110, 113, 114, 131
Newberg, Andrew, 188–90
Newton, Isaac, 11, 78, 81, 108, 110
Nichols, Robert Hasting, 20, 34, 35
Nietzsche, Friedrich, 81, 106

Origen of Alexandria, 27, 66–72, 73, 75, 76, 79, 81, 82, 85, 90, 97, 105, 116, 140, 142, 150, 156

Paley, William, 78
Parable(s), 70–71, 74, 76, 91, 99, 118, 121, 140, 141, 157, 164, 167, 183
Pascal, Blaise, 68, 92
Paul, Saint, 27, 29, 45, 46, 52, 58, 64, 84, 87, 121, 135, 143, 152, 153, 156, 166–68, 173, 182, 193
Peacocke, Arthur, 5, 130
Penrose, Roger, 119, 126
Perrin, Norman, 163
Peters, Ted, 5, 19, 79, 101, 107
Philo of Alexandria, 46
Physics
 branch of science, 15, 24, 87, 105, 108–10, 118, 127–30, 132, 166
 in Origen, 67–72, 76, 79, 86
Plato/Platonic, 84, 119, 120, 126, 183, 190
Polanyi, Michael, 5, 13, 68, 83, 85, 86, 87, 98, 117, 118, 120, 121–27, 128, 129, 132
Pope Benedict XVI, 8, 38, 42, 51
Pope John Paul II, 11, 19, 21, 85
Pope Urban VIII, 11
Purpose of life/universe, 9–10, 13–17, 63, 75, 80, 85, 99, 101, 103, 104, 112, 116, 124, 128

Rachels, James, 107, 109
Rationalism (see also Reason), 13, 21, 62, 68
Rause, Vince, 188, 190
Reason (see also Rationalism)
 as gift of God, 71–72, 75, 77–78
 as way to know God, 64, 99
 as way to truth, 40
 Faith and, 10–13, 56, 57, 59, 62, 63, 72, 74, 82–84, 87, 99, 117, 195
 God subjected to, 74–76
 world discernible by, 17
Rees, Martin, 89, 90
Reformation, 11, 27, 34, 35, 38, 49, 73, 77, 82, 92

Retribution, theology of, 147
Rolston III, Holmes, 16
Rue, Loyal, 6, 13, 16, 104, 112
Russell, Bertrand, 84, 87, 119, 126, 130

Sagan, Carl, 81
Samuel (biblical), 177
Satan/satan, 46, 146, 158, 160–63, 178
Schneiders, Sandra, 54
Schroeder, Gerald L., 88, 91
Schwartz, Jeffrey M., 191, 192
Science
  as a way to know God, 72, 87–91
  as a way to knowledge, 24
  definition of, 2
  gift to theology, 2, 4
  limits of, 84–85, 107–8
Scientific Materialism, 5, 75, 101, 103–9, 112, 114, 133, 187, 188
Segal, Alan F., 176, 177, 179, 183, 185, 191
Shakespeare, William, 55, 88, 130, 132
Shea, William R., 75
Simon, Richard, 39, 47
Simpson, G. G., 131
Solomon (biblical), 26, 48, 67, 68, 96, 145, 163
Southern Baptist Convention, 8, 34
Spinoza, Benedict, 20, 29, 38–43, 47, 48, 49, 56, 61, 62, 68, 77, 154
Stalin/Stalinism, Joseph, 32, 86, 98, 122, 123
Subjectivity, 13, 14, 17, 75, 81–84, 99, 108, 116, 125, 138, 142
Suffering, 101, 135, 145–54, 157, 175, 178, 191
Sundberg, Walter, 20, 33, 42
Symbol/symbolic/symbolism, 20, 25, 34, 66, 69–74, 76, 79, 81, 83, 91, 92, 95, 98, 99, 104, 111, 133, 136, 138–40, 142, 144, 155, 158, 165, 166, 167, 173, 192, 193

Tacit Dimension, 125, 135, 184
Timmer, Daniel C., 147
Trible, Phyllis, 95
Truth, search for, 13, 16, 17, 110, 113–15, 118, 120, 173
Tutu, Desmond, 132–33, 150

Van Biema, David, 8
Von Rad, Gerhard, 50–51, 54

Ward, Keith, 92, 106, 124, 191
Weinberg, Steven, 102, 112
Weinstein, David, 106
Wellhausen, Julius, 47, 50
Whitcomb, John C., 7, 91
Whitehead, A. N., 5
Wiesel, Elie, 149–51
Wilson, Edward O., 5, 103–7, 110, 112–15, 117, 118, 120, 121, 122, 128, 130, 131, 133, 141
Wright, N. T., 166, 169

Yates, Jenny, 184–87, 193

Zaleski, Carol, 182–87, 190, 192, 193

SCRIPTURE INDEX

Italicized numbers indicate that the reference is in a footnote.

Old Testament

Genesis
1 *91, 94*
1 94
1:2 158
1:21 *91*
1:26 16
1:26-27 57, 100
1:28 *95*
1–2 *93, 95*
1–2 6, 35, 91
1:1–2:3 93
1–3 20
1–11 93, 96
2 *93, 94*
2:4b-25 94
2:7 *79*
2:7 94
2:19 *79, 95*
2:19 70, 94
3 95
3:8 95
3:19 22
4–11 95
5:23-24 179
9:3 *95*
9:6 36
12 *93*
12:1-9 96, 178
15:6 3
18:18 96
22:1-13 46
22:2 158
22:8 46
32:29 70
35:10 70

Exodus
3:6 181
3:14 *31, 94*
3:14 172
7–8 162
8:3 162
8:15 *162*
8:15 162
14 154
14:21 154
14–15 71
14:31–15:1 *71*
15:18 *163*
20:5 *143*
20:7 *31*
20:11 *143*
21 34
31:18 162
33:19 171
34:6 149, 171

Leviticus
11 135
20:9 36
20:10 36
24:10-23 36

Numbers
11:11-12 *92*
11:12 151
15:32-36 36
21:17-18 *71*
22–24 70

Deuteronomy
5:1-4 60
5:15 *143*
6:4 60
7:1-5 *135*
7:1-5 31, 34
7:6-8 32
9:10 162
18:9-14 176
18:14 176
18:18 176
21:18-21 36
23:12-14 61
24:16 *143*
27–28 178
32:1-43 *71*
32:6 *92*
32:11 *92*

Joshua
6:21 32

Judges
5:1-31 71

1 Samuel
2:1-10 71
8:6-18 96
14:3 177
14:42 177
15:1 34
16:14-23 160
18:10-11 160
28:3 177
28:3-25 177
28:6 177
28:13 177

2 Samuel
7 96
11 143
11 157
11–12 70
11:27–12:1 157
12:1-6 141
12:23 145
22:1-51 71
24 146
24:3 146
24:14 146

1 Kings
19:8 158
19:11-13 171
22:19-23 156

2 Kings
2:11 180
21:10-15 147

1 Chronicles
16:8 71
16:8-36 71
20 143
21 146

Job
1 145
1:6 146
1:8-12 178
1:21 145
1–2 146
2:3-6 178
2:10 145
4:7-9 147
4:17-21 147
8:1-7 147
19:23-24 178
19:25-26 178
26:6 176
38 92
38:8-11 171
38:16 171
38–41 102
42:7-9 147

Psalms
2:7 158
6 148
8 35, 102
8:3-6 102
8:4 188
8:6 79
10 148
10:1 148
10:14-18 147
13 148
18 71
18:3 92
19 18, 35, 71
19:1 195
22 148, 150
22:3-5 150
22:9 150
22:10 92
23 130, 179
27:1 92
27:4 179
27:8 8
27:14 97
31:6 183
33:20-22 97
37 147
38 148
42 148, 179
42 96
42:4 179
43 148, 179
43:3 179
44 148
44:9-11 148
60 148
63 96
77:9 148
77:16 172
77:19 172
78 35, 49
78:65 30
78:65-66 92
82:1 100
84 96
85:10 97
88 175, 176
89:7 100
103:19 163
104:27-30 115
107 170
107:27-29 170
115:17 176
145:11-13 163
146:3 96

Proverbs
10:3 147
15:11 176
27:20 176
31:28 v

Ecclesiastes
1:1 116
3:18-20 79
3:19 175, 188

3:19-20 102

Song of Solomon
1:2 72
1:2-4 67
7:7-9 67

Isaiah
1:10-17 177
5:1-7 *71*
7:14 152
8:19 176
20 71
38:18 176
40:31 *97*
40–55 *172*
42:1 158
43:1-13 172
43:18-19 *115*
45:22-25 168
52:7 *163*
55:8-9 64
55:10 60
55:10-11 24
55:10-13 35
56–66 *172*

Jeremiah
1:6-7 148
2:34 *147*
5:27-28 *147*
7:1-7 178
11:18–12:6 *148*
12:7 158
15:10-21 *148*
15:18 148
16:1-2 148
17:14-18 *148*
18:18-24 *148*
19 71
20:2 148
20:7-13 *148*
20:14 148
20:14-18 *148*
20:18 148
23:21-22 156
26:8 148
31:29-30 *143*
36 35
38:6 148

Lamentations
3:38 146

Ezekiel
18 *143*
34 *92*

Daniel
4:25-27 *163*
7:13-14 *163*
9:21 *160*
10:13 *160*
12:2-3 180

Hosea
2 *92*
11:1 158
13:7-8 *92*

Amos
1–2 93
4:1 *147*
5:21-24 178
9:7 *55*
9:7 93

Jonah
1:7-16 170
1:16 170
4:11 *93*

Malachi
4:6 180

Deuterocanonical/ Apocryphal

Tobit
3:8 *160*
6:7-18 *160*
8:3 *160*

Wisdom of Solomon
7:7-9 134
10:10 *163*
11:22 1

2 Maccabees
7:28 *93*
12:39-45 27
12:40 27
12:43 27
12:44 28
12:45 28

Psalms of Solomon
17:3 *163*

New Testament

Matthew
1:23 97, 152
3:10 164
3:14-15 *157*
4 *146*
5:3-10 *147*
6:10 *164*
6:25-34 *153*
8:6-8 *168*
8:10-12 181
8:11-12 *164*
8:21 *168*
8:23-27 169
8:25 170
8:26 *153*
11:14 180
12:17 *96*

12:22-29 *146*
12:22-30 161
12:40 *141*
13:33 *92*
14:28-30 *168*
14:31 *153*
16:8 *153*
17:9-13 180
17:20 *153*
18:23-35 164
19:28 71
20:1-16 164
21:1-10 71
23:33 *176*
25:31-46 152
27:45-54 158
27:46 148
27:51-54 *143*
28:2 158
28:17 *153*
28:20 60, 97

Mark
1:9 157
1:10-13 158
1:15 164, 181
2:15-17 71
2:27 58
3:22-27 161
3:23-25 161
3:23-27 *161*
3:24-26 *161*
3:27 *161*
3:27 162
4:2 70
4:3-8 *92*
4:31-32 70
4:35-41 169
4:39 160
4:41 170
5:38 154
6:14-15 180
6:45-52 169, 171
8:11-13 *156*
8:11-13 156, 174
8:11-21 *121*
8:35 152
10:46-52 173
11:3 *168*
12:18-27 181
14:25 *164*
14:34-36 182
14:36 146
15:33-39 158
15:34 148
15:38-39 *143*

Luke
1:17 180
3:21 *157*
4 *146*
4:13 *146*
4:39 160
6:12 188
6:20-26 164
7:11-17 173
7:22 *155*
7:24-28 164
8:2 164
8:12 *168*
8:22-25 169
10:18 70
10:25-37 143
11:2 *92*
11:2-4 97
11:14 161
11:14-23 161, 174
11:17-18 *161*
11:17-18 161
11:17-23 *161*
11:19 161
11:20 *155*
11:20 162
11:21-22 *161*
11:21-22 162
12:4-5 183
12:13-21 183
12:27 71
13:1 71
13:1-9 164
13:4 *92*
13:4 71
13:16 *146*
13:31 182
15:1-2 181
15:8-10 *92*
15:11-32 141, 164
16:19-31 183
17:7-10 178
17:20-21 164
18:8 *153*
18:9-14 164
22:3 *146*
22:30 71
22:31 *146*
22:42 182
22:43-44 *182*
23:46 *183*
24:27 26
24:44 26

John
1:14 52, 59, 97
2:23-24 *121*
2:23-25 156, 174
4:26 172
4:48 *156*
6:2 *121, 156*
6:9 154
6:14-15 174
6:25-27 *156*
6:26 *121*
6:35 *172*
8:12 *172*
8:24 *172*
8:28 *172*
8:58 *172*
8:58 172
9:1 173

9:1-3 147
9:4 156
9:16 121
9:39 173
9:40-41 173
10:7 172
10:11 172
10:25 156
10:32 156
10:37-38 156
11:1-44 173
11:25 172
11:48 121
12:24 166
12:24-25 183
12:27 182
12:31 146
12:31 160
12:37 121
13:19 172
13:27 160
14:6 172
18:5-8 172
19:30 183
20:24-29 121
20:28 168
20:28 170
20:30-31 156

Acts of the Apostles
1:20 26
5:3 160
9:3 193
10:38 160
17:28 87
22:6 193
23:8 180
23:8 180, 181
26:13 193

Romans
1:18-23 49
1:19-20 64
2:27-29 46
3:20-28 29
3:21 26
3:29 55
5:6-8 53
8:19 195
8:21 195
8:21-24 152
8:23 173
8:24 173
8:35-39 71
10:13 168
12:21 153
14:17 163
15:19 156

1 Corinthians
7:29-30 182
8:6 168
10:11 45
15:50 164

2 Corinthians
1:20 96
4:6 193
5:17 193
15:50 164

Galatians
1:8-9 135
1:13 167
1:13-18 193
2:11-14 143
2:15-21 29
2:16-21 3
3:5 156
3:16 96
5:6 3
6:15 193

Ephesians
6 34

Philippians
1:21-24 182
2:6-11 168
2:7 151
2:8 170

1 Thessalonians
5:19-21 84
5:19-21 121

Hebrews
4:12 24, 35
8–10 96
11:3 93

1 Peter
3:15 55
5:8 159

Revelation
21:1 194